# Misrecognized Materialists

*Matt James*

# Misrecognized Materialists: Social Movements in Canadian Constitutional Politics

**UBC**Press · Vancouver · Toronto

15 14 13 12 11 10 09 08 07 06    5 4 3 2 1

Printed in Canada on acid-free paper that is 100% post-consumer recycled, processed chlorine-free, and printed with vegetable-based, low-VOC inks.

---

**Library and Archives Canada Cataloguing in Publication**

James, Matt, 1965-
  Misrecognized materialists : social movements in Canadian constitutional politics / Matt James.

Includes bibliographical references and index.
ISBN-13: 978-0-7748-1168-2
ISBN-10: 0-7748-1168-4

  1. Minorities – Legal status, laws, etc. – Canada – History – 20th century. 2. Constitutional history – Canada. 3. Social movements – Political aspects – Canada – History – 20th century. I. Title.

KE4395.J34 2006        342.7108'7        C2006-903286-6

---

Canadä

UBC Press gratefully acknowledges the financial support for our publishing program of the Government of Canada through the Book Publishing Industry Development Program (BPIDP), and of the Canada Council for the Arts, and the British Columbia Arts Council.

This book has been published with the help of a grant from the Canadian Federation for the Humanities and Social Sciences, through the Aid to Scholarly Publications Programme, using funds provided by the Social Sciences and Humanities Research Council of Canada, and with the help of the K.D. Srivastava Fund.

Printed and bound in Canada by Friesens
Set in Stone by Artegraphica Design Co. Ltd.
Copy editor: Matthew Kudelka
Proofreader: Sarah Munro
Indexer: Patricia Buchanan

UBC Press
The University of British Columbia
2029 West Mall
Vancouver, BC V6T 1Z2
604-822-5959 / Fax: 604-822-6083
www.ubcpress.ca

*For Lisa*

# Contents

# Acknowledgments

First thanks go to the Social Sciences and Humanities Research Council, Killam Trusts, and the University of British Columbia for invaluable research support. Thanks also to Don Blake, Ken Carty, and Sam LaSelva of the University of British Columbia Political Science Department and to Joel Bakan of the UBC Law Faculty for their helpful comments on earlier drafts of this book. Brian Elliott of UBC Sociology and Janet Hiebert of Queen's University Political Studies also provided extremely valuable feedback. Further thanks go to Barbara Arneil and Philip Resnick of UBC Political Science and to John Torpey, formerly of UBC Sociology and now of the City University of New York, for their great support. Thanks as well to Josephine Calazan, the late Nancy Mina, Petula Muller, and Dory Urbano of UBC. Joan Anderson, Avigail Eisenberg, Sherrill Grace, and Nikki Strong-Boag on the SSHRC-supported Race, Gender, and Construction of Canada project also provided wonderful help and guidance.

I want to thank two people in particular. Avigail Eisenberg was the scholar who first inspired me to want to do academic work. She has been helpful beyond words, as a stellar teacher, as a patient and astute critic of my written work, and as a treasured friend. Alan Cairns, whose writings have awakened me to so many of the things I find most fascinating and important about politics, is the other person to whom I am especially grateful. I would like to acknowledge his friendship, his generosity as an interlocutor, his unparalleled example of how to combine humanity with scholarly excellence, and, not least, his gentle impatience with dogma and cant.

I would also like to thank the friends who over countless chats and conversations helped make writing this book so enjoyable: Martin Courchaine, Rita Dhamoon, Francis Dupuis-Déri, Julie Fieldhouse, Olena

Hankivsky, the late and dearly missed Gabi Helms, Gerald Kernerman, Scott Pegg, Paddy Rodney, Tim Paterson, and Bryce Weber.

Several more people merit thanks for their help in the latter stages of the project: Emily Andrew of UBC Press for her incisiveness and tolerance; Ann Macklem of UBC Press for her easygoing professionalism; the anonymous reviewers for their perceptive criticisms and suggestions; Paul Dyck for his excellent research assistance; and Colin Bennett and Warren Magnusson of the University of Victoria Political Science department for their mentorship and assistance. I also thank the University of Victoria and the Social Sciences and Humanities Research Council of Canada for their support of my ongoing research.

Finally, two personal notes of thanks: to my parents, Bill James and Ann Maclellan, for their incredibly patient love, wonderful support, and for teaching me to love the world of ideas and books; and to my partner, Lisa Chalykoff, about whom even the most eloquent words of love would fall short. With all my heart, I dedicate this book to her.

# Acronyms

| | |
|---|---|
| AAFC | Afro-Asian Foundation of Canada |
| ACCL | All-Canadian Congress of Labour |
| B&B | Bilingualism and Biculturalism |
| BNA | British North America |
| CAVM | Canadian Association of Visible Minorities |
| CCF | Co-operative Commonwealth Federation |
| CCL | Canadian Congress of Labour |
| CCNC | Chinese Canadian National Council |
| CEC | Canadian Ethnocultural Council |
| CIO | Congress of Industrial Organizations |
| CJC | Canadian Jewish Congress |
| CLC | Canadian Labour Congress |
| CP | Communist Party of Canada |
| CPC | Canadian Polish Congress |
| FFQ | Fédération des femmes du Québec |
| FTQ | Fédération des travailleurs du Québec |
| JCPC | Judicial Committee of the Privy Council |
| LDR | League for Democratic Rights |
| LWR | League for Women's Rights |
| MP | Member of Parliament |
| NAC | National Action Committee on the Status of Women |
| NACOI | National Association of Canadians of Origins in India |
| NAJC | National Association of Japanese Canadians |
| NBCC | National Black Coalition of Canada |
| NCIC | National Congress of Italian Canadians |
| NCW | National Council of Women of Canada |
| NJCCA | National Japanese Canadian Citizens' Association |
| NUPGE | National Union of Provincial Government Employees |
| PSAC | Public Service Alliance of Canada |

QFL     Quebec Federation of Labour
TLC     Trades and Labour Congress of Canada
UCC     Ukrainian Canadian Committee
UN      United Nations

# Misrecognized Materialists

# 1
# Constitutional Politics and the Politics of Respect: An Introduction

Constitutional politics is a Canadian synonym for futility. Memories of our decades-long search for a comprehensive unity settlement spark chagrin: a "mad excursion"; a tale of "wonderful naivety" at best.[1] There can be no doubt that the constitutional turn has failed to ease the Canada–Quebec divisions it was meant to resolve and should on that key measure count as a failure. But there is also a different story to be told. This book tells that story. Bringing into focus the historic role of Canadian constitutional politics as a forum for questions that business as usual tended to exclude, it shows how the constitutional debate became an important arena for marginalized groups seeking inclusion and respect.

Significant attention has been paid to the participation of feminist and ethnocultural minority groups in Canada's high-profile and relatively recent battles over the ill-fated 1987-90 Meech Lake Accord and rejected Charlottetown amendment package of 1991-92, but more still needs to be said.[2] At the same time, what Peter Russell calls Canada's "constitutional odyssey" also includes such landmark struggles as the entrenchment of the 1982 Charter of Rights and Freedoms, Canada's mid-century transformation into a welfare state, and the 1960s confrontations over multiculturalism and dualism.[3] Social movements were key participants in these events, and this involvement merits closer analysis as well. Thus, focusing on national organizations representing women, working-class people, and ethnocultural minorities, this book studies the history of Canadian constitutional politics from a social movement standpoint, starting with the Rowell-Sirois hearings of the Great Depression and concluding with the parliamentary hearings prior to the Charlottetown Accord's convulsive referendum defeat.

The constitutional malaise of the post-Charlottetown era makes a strange window on the broader record of social movement involvement.[4] For much of the twentieth century, a combination of right-wing provincial opposition and Ottawa's reluctance to fight jurisdictional battles on behalf of outsider groups prevented equality seekers from establishing even their most elementary policy goals as significant topics of legislative discussion. Thus, when the attention of elites turned at key points to the constitutional arena, social movements responded not with cynicism or resignation but by welcoming the emergence of a venue for projects that normal politics seemed to preclude. The development of two pillars of Canadian citizenship in particular exemplified this dynamic: social programs for poor and working people, and equality rights and civil liberties for the marginalized and oppressed.

A unique feature of constitutional politics helped amplify traditionally silenced voices more generally. As Alan Cairns points out, the ultimate constitutional question – which follows from the constitution's role as an authoritative centre of nation-shaping rules and cues – is this: "Who are we as a people?"[5] When constitutional politics asked this question, the ordinarily excluded asked back: "What about *our* role in the country? What about *our* histories, contributions, and claims?" This dynamic created political space for social movement aspirations and ultimately made the polity more receptive to previously neglected identities and complaints.

Thus, Canada's constitutional debate can help us to more closely examine key aspects of social movement struggle. The constitutional record reveals movements wrestling with a fundamental aspect of democratic politics: the use of civic dialogue to shape the perceptions of nonsupporters. For resolute Marxists, unlettered trade unionists, dedicated feminists, and uneasy ethnocultural minorities, constitutional participation meant engaging interlocutors whose identities and affiliations could scarcely have been more different. At the same time, the constitution's role as an authoritative transmitter of civic messages and cues provided a platform from which groups seeking inclusion and respect could reach the political community as a whole. How equality seekers grappled with these opportunities and exigencies is the focus of this book.

To some, constitutional politics was the indulgent diversion of misguided elites, a world of "pretentious high-mindedness" and "words for the pleasure of words."[6] But from the vantage point of social movements, it was something else: it offered citizens the chance to force onto the national agenda some of the most serious problems of their day – unemployment and poverty; state repression and harassment; disfranchisement and internment; and the myriad forms of discrimination visited on women and racialized minorities.

These were not usually the issues on which dominant groups wanted to focus. Indeed, when citizens tried to make these complaints the focal points of civic discussion, authorities often replied with disrespectful diversions that aimed to foreclose even the possibility of consideration or debate – evasive and trivializing digressions, intimidating attacks, and other assorted signals to "mind one's place." These tactics, which remained common into the 1970s and were occasionally seen during the 1980s' Meech Lake debates, made it difficult for marginalized groups to articulate their political concerns. Equality seekers responded by becoming more attuned to issues of voice, status, and prestige – to the question of honourable inclusion in dominant representations and understandings of the Canadian political community. This book explores the origins and development of this response in the Canadian constitutional arena.

The book also describes the impact of this response on Canadian constitutionalism. The entrenchment of the Charter of Rights and Freedoms, the development and constitutional enshrinement of official multiculturalism, and, more diffusely, the creation of a more meaningful national citizenship through the construction of a welfare state – these innovations had an importance beyond the immediately practical or merely legal. They infused Canadian constitutionalism with new currents of meaning and purpose and in this way helped movements to pursue their often ignored aspirations and concerns.

The significant venues featured in this book are parliamentary committees and Royal Commissions on key issues of constitutional change between 1938 and 1992. The movements discussed are rooted in both the traditional left and the new social movements; they include organizations based in trade unionism, socialism, feminism, antiracism, and multiculturalism.

Canadian women's movements are represented by two main groups: the National Council of Women of Canada (NCW), and its more recent counterpart, the National Action Committee on the Status of Women (NAC). This study also includes the leading national organizations representing Canadians of African, Chinese, East Indian, Italian, Japanese, Jewish, Polish, and Ukrainian ancestry. The traditional-left groups examined are the main national trade-union umbrella organizations and the Communist Party of Canada (CP). Although the Party is now irrelevant, its significance in the past and its dogged focus on questions of class warrant its inclusion in a study of organizations representing marginalized constituencies.

By contrast, the Co-operative Commonwealth Federation and the New Democratic Party are omitted because their basic concern – to draw electoral support from across class lines – led to a much more varied focus. Social welfare organizations are excluded because, except for the relatively recent case of the National Anti-Poverty Organization, which participated only sporadically in the constitutional arena, they tend to represent social welfare as a cause rather than poor people as a constituency. In addition, they have generally been led by social work advocates rather than by poor people themselves. For their part, lesbian and gay organizations do not appear because they made only one formal presentation to a parliamentary committee on constitutional change between 1938 and 1992; thus, there is not enough lesbian and gay participation as such for me to make meaningful generalizations.[7]

Also excluded from coverage are organizations representing indigenous peoples and francophone Quebecers, whose struggles cannot adequately be treated in a study that focuses on groups seeking inclusion in an overarching Canadian citizenship. These actors have instead tended to search for group-differentiated arrangements to honour their historically anchored national claims. However, the Quebec-based League for Women's Rights (LWR), which appeared before the Rowell-Sirois Commission to advocate the enfranchisement of Quebec women (who could not vote provincially until 1940), does make a brief appearance. Its suffragist focus provides insights into the broader history of women's constitutional engagement that the temporal parameters of this book would otherwise preclude.

### Symbolic Capital, the Citizens' Constitution, and New Politics Theory

Although recognition struggles are often seen as campaigns for self-esteem and cultural authenticity, this book takes a more materialist approach.[8] It treats recognition as a problem of symbolic capital, which is sociologist and cultural theorist Pierre Bourdieu's term for a potent social product produced in fields of unequal power.[9]

Unlike the notion of social capital popularized by the political scientist Robert Putnam, Bourdieu's term shares some of the critical bite of Marx's conception.[10] Evoking Marx's view of capital as a technology of exploitation, Bourdieu stresses that advantages and attributes such as network membership and "good taste" operate as bases of sociopolitical power, silencing some agents while privileging others. These two examples are instances of what Bourdieu calls social and cultural capital, respectively; along with Marx's economic capital, they qualify as species of symbolic capital whenever their tendency to function as power goes unrecognized.[11]

This emphasis on the "symbolic" in symbolic capital highlights the role of processes of symbolization and representation in securing relations of deference, naturalizing privilege, and masking the pursuit of self-interest. These processes are politically significant because they help actors exercise powers that might otherwise be blocked or contested. Perhaps most notably, therefore, Bourdieu emphasizes the concept of symbolic capital as a theoretical corrective for one-sidedly economistic approaches to inequality and power – approaches that sometimes constitute the symbolic as "noneconomic, and therefore disinterested," "as lacking concrete or material effect, in short, disinterested but also useless."[12] Accordingly, Bourdieu's concept emphasizes that all but the most directly and immediately coercive instances of power depend on symbolically mediated processes of social interaction and exchange – processes that are also a key focus of this book.

Symbolic capital is often conferred by institutions. Framed as matters of established rules and procedures, institutionally sanctioned acts and discourses assume an aura of propriety that tends to mitigate potential appearances of arbitrariness or self-interest. Thus, as social theorist John Thompson states in his commentary on Bourdieu's work: "Individuals [can] possess more or less ... [symbolic] capital in so far as they are in a position to mobilize more or less of the authority delegated by an institution."[13] This brief account suggests a useful schematic perspective on the constitutional participation of Canadian social movements.

In Canada as in many other countries, women, working-class people, and ethnocultural minorities have often experienced profound disrespect. Stigmatized as categorically inferior, they have been systematically denied economic, educational, and social opportunities and occasionally even singled out for legally sanctioned demonization and abuse. At the same time, they have faced profound barriers to raising these problems in the political arena; their claims and indeed their very voices have been dismissed routinely as out of place, irrelevant, or unacceptably idiosyncratic. Over the course of the twentieth century, equality-seeking movements sought to confront these elementary problems of voice by struggling to change traditional distributions of respect – that is, by striving to make symbolic capital work for rather than against them. In the Canadian context, constitutional recognition became an especially valued source of symbolic capital – of sanctioned, "in place" discourses for bringing long silenced concerns to the attention of an indifferent and sometimes hostile polity.

This book's focus on constitutional symbolism also draws on the work of Alan Cairns, whose pioneering writings on post-Charter constitutional politics mark a signal break with Canadian political science's earlier lack of interest in the politics of recognition. This work – and particularly its interpretive response to the 1980s controversies over the Meech Lake Accord – has established the constitution's new importance as "the central arena within which the groups of an increasingly plural society ... vie with each other for recognition and acceptance": Canada's "supreme instrument of social recognition and its denial."[14]

Most importantly, Cairns suggests that the identification of particular axes of social difference in the 1982 Charter, such as gender and ethnic origin, has made "Charter Canadians" out of those who value their newfound recognition and rights.[15] Yet the architects of the Meech Lake Accord seemed unaware of this transformed constitutional orientation. In proposing to subordinate Charter rights to a prior clause recognizing Quebec as a "distinct society" – a clause they sought to entrench through the traditional elitist methods of executive federalism – the first ministers failed to grasp what Cairns identifies as the elementary political reality of the new Charter-identifying groups: "The constitution that gives them status matters to them."[16] Cairns' work has stimulated interest in social movements among Canadian political scientists. His account of the constitution's contemporary role as a source of symbolic recognition, known as the Citizens' Constitution theory, has expanded the traditional parameters of the field and prompted a generalized disciplinary awareness of the "new constitutional players" and "new Canadian constitutional culture."[17]

Of course, Cairns' theory has also left a number of gaps to fill. Some writers have begun to explore the broader constitutional histories of particular equality-seeking movements, showing that social movements have pursued concerns beyond the "Charter Canadian" preoccupations emphasized by Cairns.[18] For their part, scholars dissatisfied with the temporal and spatial restrictions of the Citizens' Constitution theory have investigated the origins and meaning of the new movements' emphasis on recognition – an important emphasis throughout the modern world. For many such scholars, American political scientist Ronald Inglehart's New Politics theory provides precisely the broader comparative and historical perspective required.

Drawing on a sophisticated long-term project of international opinion research, New Politics theory has charted the sources and contours of a long-term transformation in Western political culture.[19] Inglehart calls this transformation a "culture shift": a constellation of far-reaching changes in values stemming from the increased peace and prosperity enjoyed in many nations since the Second World War.[20] These changes have enabled growing numbers of citizens to set aside the materialist preoccupations of physical safety and economic security that dominated earlier eras, in favour of what New Politics writers call a "postmaterialist" focus on esteem, belonging, and the overall quality of life.[21]

Many Canadian scholars, including F.L. Morton, Rainer Knopff, Neil Nevitte, and Ian Brodie, have thus found in New Politics what Cairns' approach lacks: a broader account of the sources and aspirations of today's politics of identity and recognition.[22] The New Politics perspective has been especially useful in helping situate the social movement dimension of Canada's recent constitutional experience as a particularly sharp manifestation of more subtle, long-term changes affecting political culture and behaviour in all of the advanced democracies.

More recently, and looking beyond the constitutional arena, Nevitte's influential *The Decline of Deference* shows how the changes in values associated with postmaterialism have fostered an "elite-challenging" ethic that is shaking Canada's traditional practices of brokerage and elite accommodation to their core.[23] Similarly, Morton and Knopff's *The Charter Revolution* suggests that advantages of education and class location have helped newer generations of activists to bring New Politics values to bear on the courts.[24] These and other New Politics–influenced works have contributed significantly to our understanding of Canadian social movements. As this book will go on to suggest, however, the New Politics approach is in some respects a vision in need of a corrective. I will outline this concern after looking more closely at the vision itself.

**New Politics: A Closer Look**
New Politics theory addresses a remarkable array of themes, including the changed distribution of political skills, shifting notions of left and right, the increased protest potential of Western publics, and transformations in the bases of party choice. In several influential works over the past three decades, Inglehart has elaborated the social-psychological model behind the New Politics approach in three major ways.

First, he has advanced the scarcity hypothesis, which posits that "one places the greatest subjective value on those things that are in relatively short supply."[25] The scarcity hypothesis suggests that postwar environments of economic security and personal safety have heightened people's interest in goods that prosperity and peace cannot on their own provide, such as free expression and a clean environment. Second, he has argued that changes in the distribution of political skills have made citizens better placed to pursue their civic goals than were members of earlier generations. In particular, he has noted that advances in access to higher education have enabled more and more people to acquire cognitive and communications skills that help them to articulate and amplify their demands. Thus, New Politics scholars link the postwar increase in "unconventional participation" – such as petitions, protest marches, boycotts, and sit-ins – to the heightened political literacy that university and college graduates tend to enjoy.[26]

The third and core element of New Politics theory is its emphasis on a shift toward postmaterialist values. This emphasis draws on the psychologist Abraham Maslow's notion of a needs hierarchy, which distinguishes between the "lower-order" physiological needs essential to human survival and the "higher-order" psychological and aesthetic concerns of the sort that individuals tend to emphasize once basic security has been achieved.[27] Postmaterial value change is thus said to occur when large numbers of people begin moving up the needs hierarchy – a process that according to Inglehart's research began in earnest in most Western countries in the 1960s. To be clear, New Politics does not assert a simplistic correspondence between changed economic conditions and shifts in individual values. It holds, rather, that a postmaterial change in values involves a long-term process of intergenerational population replacement, which occurs as successive cohorts come to political maturity after having been raised in conditions of prosperity and peace.[28]

Thus, New Politics theorists use the notion of postmaterial value change to illuminate conflicts that are reshaping political landscapes around the world. Material disputes over questions of public order and the distribution of wealth remain; but at the same time, new, postmaterial questions of belonging, esteem, and quality of life have come to the fore. The key political actors in this process are new social movements; just as trade unions and social democratic parties in earlier phases of industrialism articulated unrealized material needs, so movements such as feminism, environmentalism, and multiculturalism are highlighting unmet postmaterial concerns today.[29]

This contrast between materialism and postmaterialism has similarities to a European body of work, New Social Movement theory, which also traces a shift from an industrial society focusing on class politics toward a post-industrial society emphasizing a politics of self-realization and identity.[30] However, because the European theories are designed specifically to counter Marxist understandings of social development and human action, they speak less directly to those political and academic contexts in which Marxism's impact has been less intense.[31] For its part, an American approach, Resource Mobilization theory, shares the New Politics emphasis on how postwar affluence has enhanced the availability of goods and skills that help movements to proliferate.[32] What distinguishes New Politics from Resource Mobilization theory is the argument of the former that new social movements reflect and promote changes in political culture stemming from the spread of postmaterialist values.

Critics often raise methodological questions that emerge from New Politics theory's quantitative dimension. They ask, for example: "How are we properly to discern materialist from postmaterialist value orientations among survey respondents?" and "Do Inglehart's survey questions tap values, or do they tap attitudes and beliefs?"[33] A different set of disputes turns on whether postmaterialist values arise primarily from formative experiences of security (as Inglehart contends) or from increased access to higher education or other non-economic sources.[34] Finally, critics argue that postmaterialism can fuel a variety of political orientations, and not just the New Left outlook on which Inglehart and his colleagues tend to focus.[35] This book does not address these debates.

This book also respects as important the core empirical findings of New Politics survey research. This research suggests that support for postmaterialist priorities tends to be correlated with rising levels of education and economic security and that individuals who back causes such as feminism and antiracism tend to support these priorities.[36] It is no surprise, then, that this book's story is in many ways consistent with a New Politics approach. It suggests, as does New Politics, that the long postwar boom provided a context in which social movements could take root and grow; that the rise of movements such as feminism and multiculturalism was accompanied by a proliferation of symbolically focused struggles over esteem and belonging; and that these changes altered the character of political conflict, in particular by changing the shape and voice of the left.[37]

## The Politics of Respect and the Instrumental Significance of Symbolic Goods

Yet the chapters that follow also highlight themes that fit less easily with the New Politics account. Empirically, for example, they show that mid-century socialist groups and trade unions were keenly interested in symbolic questions of honour and dignity. By the same token, feminist and antiracist groups often prioritized distributive concerns such as equal pay, opportunity in employment, and access to social programs. This difference regarding how to characterize movements' priorities is partly a matter of emphasis; a more in-depth focus on actual movement participation will inevitably capture nuances that an opinion research lens tends to miss.

Nevertheless, the book's emphasis on the mixed and overlapping character of movement priorities is a useful reminder that the materialism–postmaterialism distinction – a staple in textbook accounts of new social movements – can easily be pushed too far.[38] As Miriam Smith observes, for example, the postmaterialist label often obscures the fact that many new social movements, such as feminism, antiracism, and lesbian and gay rights, represent groups with "strong material interests in equality."[39] Their focus on physical threats such as forced childbirth, spousal assault, and hate crime adds warrant for further caution in this respect.

However, this book's purpose in questioning aspects of the New Politics approach is not to pile up illustrations in support of "the small academic cottage industry that has grown up around the project of proving that [the new social movements] are not really new."[40] In focusing historically on the participation of Canadian social movements, it is concerned more positively with illuminating Canadians' constitutional struggles over esteem and belonging. At the same time, by engaging critically with the postmaterialism thesis, it hopes to make a modest contribution to the larger scholarly project of analyzing and interpreting the social movement politics of recognition and respect.

To this end, I suggest that the postmaterialism thesis overemphasizes two features of contemporary recognition struggles in ways that tend to obscure other, equally important aspects. The first feature is the link between postwar prosperity and the politics of esteem and belonging; in New Politics scholarship, this emphasis tends one-sidedly to depict new movements and their supporters as the lucky beneficiaries of affluence. Second, the theory's classification of esteem and belonging as "higher-order" needs frames new movements' concerns as esoteric departures from more comprehensible preoccupations. These emphases combine to provide an unduly partial and at times misleading narrative of the politics of recognition and respect.

This narrative features prominently in Canadian laments over the "problems of governability" in post-Charter constitutional politics.[41] Nevitte's account in *The Decline of Deference* is one example; by linking "the turmoil facing Canadians since the early 1980's" to the rise of postmaterialist movements "not filled with those who suffer from any personal deprivation," it portrays the movement concerns involved as somewhat trivial.[42] More directly, an emphasis on the "higher-order" character of postmaterialist aspirations paints new movements' objectives as cultural cum emotional desires, in contrast to more evidently rational concerns. Thus, Janet Ajzenstat asserts that "the demands of 'new politics' groups are less amenable to conciliation through the bargaining and trade-offs that are a feature of quantitative who-gets-what-when-and-how politics ... New politics adds a further dimension of intolerance to the contestation in the arena of constitutional debate."[43] Leslie Pal's discussion of the "sorry history of Canadian constitutionalism" puts the postmaterialism concept to similar use: "Citizens and policymakers are willing to compromise on material interests, but ways of life are intrinsically more precious and less negotiable. The result is new difficulties ... a certain prickliness on the part of significant segments of the public who feel that public policy should not merely confer benefits but also afford dignity, recognition, and support."[44]

In the Canadian constitutional context, "postmaterialism" has in this way become a shorthand designation for the symbolic and emotional aspirations of a privileged activist minority whose struggles leave upset in their wake. Indeed, in some uses the term itself is self-evidently negative, as in Anthony Peacock's "anti-majoritarian ... post-materialist ... constitutional cognoscenti," or Knopff and Morton's "postmaterialist ... knowledge class ... fatally removed from ... the reality inhabited by ordinary men and women."[45] While obviously polemical, these usages reflect the concept's more general tendency to frame movements such as feminism and multiculturalism as "lifestyle" movements in search of "self-fulfillment," but not as political campaigns for employment opportunity or freedom from violence.[46]

This book is not a critique of New Politics theory; its aim is more modestly corrective. Nor does it suggest that Canada's social movement struggles have been salutary in every possible respect and that criticisms are therefore inevitably unwarranted. It seeks instead to illuminate dynamics and problems that the notion of postmaterialism tends to obscure. Focusing historically on the constitutional participation of Canadian social movements, it explores the significance that esteem and belonging tend to assume when disrespected groups seek to focus political discussion on their traditionally neglected needs. The postmaterialism lens misses this significance by taking an exclusively expressive view of esteem and belonging. According to this view, esteem and belonging are aesthetic, cultural, and psychological goods valued for the intrinsic satisfactions they bring. Of course, the expressive view has considerable general validity; the emotional and psychological importance of esteem and belonging indeed makes them ends-in-themselves. However, researchers must also attend to their instrumental significance if they are to understand the problems, motivations, and achievements of equality-seeking movements.

Thus, by emphasizing the instrumental dimension, the chapters that follow foreground what the New Politics approach tends to miss. Highlighting the practical and political aspects of esteem and belonging through a series of concrete cases and examples, they show how problems of stigmatization and disrespect presented marginalized groups with significant problems of security and safety. Furthermore, they show how groups seeking to confront these problems in the constitutional field became increasingly engaged in struggles for recognition and respect. From this account emerges the main message of the book: social movements have not participated in Canadian constitutional politics as the fortunate postmaterialists of New Politics theory, but rather as "misrecognized materialists" – as groups seeking esteem and belonging in order to focus their political community on traditionally neglected needs for security and safety. To these struggles we now turn.

# 2

# Searching for a Forum: Social Movements at the Royal Commission on Dominion-Provincial Relations

By the mid-1930s the disorder and suffering unleashed by the Great Depression had finally placed the left's long-standing demand for a national system of social security and worker protection on the mainstream political agenda. In a classic instance of deathbed repentance, Conservative Prime Minister R.B. Bennett introduced federal legislation addressing issues such as unemployment insurance, the minimum wage, and maximum hours of work. Yet Bennett's party was promptly defeated by William Lyon Mackenzie King's Liberals in the general election of 1935.[1] King, whose cherished self-image as a labour-friendly reformer was matched only by his electoral dependence on ultramontane Quebec, then referred Bennett's "New Deal" legislation to the courts.[2] At issue was whether the Bennett package violated Section 92 of the British North America Act, which allocated jurisdiction over "property and civil rights" to the provinces.

In a landmark 1937 ruling, the British Empire's highest court, the Judicial Committee of the Privy Council (JCPC), concluded that the Depression crisis was of insufficient importance to allow Ottawa to act in areas constitutionally assigned to the provinces.[3] Canadians seemed stuck with laissez-faire forever; progressive social legislation was proscribed federally, yet at the same time the provinces lacked the necessary tax powers and fiscal capacity to implement their own reforms.[4]

The Royal Commission on Dominion-Provincial Relations (1937-40) was established to address this crisis of economic chaos and jurisdictional inflexibility. The first official forum of any significance to offer Canadians the chance to convey their views on constitutional issues, the Rowell-Sirois Commission (as it came to be known in honour of its two chairmen) constituted a significant political opportunity for progressive forces.[5] Although political economists and constitutional scholars enjoyed a special prominence in the commission's deliberations,

trade unions and socialist activists gained uncustomary political leverage from the era's novel atmosphere of working-class protest.[6] Even the
notorious vacillator King feared that continued inaction might lead
popular unrest to "assume alarming proportions at any time."[7] This
context made the commission's public hearings a unique venue for actors seeking to transform their political community.

Although economic and social policy concerns were central, histories
of struggle against a closed and often repressive political system encouraged a strong democratizing emphasis in the presentations of equality-
seeking social movements. Trade unionists and socialists, in particular,
argued for a robust system of civil liberties and an expanded menu of
opportunities for political participation as the means by which citizens
could best pursue their economic-security interests against the opposed
positions of dominant elites.

Despite this controversial stance, the Royal Commission seemed to
recognize the male-dominated organizations of Canada's traditional left
as significant partners in its novel enterprise of national inquiry and
civic dialogue. By contrast, women's democratic and social policy claims
tended to be shunted aside – to remain unheard even as they were being made. Studying these divergent experiences is an appropriate way
to begin exploring how questions of prestige and respect have shaped
the participation of traditionally disrespected actors in the Canadian
constitutional arena.

### The 1938 Royal Commission on Dominion-Provincial Relations

#### Craft Unions and Communists
The Communist Party of Canada (CP) and the Trades and Labour Congress of Canada (TLC) both expressed keen support for the commission's
mandate, which was to re-examine "the economic and financial basis
of Confederation and of the distribution of legislative powers in the
light of the economic and social developments of the last seventy years."[8]
On behalf of the Moscow-affiliated CP, Secretary-General Tim Buck ap-
plauded the commission "as an historic step forward."[9] President P.M.
Draper of the TLC, a craft-union umbrella group whose 1886 founding
was intended to give Canadian unions a more effective presence in the
corridors of government, called the hearings "most certainly welcome."[10]

This enthusiasm for constitutional politics reflected frustration with
the jurisdictional obstacles that were blocking economic and social reform.[11] Finding it a "cause of surprise that seventy years [had been]
allowed to elapse between the passing of the British North America Act
and this first enquiry into its operations," the TLC proposed holding

regular public hearings at ten-year intervals "to give all sections of the public a hearing on Dominion-Provincial Relations and constitutional questions."[12] Draper argued for this proposal by reciting a list of sixteen different legislative measures that the TLC had sought without success at the federal level for almost fifty years, and concluded that "the general resulting situation is to be deplored."[13]

Left-wing leaders also deplored the repressive tactics – including police brutality, state-sanctioned mob attacks, and pre-emptive round-ups of activists – that were being deployed routinely against the protesters, strikers, and organizers of the day.[14] In an innovative response, the CP and TLC both proposed a bill of rights that would protect the liberties of speech, assembly, religion, and trade union membership. Although neither group could be accused of an undue preoccupation with institutional detail, each sought a constitutional charter that would bind federal and provincial governments alike. In doing so they became the first social movement actors to call publicly for a Canadian charter of rights.[15]

Focusing on the right of union membership, Draper argued that "if workers cannot join a union without fear of dismissal, their rights are being stopped by economic pressure." Rights such as those to free speech, he added, were also "necessary in a true democracy and ... should be given definite, legal standing."[16] The CP was more emphatic. Speaking as a recently released political prisoner, Buck declared: "Civil liberties have been trampled underfoot. The present situation shows the need for a Canadian bill of rights and for a procedure giving the citizen redress when those rights are invaded."[17]

Though they agreed broadly on civil liberties, social welfare, and trade union freedoms, the TLC and CP framed their arguments differently. The CP was eager to identify the Canadian enemies of social progress. "It is not accidental," Buck asserted, that the "provincial governments which are leading the fight to prevent [a national welfare state] are at the same time seeking to abrogate the rights of labour to organize." Citing Mitchell Hepburn's Ontario and Maurice Duplessis' Quebec as the most glaring examples, Buck called the provinces "strongholds of reactionary finance in [their] fight against reforms demanded by the Canadian people."[18]

In contrast, the TLC elected to blame the JCPC for Canada's stalemate in social policy. The Imperial court's jurisprudence was unduly formalist, Draper complained: it had made "the interpretation of the law of first importance and the interests of those to be dealt with under the law of minor importance."[19] Attacking the formalism of the English law lords was safe political rhetoric, for it allowed the TLC to express its respect for Canadian institutions. The TLC proposed that JCPC appeals be abolished on the grounds that "our judges enjoy a high reputation for integrity and their knowledge of the law has never been shown to be less than judges elsewhere."[20]

This decorous approach reflected the craft unions' conviction that influencing government required social respectability and political moderation.[21] The rhetoric of respectability had gained force during the 1930s as craft unions sought to fend off rival "industrial union" groups proposing to bring ordinary labourers and accomplished craftsmen together within a single framework.[22] The craft unions responded by proclaiming their disdain for "riffraff," "good for nothings," and "rubbish," emphasizing the Victorian distinction between the respectable and the rough working classes.[23]

The TLC saw its long history and its links to the "honourable" working-class trades, such as carpentry, machining, and printing, as badges of organizational distinction.[24] Although it shared a common platform of civil liberties, trade union recognition, and national social welfare programs with its competitors in the industrial unions, the TLC believed that packaging was important.[25] It framed its Rowell-Sirois presentation as "the outgrowth of more than fifty years of experience of Canada's organized workers," as a "common sense" program that "would improve employer-employee relations" while protecting "the welfare of the masses."[26]

Yet even the CP was sensitive to its image, and it too wanted respect. Thus, it showed a surprising willingness to sacrifice key Marxist tenets to the nationalism and social conservatism of the dominant English-Canadian society. For example, it set aside Marx's dictum that "working men have no country" in favour of calling for "national unification"; it criticized "the provincial dismemberment of the nation"; and it saluted civil liberties as "the special tradition of all British people for all generations."[27] And though Marx would have scoffed at such "bourgeois claptrap," the CP also positioned itself as the traditional family's saviour. Complaining of "impaired moral standards" and "children ... running wild," Buck argued that the Depression had "precipitated situations ... threatening to cause the break-up of the home," with "the father [having] actually deserted" in many cases.[28]

Thus, during the decade that historian Ruth Roach Pierson calls Canada's time of "masculinity in crisis," the CP capitalized on the widespread contemporary understanding of the Depression as a special catastrophe for men.[29] This approach framed an otherwise radical program in strikingly wholesome terms. It encouraged Canadians to embrace social insurance programs, extensive income redistribution, and the nationalization of major industries as conservative measures for restoring patriarchal authority and conventional family relations. Communists were simply trying to help Canada's breadwinners "save their farms and homes and protect their families": to rescue them "from the demoralizing situation in which they ... find themselves and [give] them an opportunity ... to find a place in life in which they could hold up their heads and feel as if they were really part of Canada."[30]

**Separate Spheres: Women's Groups and the Rowell-Sirois Commission**
Like their Communist and craft union counterparts, the National Council of Women of Canada (NCW) and the Quebec-based League for Women's Rights (LWR) both welcomed the unprecedented opportunity to appear before a body charged with considering fundamental changes to the Canadian constitutional order. Because women were prohibited from voting or standing as candidates in Quebec provincial elections, the opportunity was especially important for the LWR. Its key demand was that the following amendment be added to the BNA Act: "No law of Canada or of any province thereof shall disqualify any person by reason of sex from the exercise of any political rights or public function."[31]

The LWR delegation spent most of its time before the commission emphasizing the economic impact of disfranchisement on its constituency. President Thérèse Casgrain, who as the future leader of the Quebec CCF would become the first Canadian woman to lead a political party, argued that Quebec women's "vote-less condition" was exposing them to a host of unfair financial burdens.[32] One burden was that Quebec's women teachers were among the lowest paid in Canada. Another was a network of provincial and municipal regulations that made any woman in Quebec not living under the direct supervision of a husband ineligible to receive relief payments.[33] Also harmful was the Quebec government's decision to essentially exclude women from the benefits of recent federal grants-in-aid for worker retraining.[34] Casgrain concluded: "It is clear that the disfranchisement of women in the Province of Quebec has been an important factor in allowing such discriminatory measures to be adopted against women."[35]

When asked by commissioner Harry Angus whether transferring social policy jurisdiction to Ottawa might allay some of the LWR's concerns, Casgrain insisted on the distinct importance of democratic voice for women. Although the LWR welcomed the prospect of new federal programs, it saw enfranchisement as a more reliable approach: "If you have no power behind your demands you cannot get very far, and that is why we are insisting very much on this point."[36]

In an attempt to defuse potential objections that its suffrage proposal fell outside the commission's mandate, the LWR argued that the status of women in Quebec posed important problems for Canadian federalism as a whole. As Casgrain explained, absent a change in the suffrage law, each of the two main alternative directions being considered by the Rowell-Sirois Commission would have the effect of intensifying sex discrimination in Quebec. If the commission recommended expanding provincial tax powers to allow the provinces to meet their constitutional responsibilities, Quebec women would experience increased levels of taxation without representation. But if the commission recommended an expanded use of the grant-in-aid device to promote provincial action on social security, Quebec women would likely face "further discriminations of the type to which we have referred when discussing the distribution of relief funds."[37] In either case, the commission and the federal government would be promoting, "indirectly, discrimination against women in Quebec which [they] would not presumably authorize directly."[38]

The LWR also addressed the potential objection that acting against Quebec's suffrage regime would violate the terms under which Quebec entered Confederation. Casgrain explained that because the disfranchisement was rooted in statutory law, her proposals left untouched the sanctity of the Quebec Civil Code as guaranteed by the BNA Act.[39] Whatever the logic and ingenuity of these arguments, they failed to persuade the commissioners that the suffrage issue was in any way relevant to their deliberations.

Acting chairman Joseph Sirois (who replaced the ailing N.W. Rowell) began the LWR's question period by declaring flatly: "Of course, there are quite a number of your proposals which are outside the scope of our enquiry."[40] Commission legal advisor and future prime minister Louis St. Laurent then cited a recent court decision upholding British Columbia's disfranchisement of persons of Chinese ancestry. He asked rhetorically: "We still have to admit, have we not, that it is within the jurisdiction of the provinces to restrict the rights of citizenship?"[41] The LWR's legal counsel, Elizabeth Monk, responded by reminding St. Laurent why the commission had been summoned in the first place: "I take it that this Commission has been appointed because the Governments are not satisfied with the interpretation which has been placed upon the BNA Act in the past both by the Judicial Committee and by our own courts."[42] St. Laurent ignored her response.

Thus, a commission charged with re-evaluating Canada's distribution of legislative powers invoked formalistic jurisdictional arguments to avoid substantive debate. The contrast with its treatment of male social movement witnesses is significant. For example, the commissioners engaged Buck of the CP at length on the history of international communism and the desirability of violent revolution – topics arguably further from their mandate than was the Quebec suffrage question. Yet acting chairman Sirois, who advised the LWR that its concerns were "outside the scope of our enquiry," told Buck to "take all the time you need."[43] True to their word, the commissioners engaged Buck in a wide-ranging and respectful question period, the transcript of which ran a remarkable sixty-one printed pages. Indeed, Communist planks such as extensive wealth redistribution and the nationalization of industry had much broader implications for provincial jurisdiction than did the single constitutional amendment requested by the LWR.

So why was the LWR received so dismissively by the Royal Commission? As we have already seen, policy makers as well as leaders on the traditional left viewed the Great Depression as a particularly male tragedy; public discussion revolved around men's diminished capacity to serve as breadwinners and tended to neglect the specific economic problems facing women.[44] Furthermore, in deciding to protest this neglect, the LWR faced an additional difficulty. As Catherine Lyle Cleverdon's pioneering study of Canadian suffragism reports, an era that equated acceptable femininity with submissiveness also derided politically minded women as "old harpies, invariably childless and detesting babies."[45]

The LWR aimed to pre-empt this type of silencing tactic by striking a posture that the sociologist Erving Goffman sometimes finds among dominated groups in rigidly hierarchical settings: "strategic modesty."[46] Although Casgrain would write angrily in her memoirs of "the scornful and haughty attitude of our masculine elite towards women," she concluded her presentation with a demure appeal to the chivalry of the commissioners: "We would ask for your kind consideration in view of the fact that we are very sincere."[47] And while the LWR presentation had begun by calling for a women's equality "clause [to] be inserted in the ... BNA Act," strategic modesty led Casgrain to conclude on a contradictory note: "We would like to say that we are not trying to force any amendment to the BNA Act."[48]

The LWR also tried to harmonize its platform with conventional gender norms by invoking the maternal-feminist position that women's unique experiences as mothers could bring significant benefits to political life. As historian Alison Prentice and her co-authors note, one riposte to the insistence that women's delicate nature made them unsuited to politics was that women "had special experience and values that would ... establish order and well-being ... for the country."[49] LWR delegates took this position when they argued that Quebec suffered from a general backwardness in social policy that only women's enfranchisement could remedy. In particular, both league presenters spoke at length about Quebec's high rates of infant mortality, a discussion that Monk summarized in the following terms: "We have collected these vital statistics [on infant mortality] not only because they were so horrifying but because ... it is part of our thesis ... that in countries in which women have the vote ... a great deal of attention is given to questions like these, and social questions immediately come into prominence."[50]

However, the commission used this maternal appeal as a warrant for diverting the discussion away from political rights for women. Monk, after besting St. Laurent over the question of the commission's mandate and scope, had raised the issue of infant mortality as a conciliatory way of restating the case for enfranchisement. St. Laurent seized this opportunity to conclude the LWR's question period on a less threatening topic. Noting that Ontario had recently adopted the practice of "enforcing [the] pasteurization of milk," which experts believed beneficial for infant health, he asked: "Has the league any opinion as to the possibility of a similar measure in the province of Quebec?"[51] Although milk pasteurization was unambiguously a topic of provincial jurisdiction, it evidently fell within what St. Laurent regarded as the appropriate domain of his witnesses.

The presentation of the other major women's organization to appear before the commission, the NCW, focused exclusively on the constitutional position of marriage law in Canada. As that group's representative explained in detail, the treatment of marriage under the 1867 division of powers was causing considerable confusion. The BNA Act gave Ottawa the exclusive power to legislate in relation to the validity of marriage, yet it gave the provinces legislative authority over the solemnization of marriage.[52] The NCW's main complaint about this state of affairs was that Quebec authorities were using the solemnization provision to annul inter-religious or "mixed" marriages involving Catholic Quebecers if those marriages had not been performed by a Catholic priest. Thus, the NCW requested that the BNA Act be amended so that any marriage that had been duly solemnized anywhere in Canada would be legally valid throughout the country.[53]

The historian Veronica Strong-Boag recounts that "faith in ... women's maternal nature ... justified the Council's very existence and every intervention of women outside the home." Yet she also notes that the women of the NCW were "reformers" and "apprentice social critics."[54] For example, during the Great Depression the council advocated federal legislation on wages, hours, and working conditions, the equal right of women to unemployment relief, and the right of married women to seek employment.[55] Explaining why the records of the NCW's presentation do not convey this progressive focus will require some elaboration.

The council's Rowell-Sirois brief was the product of considerable labour. Minutes of the 1938 NCW convention reveal that the council executive had not "realized in deciding to send forward such a brief, the amount of work entailed in preparation." The brief's title, "The Political and Civil Status of Women," also conveyed a more ambitiously political focus than anything seen in the NCW's earlier years.[56] However, because the Rowell-Sirois Commission's transcripts of citizen testimony are of briefs as read, not as submitted, only the council's position on what it called the "marriage question" is available for analysis. Yet the choice to focus exclusively on marriage was made neither by the commission nor by the council. It was instead made by the NCW's honorary solicitor, Everett Bristol, who presented the organization's brief on behalf of the council's absent executive members, who on the day of their scheduled appearance were attending the annual NCW convention in Vancouver.

Bristol began his remarks by depicting the NCW women as dilettantes for whom politics was a diversion. He confessed to having had "very limited opportunity" to discuss with his "fair clients" the council's brief, "which they themselves have prepared." This lack of consultation did not prevent him from suggesting that "a number of the submissions in the brief are probably not within the purview of the Commission."[57] The issues that he deemed irrelevant included "such matters as the political status of women, their position in the civil service and under the Bankruptcy Act, and so on." Bristol also described the council's demand for federal legislation on wages, hours, and conditions of work as a matter upon which he "need not dwell."[58] Explaining that the "commission [had] undoubtedly received representations from other bodies" on the subject, he seemed to suggest that the views of male-dominated organizations could easily substitute for those of his clients.[59] Yet the council was urging legislation guaranteeing women equal pay and the equal right to work; clearly, it believed that women's economic interests required independent advocacy.

The council's convention minutes touched with a secondary emphasis on "the resolution being submitted on the marriage question"; yet Bristol transformed their brief on the "Political and Civil Status of Women" into one dwelling exclusively on marriage.[60] Much like St. Laurent, Bristol seemed less interested in respecting the mandate of the commission than in policing the purview of women. The marriage issue, Bristol declared, "goes to the root of the basis of our national life, the home, the family, and therefore is most important to women."[61] Thus, marriage law joined infant mortality rates and milk pasteurization as topics on which male elites seemed prepared to countenance women's opinions. Bristol's approach testifies further to the confining nature of maternal-feminist appeals; the symbolic capital that was most readily available to women also served as men's opportune justification for restricting their political input to a narrow list of acceptable issues.

### The Rowell-Sirois Hearings: Voice, Security, and the Attractions of Constitutional Politics

Social movements representing women and working-class men participated enthusiastically in a Royal Commission charged with reconsidering the fundamentals of Canadian governance. Eager to revisit the country's "economic and financial basis [and] distribution of legislative powers," progressive actors welcomed this unprecedented opportunity to press for a national welfare state.[62] A policy-minded observer might lament the relative inattention paid to matters of program financing, design, and implementation in these presentations. However, equality seekers had virtually no experience as policy community participants in what was then an embryonic and utterly business-dominated system of sectoral representation.[63] As a result, marginalized groups came to view constitutional politics as a new forum of civic voice for the unheard and the oppressed.

It is crucial to emphasize the extent to which histories of exclusion and disrespect determined the content and style of the social movements' presentations. In terms of content, for example, long-standing problems of employer coercion and state oppression forced both the TLC and the CP to dwell on considerations that were essentially preliminary to the economic advocacy that was the top priority for working-class organizations during the Depression. Proponents of welfare state solutions in the 1930s all had to grapple with a range of obstacles, including constitutional interpretation, federal-provincial relations, Quebec nationalism, and the role of the JCPC. That said, socialists and trade unionists faced barriers that were more dangerous as well as more fundamental.

In a polity that often denied them the elementary freedoms of speech, association, and assembly, left-wing activists encountered extraordinary difficulties in promoting their economic agendas, and sometimes even in just meeting to discuss them. This reality meant that only the most ineffectual of representatives would have seen their task before the Rowell-Sirois Commission as a matter of reciting the contents of the traditional left's favoured industrial and social policies. Instead, the TLC and CP spokesmen were equally concerned to advance a democratizing agenda of trade union recognition, civil liberties, fundamental freedoms, and political participation.

Women and working-class men also faced more subtle participatory barriers rooted in their stigmatization as somehow unfit to share fully in the exercise of political power. Keenly aware of these barriers, equality-seeking movements paid close attention to stylistic and rhetorical concerns of the sort that Goffman calls matters of "impression management."[64] For instance, the impeccably respectful TLC positioned itself as the voice of Canada's skilled craftsmen as against the less reputable entities of mere labourers. And even the radical CP, by emphasizing the male breadwinner's fight to protect home and hearth from the forces of the Depression, took care to harmonize its approach with mainstream understandings of gender and duty.

The TLC and the CP were marginalized groups in the broader Canadian scheme of things, yet the commission accepted them as important participants in a crisis defined as men's business. Women's problems of impression management were more daunting. The LWR and NCW were accepted as speakers on infant mortality and marriage law; but their male interlocutors – and, in the case of the NCW, their male representative as well – refused to consider seriously any of the core positions that women themselves sought to discuss.

Women's uniquely weak position in Canada's first public constitutional debates can be underscored by noting the counterproductive character of maternalism as a source of symbolic capital. When the LWR invoked women's maternal expertise, it only made it easier for the commissioners to ignore Quebec women's disfranchisement and economic hardship in favour of discussing the evidently more congenial topics of milk pasteurization and infant mortality. The NCW's own solicitor used maternalism to similar ends, thus relieving the commissioners from having to undertake the avoidance tactics they had used against the LWR delegation. From the standpoint of framing strategies, women's social movements were trapped in a dilemma. Because maternal domesticity was prized as a civilizing bulwark against the "competition, self-interest, and economic aggression" of public life in capitalism, eschewing maternal-feminist appeals would have meant threatening men's "haven in a heartless world" while sacrificing the only socially acceptable language with which they could speak to a predominantly anti-feminist society.[65]

This chapter has shown that social movements were frustrated by an elitist and closed political system. They had been silenced routinely by problems of oppression and disrespect and were therefore enthusiastic about the new opportunities to participate in constitutional politics. The main conceptual point I want to draw from this account is that the themes which analysts have sometimes treated as distinctly contrasting dispositions associated with distinct movement types are in fact closely interconnected. Most notably, New Politics theory rests on a "basic distinction between the material needs for physiological sustenance and safety and nonphysiological needs, such as those for esteem, self-expression, and aesthetic satisfaction." Scholars use this distinction to contrast a materialist or traditional-left focus on matters of economic and physical security with a postmaterialist or "new" social movement emphasis on "free speech," "participation," and "belonging, self-expression, and the quality of life."[66]

The movement interventions considered in this chapter do not map easily onto the distinction between materialism and postmaterialism. For example, the presentations by the TLC and the CP consistently raised issues of civil liberties and political participation despite the obvious economic urgency of the Depression context. And feminists undoubtedly prioritized women's civic belonging and self-expression, but they also strongly emphasized economic issues such as women's access to employment opportunities and social programs.

Although one response to this apparent puzzle is to say that interwar Canadian social movements pursued an eclectic range of concerns, this chapter has found a coherence in the various presentations that belies any claim of eclecticism. The key to understanding this coherence is the foundational character of equality-seeking movements as responses to exclusion and disrespect. By focusing on this character, this chapter has highlighted key interrelationships among themes that the New Politics approach tends to treat as conflicting alternatives. For example, when Communists and trade unionists argued for enhanced opportunities for participation and a national charter of rights, they were not departing from or modifying an otherwise materialist position. Rather, they were focusing on civil and political rights in order more effectively to pursue left-wing economic solutions in a polity that often denied workers the elementary freedoms of speech, association, and assembly.

Thérèse Casgrain made a similar point about interwar feminist politics when one commissioner suggested that future federal action on social policy might resolve some of the LWR's complaints about the economic position of women in Quebec. Unwilling to entrust women's concerns to male elites, Casgrain emphasized democratic empowerment as a basis of women's economic security: "If you have no power behind your demands you cannot get very far, and that is why we are insisting very much on [enfranchisement]."[67] Of course even enfranchised women faced great difficulties in bringing their economic concerns to the civic arena. An evident belief that women had little to offer on such matters – a belief enforced in this case by the group's own solicitor – meant that the NCW's proposals on women's social security, employment rights, and workplace conditions were not even heard, let alone discussed, by the Rowell-Sirois Commission.

These findings suggest that the New Politics distinction between aspirations for economic security and aspirations for participatory self-expression can sometimes be a faulty approach to understanding social movement struggles in contexts of civic marginalization. Whether it was a feminist group suffering exclusion or a traditional-left organization facing state and police repression, the group's platform stressed democratic voice – not as a departure from concerns about material security, but rather as a vital starting point from which to pursue those concerns. The NCW's presentation amounted to an exception that proved the rule; its enforced silence on both economic matters and women's political participation contradicted the group's own written brief, which stressed economic security and political participation.

Thus, the larger point remains. Focusing on democratic voice as a basis of security – and democratic voice is something the NCW signally lacked – can lead to a richer understanding of social movements' behaviour than distinctions between materialist and postmaterialist movements might sometimes allow. The following chapters will focus particular attention on the important link between social esteem and democratic voice for marginalized groups seeking economic and physical security. Doing so will show that the Canadian constitutional arena was a key venue in which disrespected groups have grappled with problems of esteem and prestige, opening new windows on the Canadian constitutional experience in general and on the contributions of equality-seeking movements in particular.

# 3
# Wartime: Social Esteem and Social Citizenship in the Reconstruction Debates

At the outset of the Second World War, Canada's division of powers and social policy regime seemed much as the Rowell-Sirois Commission had found them. The obvious initial exception was the January 1940 amendment establishing unemployment insurance (UI) as an area of exclusive federal jurisdiction. The biggest expansion of the federal government's social responsibilities since 1867, UI gave millions of workers a more dignified and remunerative alternative to private charity and municipal relief.[1] UI alone thus brought about a major transformation in Canadian citizenship. As historian James Struthers notes: "Whether searching for work or cashing their insurance cheques, Canadians could no longer regard Ottawa in the same way as before [the program's introduction on] 1 August 1940."[2]

Formal changes aside, wartime Canada was moving decisively toward becoming a welfare state. Employing the heightened working-class bargaining power of a military economy and a heady discourse of "reconstruction," which envisioned "a new, more humane ... era in which capitalism was subordinated to social needs," the Canadian left made future egalitarian intervention the sine qua non of domestic political discussion.[3] Interventionist assumptions in fact became so widespread during the war that a new constitutionalism would soon arise to put some of their policy corollaries into effect.[4] Between 1945 and 1968 the weight of voter expectations and the inducement of the grant-in-aid device combined to compel the provinces to accept federal leadership in the construction of a national welfare state.[5] The network of shared-cost programs that emerged from this project strengthened considerably the egalitarian and national dimensions of Canadian citizenship. The era of laissez-faire and classical federalism was over.[6]

To understand the contribution that social movements made to Canada's pivotal reconstruction debates, this chapter studies the hearings of three separate but thematically linked parliamentary committees: the 1940 House of Commons Special Committee on Bill No. 98 Respecting Unemployment Insurance; the 1943 House of Commons Special Committee on Reconstruction and Re-establishment; and the 1943 House of Commons Special Committee on Social Security. Taken collectively, the printed transcripts of their hearings point to the growing power of left-wing reconstruction discourse in the wartime context. As Ottawa positioned its postwar planning as a "morale-building device for war-weary Canadians" – affixing the word *reconstruction* to at least three parliamentary committees, two cabinet advisory committees, and a high-profile government ministry – progressive voices acquired unprecedented political force.[7]

Yet not all progressive voices were equal. The prevailing view of war as an arena of male sacrifice helped the traditional left amplify its reconstruction demands; however, female participants fared no better than they had in front of the Rowell-Sirois Commission. The two political contexts were hardly identical: women's service as war-industry workers and military personnel provided a potential new source of symbolic capital and helped nourish a more oppositional feminist consciousness. However, women had gained no discernible political advantage from what was seen as a temporary and exceptional departure from their proper domestic place.[8]

Discussing the resiliently gendered character of Canada's reconstruction debates will help establish two key points: first, masculinity was an indispensable political resource for the traditional left; and second, the mid-century political role of masculinity – a veritable prerequisite for participating in official discussions on economic policy, income security programs, and postwar planning – reflected a patterned allocation of civic respect that visited significant negative material consequences on women.

Women were treated with remarkable disregard and were often deliberately excluded from the wartime reconstruction debates. Furthermore, they entered the postwar era facing the near certain loss of their wartime jobs, the closure of a promising system of public child care facilities, and virtual exclusion from a UI program that had been crafted to reinforce their economic dependence on men.[9] As a consequence, women and men joined Canada's postwar citizenship regime on unequal footings.[10] Exploring the wartime political origins of these distinct citizenship standings is both an instructive undertaking in its own right and a necessary step toward understanding the later participation of feminist and traditional-left organizations alike in the processes of constitutional reform.

## The 1940 House of Commons Special Committee on Bill No. 98 Respecting Unemployment Insurance

### Trade Unions and the Male Worker's Dignity

The July 1940 hearings of the House of Commons Special Committee on Bill No. 98 Respecting Unemployment Insurance gave witnesses the opportunity to comment on a bill that would become law just one month later. Although UI's design had been essentially settled, the bill itself was the fruit of persistent efforts on the part of Canadian workers' movements.[11] The established craft body, the Trades and Labour Congress (TLC), and its younger rival the All-Canadian Congress of Labour (ACCL), a grouping of the nascent industrial unions, had been calling for a nationwide scheme since 1921 and 1927 respectively.[12] Although a wartime ban had prevented it from appearing at any of the parliamentary hearings of those years, the Communist Party (CP) had already conveyed its "keen desire to get the unemployment amendments through."[13] No women's organizations appeared before the committee.

The bill before the House Special Committee on UI proposed a contributory scheme – one that would base contributions and benefits on the worker's employment income.[14] Adopting the social insurance model was not simply a technical choice; tying benefits to income deliberately brought market notions of differential reward into the program. This approach made UI an inadequate source of income security for low-paid individuals; even so, many workers supported it on the grounds that it framed benefits as a right earned rather than as a stigmatizing form of relief.[15]

At the same time, deviations from the social insurance model were required to satisfy a further set of psychological cum moral concerns. Thus the bill combined special supplementary allowances for claimants with dependants – a category that included wives as well as children – with a number of special restrictions to inhibit women's use of UI. As Ruth Roach Pierson explains, by ensuring that "women's principal access to benefit[s] would be through the indirect channel of dependants' allowances" paid to husbands, these provisions were designed to shore up the breadwinner status of men.[16]

Both the craft TLC and the industrial ACCL supported the long-awaited UI legislation.[17] Yet the two groups used their time before the House committee differently. TLC President Tom Moore, whose organization "nurtured its connections with government," accepted from the outset that critics would find shortcomings "in this measure or perhaps any that could be drafted."[18] Accordingly, when a committee member asked about the bill's provisions for denying benefits to workers for reasons of strike involvement or job loss due to misconduct, Moore signalled his trust in the UI Commission that would be charged with adjudicating contested claims: "It is built up out of a mass of experience over a period of time, and that has been found much more effective than attempting to devise strict regulations."[19] On this and other questions, the ACCL took a more critical course, reflecting its propensity to launch "slashing attacks on any government which failed to follow what was thought to be the proper course." Thus it vowed to "watch carefully the application" of the disqualification rules, particularly "regarding Trade Union Activity."[20]

Although labour historians disagree on the extent and political implications of the difference, craft and industrial unionism embodied distinctive visions of labour organization.[21] Craft unions were content to represent the "respectable" segment of the working class; their more ambitious industrial counterparts aimed to "organize the unorganized."[22] During the UI debates this difference manifested itself as a disagreement over the character of UI as a tool of social policy. The upstart ACCL hoped to turn UI into an explicitly redistributive program providing special assistance for low-wage earners; for its part, the TLC urged that the plan be "actuarially sound" – that it be run strictly as an insurance program, with benefits pegged to claimants' contributions.[23]

The TLC underlined its opposition to a redistributive scheme by recalling the humiliation associated with Depression-era relief programs. As Moore explained: "This Act does not take into account the social need. But in my opinion the worker would sooner take the benefits under unemployment insurance and maintain his independence in getting them as a right than take the higher rate and have to prove his destitution and disclose all his family affairs to investigators and be subject to general scrutiny."[24] This was no mere rhetoric: Moore's stance reflected an attitude common among skilled men from the upper reaches of the working class, a group whose "testy sense of manhood, dignity, and sturdy independence" had even stood as a barrier to accepting relief in times of need.[25]

However, the more solidarity-minded ACCL was not indifferent to questions of masculine dignity. It sought to explain how UI could redistribute income without stigmatizing its beneficiaries. Stressing that "the

individual workers are not responsible for unemployment," ACCL President Norman Dowd began his presentation by invoking the principle
that "the cost of maintaining unemployed workers should be a direct
charge upon industry" rather than a matter of public charity.[26] Acknowledging that business was unlikely to accept this scheme, he then introduced the ACCL's fallback proposal for a redistributive UI program. In
this more modest vision, low-income workers could receive benefits but
would be exempt from paying premiums, so long as industry – "as now
organized," in Dowd's cocky phrase – refused to accept its responsibility.[27] In effect, the ACCL was proposing an enriched scheme of social
assistance benefits for unemployed low-wage earners that would spare
them the indignity of having to appear before relief officers as charity
cases.

Yet the otherwise bold and energetic young organization expressed
no similar interest in women's dignity and autonomy. For example,
although the proposed UI Act explicitly denied coverage to workers in
such female-dominated professions as schoolteaching, nursing, and
domestic service, the ACCL presentation focused on the exclusion of
"lumbering, logging, and the like."[28] Indeed, far from seeking to promote women's independent access to UI, the ACCL treated women's
interest in economic security solely as a matter of increasing the special
dependants' allowances for breadwinners. As Dowd explained: "The
differentials in benefits payable to single and married workers are not
regarded as adequate." Thus, while the ACCL wanted UI to be "of assistance to the family as a whole," it reserved its concerns about dignity
and autonomy for men.[29]

### The 1943 House of Commons Special Committee on Reconstruction and Re-Establishment

Trade Unions: Demanding Their Due
Three years of tremendous change separated the public hearings of the
House UI Committee from those of the 1943 House of Commons Special Committee on Reconstruction and Re-Establishment. As indicators
of political transformation, two developments stand out in particular:
the year 1943 set a Canadian record for number of strikes and total
number of workers involved and the social democratic Co-operative
Commonwealth Federation (CCF) had become a serious contender for
government.[30] Intensifying this atmosphere of political ferment was
Ottawa's ongoing failure to address labour's growing list of concerns.
Although workers had launched bitter protests over their long hours,

their inadequate wages (which had been frozen at 1929 levels), and their employers' refusal to engage in bargaining over these issues, in each case the imperative to maintain war production had led the federal government to side with the employers.[31]

This explosive situation led even the respectable TLC to start questioning its customary posture of deference and official non-partisanship.[32] For instance, its 1943 presentation to the Reconstruction Committee used phrases such as "architects of depression" and "gross mismanagement" – pejoratives absent from the TLC's UI Committee and Rowell-Sirois appearances.[33] Perhaps this changed behaviour also reflected frustration with the King administration's growing openness to the craft organization's competitor, the new Canadian Congress of Labour (CCL). Shortly after a fall 1940 merger between the industrial-union ACCL and the like-minded Congress of Industrial Organizations (CIO) created the CCL as the largest trade union umbrella group in Canada, the TLC began losing its long-standing monopoly over labour representation on federal boards and agencies.[34]

The newly truculent TLC focused considerable energy on one of labour's traditional concerns: the worker's need for dignity and respect. The TLC's wariness toward the extensive network of social programs outlined in the much-discussed Marsh Report, which Ottawa had commissioned as part of its reconstruction plans, exemplified this focus. Although the Marsh Report was "better than nothing at all," the TLC preferred "social security in its full sense": employment for "every citizen of Canada [who is] able and willing to work."[35] Furthermore, TLC Acting President Percy Bengough warned the committee that his members would not accept public works programs that reflected the 1930s philosophy that "twice as many could be put to work if a half-sized shovel was used." He concluded: "We can state emphatically that the workers of Canada want no more of that kind of treatment ... They want, and have a right to expect, useful creative employment with a decent standard of living."[36]

These remarks irked the pro-business majority on the Reconstruction Committee. For instance, Mr. McDonald disputed Bengough's assertion that labourers on public works projects deserved the benefits of automation: "During the period of depression I noted some cases where unemployment work was being carried on ... where the machine was doing the work and the men stood looking on, drawing relief payments at the same time." A similarly affronted Mr. Purdy satirized the TLC's reconstruction demands by asking, "You have no formula for regulating the weather ... have you?"[37]

Bengough's claim that "gross mismanagement" and "architects of depression" were to blame for the past decade's economic catastrophe was especially provocative.[38] Mr. McDonald demanded proof that "anybody benefited financially from the last depression" and was not satisfied with the reply that "if people sit down to a game, they cannot all lose. Somebody has to win."[39] Bengough then attempted to explain his larger point – that depressions could be averted through deliberate government action – by relating an apocryphal tale about how the repeated circulation of a fake ten-dollar bill had saved a small town from economic decline.[40] Fearing that the TLC presentation was not serving the cause of social democracy well, CCF members on the committee began to offer their assistance. Most notably, Clairie Gillis, a "tough, eloquent miner" from Cape Breton, offered a critique of capitalism that proceeded for five pages of print, with occasional interruptions from incredulous Liberal and Tory members but none from a silenced Bengough.[41] When the chairman pointed out that "we have a witness here and he is an audience rather than the one giving testimony," Gillis defended the CCF intervention: "We are merely trying to help him out. We belong to the same class."[42]

Although the reconstruction platforms of the craft TLC and the industrial CCL were virtually identical, the latter's presentation was the more successful by far. Like the TLC, the CCL argued for sustained federal economic intervention to achieve full employment, an extensive program of public works, and a comprehensive social welfare regime. One theme seemingly unique to the CCL was its emphasis on worker participation. Yet the TLC's official 1943 reconstruction pamphlet demanded that labour be recognized as "an equal partner in industry and that representatives be appointed, after consultation with organized labour, on such boards, commissions ... already established, or those which in future may be set up."[43] Perhaps the diversion caused by his inability to substantiate the "architects of depression" remark prevented Bengough from attending adequately to the rest of his organization's platform. In support of this assumption, we can observe that the CCL's new director of research, the constitutional expert and future senator Eugene Forsey, enjoyed a full fourteen pages of presentation time before submitting to the committee's examination, while the beleaguered Bengough managed just over three.

Forsey spoke at length about the importance of democratic administration in the future postwar order, an emphasis that reflected labour's deep discontent with the wartime regime of wage and price controls. As Forsey explained, "in almost every case it is the business men themselves who have operated the controls." Accordingly, the CCL insisted on the democratization of the existing controls, of the anticipated postwar works program, and of the expected interventionist activities of future federal governments more generally.[44] As Forsey put it, workers would no longer "submit to being pushed round ... They will accept the necessary [postwar economic] controls only if those controls are in the hands of their own representatives." "Perhaps no single measure," he concluded, "would do so much to restore labour's waning confidence in government."[45]

Whereas Bengough faltered in the face of the committee's indignation, Forsey received an almost deferential response. The difference was certainly not the result of any delicacy on Forsey's part: he suggested that "the basic distinction between capitalists and non-capitalists is between those who won't starve if they don't work and those who will starve if they don't work"; he boasted that "strong trade unions ... are likely to be far more effective guardians of freedom than the modern corporation"; and he compared "the existing ... capitalist state" to the "very fascism we are now fighting to destroy."[46]

Yet the same committee that chastised the TLC presenter offered quite muted objections in responding to his CCL counterpart. For example, Mr. Hill agreed with Forsey "that there has been a lot of monopoly of capital" and merely suggested that "monopolistic unions ... are using the same power."[47] Whereas Mr. Purdy had accused the TLC of wanting to "regulate the weather," Mr. McNiven simply noted that no government could address "unemployment due to climatic conditions." And although Mr. McDonald had accused the TLC of wanting machines to "do the work" while men drew "relief payments at the same time," his only criticism of the CCL presentation was that its objective of full employment would become impossible once industry caught up "with all the orders for the wants of the people."[48]

A crucial difference between the TLC and CCL appearances was Forsey's masterful performance as a presenter. Bengough recited a list of demands interspersed with homespun anecdotes; in contrast, Forsey offered reasoned positions backed with a blizzard of citations, which he seemed to invoke as weapons for threatening a committee of whose inferior logical and argumentative skills he was certain.[49] This performance intimidated potential critics with the threat of public humiliation.

But performance skills were not all; the mere fact of Forsey's elite status also seemed to play a role. For example, while Bengough was frequently and harshly interrupted, Forsey presided over a parade of honorifics. Members repeatedly addressed "Dr. Forsey," with one member even prefacing his questioning with two "Dr. Forseys" and one "doctor," and the chairman closed the CCL presentation with a "Thank you, Dr. Forsey."[50] Thus, while the CCL and TLC both dispatched representatives to defend the dignity and security of their members, Forsey's academic credentials, intellectual skills, and professional polish garnered his presentation the respectful attention that Bengough's was denied.

## The 1943 House of Commons Special Committee on Social Security

### The National Council of Women: Pigeonholed and Ignored

The 1943 House of Commons Special Committee on Social Security was charged with evaluating a set of public health insurance proposals that Ottawa's reconstruction planners had commissioned from Assistant Deputy Minister of Pensions and National Health, Dr. J.J. Heagerty. Most notably, the Heagerty Report called for a joint federal-provincial program of public health insurance that would require all but indigents to pay a flat-rate annual premium.[51] Like reconstruction planning in general, the hearings on social security provided the King administration with an opportunity to boost flagging morale by demonstrating Ottawa's commitment to postwar reforms.[52] But the hearings also served to channel women's participation into a comparatively narrow sector of demobilization planning, one that male parliamentarians viewed as an appropriate arena for women's involvement.

While the National Council of Women of Canada (NCW) was indeed invited to appear before the Health Insurance Committee, not a single women's group participated in either the House Reconstruction or the UI hearings.[53] The reasons why not are difficult to ascertain, but it seems likely that women's groups had failed to meet the official standard for appearing before a House Committee: "No witness shall be summoned to attend before any committee of the House unless a certificate shall first have been filed with the chairman of such committee, by some member thereof, stating that the evidence to be obtained from such witness is, in his opinion, material and important."[54] The availability of at least one women's group for the hearings on reconstruction was not at issue. The NCW noted at its 1943 annual meeting that "the fact that the National President is resident in Ottawa gives our Organization great opportunity to be called upon at very short notice."[55] Furthermore, as will be seen below, the federal government's past record of excluding women from postwar planning suggests that their exclusion from the UI and reconstruction hearings was simply par for the course.

Women had complained about their absence from Ottawa's reconstruction activities as early as 1941. As historian Gail Cuthbert Brandt recounts, the Canadian Federation of Business, the Professional Women's

Clubs, and the League for Women's Rights (LWR) each wrote to Ottawa that year outlining "the importance of the contribution which Canadian women were making to the war effort and their keen interest in post-war planning."[56] However, instead of inviting women's groups to participate in any of the established reconstruction venues, Cabinet responded by creating a separate Advisory Committee on the Post-War Problems of Women. The narrowly defined role of this committee was to compile information about women workers and then report to the Cabinet Advisory Committee on Reconstruction. As Brandt explains, moreover, the parent Advisory Committee submitted its final report to Cabinet before bothering even to hear from the Women's Subcommittee, whose work was thus "pigeon-holed and forgotten."[57]

Although it did not send one of the 1941 letters, the NCW was certainly interested in postwar reconstruction. Historian N.E.S. Griffiths notes that "one of the most important events" of 1943 for the NCW was the development and circulation of its Program for Post-War Planning.[58] Drawn up by a Special Committee of Council on Reconstruction after a series of consultations with the national organization's local councils, this program contained eleven sections. It called for future international initiatives to prevent war, further consideration of the Rowell-Sirois Report, a postwar scheme of social security, the eight-hour day, a national minimum wage, more appointments of women to federal boards and agencies, and women's right to equal pay for equal work.[59] Thus, women's exclusion from the reconstruction debates makes the complaint in Mrs. Edgar Hardy's 1943 NCW Presidential Address seem particularly apt: "We hear often, generally from men, the remark that 'after the war women will go back to the kitchen' ... We are in effect being told what we are to do before we have been given the chance to express what we intend to do."[60]

One way of sidetracking aspiring female participants was by assigning them the fruitless task of compiling information for an indifferent Cabinet Advisory Committee: the House Social Security Committee served a roughly analogous function. As will be seen below, the members of what amounted to Canada's sole parliamentary venue for women's input on matters of reconstruction saw the NCW's appearance as a token formality requiring neither debate nor even opportunity for argument.

Hardy began her brief testimony by restating the health insurance recommendations from the NCW's Program for Post-War Planning. As she explained, the NCW "asked for ... Dominion leadership" in establishing a three-tiered scheme, which would feature private coverage for the wealthy, contributory public insurance for those of medium and low incomes, and publicly financed insurance for those "unable to pay."[61] In what was perhaps a subtle gesture of defiance, she then noted the broader focus on "other social insurances" in the NCW's official reconstruction platform, which her group had been unable to discuss with the Reconstruction Committee. She suggested that Canada's public health objectives could be furthered by "an extension of benefits under the Unemployment Insurance Act [and by the] establishment of a national plan of contributory old age pensions."[62]

Here, the NCW was staking out two possible areas of discussion; it was disagreeing with the Heagerty proposals for a universal insurance scheme, and it was arguing that measures to improve living standards were essential to national health. However, the House Social Security Committee declined to engage the council on either point. Indeed, no member of the committee saw fit to involve the NCW delegation in any exchange of dialogue at all. The committee's record of proceedings reads: "*The Chairman:* 'Are there any questions?' *Witness retired.*"[63]

Yet it must be noted that Hardy was a rather feckless witness. For example, she confessed to her audience that she had "not yet studied the report of the Health Insurance Committee; I am trying to read it, but it is quite a long volume."[64] She also signalled her apparent willingness to forgo the committee's examination, stating that the NCW would "support any plan in principle which will secure for Canada an adequate national health plan."[65] This was a curious stance for her to take, considering that her organization disagreed with the proposals before it and had published its own position under the rubric "National Health and Nutrition" in its Program for Post-War Planning. Hardy's reticent posture is also difficult to square with her 1943 Presidential Address, which proclaimed "aroused indignation" at men's disrespect.[66]

It would seem that qualms about exposing a male audience to feminist indignation dictated a more compliant pose. As Erving Goffman explains in his classic work on the dynamics of social stigma, "the very anticipation" of experiencing negative reactions in social encounters can lead "the stigmatized to arrange life so as to avoid them."[67] Thus, Hardy's variation on this common tactic for pre-empting anticipated disrespect reflects the depth of women's marginalization at the founding of Canada's welfare state.

## Social Esteem, Civic Voice, and Canada's Nascent Welfare State
By mid-war the beginnings of a Canadian welfare state were clearly in view. While a series of parliamentary committees explored new visions of social security and national reconstruction, the path-breaking 1940

UI Act set the stage for such future achievements as collective bargaining, Old Age Security, the Canada Pension Plan, and universal public health insurance. The trade union movement was a significant contributor to these developments. By picketing, protesting, and joining intellectuals and farmers in the freshly invigorated CCF, unionists helped forge a new Canadian citizenship regime that recognized – albeit hesitantly, unevenly, and imperfectly – the claims of working people to equal community membership.

The traditional left's materialism was not narrowly economistic. On the contrary, we can understand its vision of economic security only by grasping its emphasis on autonomy and esteem. Notwithstanding the significant ideological and stylistic differences pitting craft against industrial unionism, both movements advocated a welfare state that would uphold the dignity and social respect of workers. The craft union TLC preferred a strictly contributory UI program to a more financially generous but potentially demeaning plan of enriched assistance; the industrial ACCL designed its redistributive scheme to protect the privacy of low-income beneficiaries. This focus on dignity and respect informed the broader trade union visions of postwar reconstruction. Suspicious of officialdom's new enthusiasm for income assistance programs and public works schemes, the TLC insisted that workers did not want handouts; they preferred "useful creative employment with a decent standard of living."[68] The ACCL's successor, the CCL, had similar worries about technocratic and paternalistic approaches to planning, and warned its parliamentary audience that labour would not "submit to being pushed round."[69]

As the UI debates made particularly clear, the trade unions' emphasis on dignity, autonomy, and respect did not tend to encompass women. The TLC's presentation depicted the male breadwinner as the sole figure whose preferences were to be considered; its president, Tom Moore, assured the committee that "the worker would sooner ... maintain his independence" and refuse benefits under a redistributive scheme than "have to prove his destitution and disclose all his family affairs to investigators and be subject to general scrutiny."[70] The ACCL placed more emphasis on women's needs, yet in advocating a program that "would be of assistance to the family," it shared the TLC's gendered assumptions about respect. Its proposal to increase the "benefits payable to ... married workers," which relied euphemistically on gender-neutral language, suggests that the ACCL viewed women as faceless dependants.[71]

The reconstruction debates were structured around the economic, psychological, and status needs of men; as a result, women found it almost impossible to convey their political aspirations and complaints. Largely excluded from the main hearings on economic policy and post-war planning, they were diverted to afterthought venues like the Advisory Committee on the Post-War Problems of Women, which the parent Cabinet Advisory Committee on Reconstruction chose to ignore. At the same time, authorities continued the Rowell-Sirois tradition of attempting to confine women's political input to matters such as childbirth and health. Thus, the NCW was invited, as were the Canadian Nurses Association, Fédération des femmes Canadiennes françaises, the Catholic Women's League of Canada, and the Victorian Order of Nurses, to participate in the relatively inconsequential House Social Security Committee deliberations on public health insurance. Yet even in this ostensibly sanctioned arena of women's involvement, Canada's leading national women's organization was not accorded the customary opportunity to answer parliamentarians' questions and engage in debate.

It is reasonable to assume that the indifference of the male-dominated traditional left and the exclusionary tactics of federal political elites had negative material consequences for Canadian women. After all, these factors virtually guaranteed that the wartime feminist emphasis on women's rights to work, equal pay, social program benefits, and child care programs would not figure in official political discussion.[72] Feminist students of the welfare state have certainly noted the phenomenon. As the sociologist Ann Shola Orloff notes, "if women do not participate in [its] formation ... social policy ... is unlikely to translate into women's social citizenship."[73] Yet despite their importance, the dearth of opportunities for formal participation was only one part of the problem. As this chapter has shown, although Canadian women complained of their exclusion from reconstruction planning and condemned sexism at their own meetings, the actual participation of Canada's leading national women's organization bore the self-defeating hallmarks of adjustment to a demeaning civic status.

Hardy's interactions with her parliamentary audience could not have been more different from those of her male counterparts. Although unversed in the details of economic policy, the TLC's Bengough did not hesitate to speak in a frankly confrontational way. And while many members considered his analysis outrageously uninformed, they still engaged him in a spirited debate. Similarly, Forsey's professional credentials and self-confidently technical arguments conveyed his status as an expert. The committee's majority was not friendly to the CCL research director's social democratic views; even so, they responded with a highly respectful round of questioning, acknowledging that their witness was "well travelled and well versed in this matter."[74]

This is not to say that men invariably prevailed simply because they were male. The House Reconstruction Committee responded to the aggressive 1943 TLC presentation with disrespectful attacks that virtually silenced Bengough. The far more positive reception accorded to Forsey's almost identical complaints reflects both the benefits of the confident polish of professional status and the symbolic and interactional disadvantages that working people can often face in the civic arena. Nevertheless, whether they were unschooled critics or polished experts, the male participants expected and received the basic courtesy of questioning, argument, and debate.

At least in theory, the shock value of Bengough's outrage and the intellectual force of Forsey's erudition were both potentially available political resources for the NCW. As her Presidential Address confirmed, Hardy did not lack "aroused indignation."[75] Griffiths has observed more generally that a "note of independence and conviction ... was present throughout the Council deliberations of 1943."[76] And with a membership structure that included the Canadian Dietetic Association, the Health League of Canada, the University of Toronto Medical Alumnae, and the Victorian Order of Nurses, the NCW certainly possessed ample expertise in the health care field.[77] Yet profound problems of marginalization and disrespect led Hardy to downplay her organization's concerns and perspectives almost to the point of silence.

Little wonder that the male-dominated organizations of the traditional left placed such heavy emphasis on the breadwinner's dignity and social esteem. In a context that defined problems of unemployment, demobilization, and income security as "men's business," maleness was a crucial prerequisite for successful civic participation. As we have seen, citizens without this elementary attribute tended to become the voiceless subjects of the unchecked decisions of others.

# 4
# The Postwar Identity Emphasis: Rights, Universalism, and Virtue

With a new consensus on federal intervention in place, the work of building a Canadian welfare state fell to a growing corps of line department bureaucrats and intergovernmental relations specialists.[1] However, Canadians soon encountered a fresh set of constitutional controversies, which addressed questions of rights, diversity, and identity in a postwar context of modernizing Quebec nationalism, declining imperial prestige, and rising immigration from eastern and southern Europe. The new focus heightened constitutional awareness and involvement among ethnocultural minorities, whose ensuing advocacy stamped Canada's postwar citizenship regime with a pioneering emphasis on multiculturalism and human rights.

The early postwar development of this emphasis is a prominent theme in this chapter's analysis of the following three arenas of constitutional debate and reform: the 1950 Senate Special Committee on Human Rights and Fundamental Freedoms, the 1960 House of Commons Special Committee on Human Rights and Fundamental Freedoms, and the Royal Commission on Bilingualism and Biculturalism ("the B&B Commission"), which held public hearings between 1963 and 1965.

Many of the key structural factors behind Canada's postwar shift toward a constitutional politics of rights, diversity, and identity feature in the New Politics account of a transition from a materialist focus on safety and security to a postmaterialist politics of esteem and belonging.[2] The absence of war and Depression opened space for new political concerns; and as a consequence, successive generations grew more confident in their personal fortunes and less authoritarian and chauvinistic in their attitudes. At the same time, a dramatic expansion of opportunities for postsecondary study in the social sciences and humanities – itself a result of the era's unprecedented prosperity – provided vital institutional support for an ethic of individual freedom and respect for difference.

The postmaterialism narrative is less helpful when it comes to the more specific ideational and political context surrounding the immediate postwar focus on human rights. A slowly but steadily growing Holocaust awareness promoted a revivified Enlightenment ideal as a shield against future totalitarian calamity, providing anti-discrimination themes with a political force that the morally inert fact of prosperity could not. The touchstone for this new politics of memory was the 1948 United Nations Universal Declaration of Human Rights, which proclaimed that the "recognition of the inherent dignity and of the equal and inalienable rights of all members of the human family is the foundation of freedom, justice, and peace in the world."[3]

The clearest early outcome of this emphasis was a growing commitment to formal equality, which, to offer some Canadian examples, led to the enfranchisement of Asian Canadians in 1947, of Inuit in 1950, and of Status Indians in 1960.[4] Many commentators have characterized this trend as part of a longer-term Western shift away from allocating rights in accordance with stereotyped views of citizen virtue and toward regimes of what the critical theorist Axel Honneth calls "legal universalism."[5] However, actually using one's citizenship rights to participate in the postwar public sphere could still be a different matter. As this chapter will show in the Canadian case, the social esteem accorded to individuals on the basis of their group membership continued to be a significant basis of informal political distinction. Members of disrespected groups were often slighted, ignored, or insulted in civic interaction, and faced an array of discursive tactics oriented toward enforcing their customary role as the silenced subjects of their putative betters.

By examining the postwar constitutional participation of Canadian marginalized groups, this chapter will raise questions about the New Politics interpretation of the increased postwar emphasis on esteem and belonging. That interpretation contrasts the traditional left's materialist struggles for safety and security with a more recent, postmaterialist focus on esteem and belonging, and it explains the shift to the latter focus by arguing that increased economic and physical security allowed a distinctly novel set of priorities to emerge. As this chapter will show, Canadian minority leaders, in particular, responded to persistent problems of exclusion and marginalization by developing a politics of esteem and belonging that stressed the unappreciated virtues of their constituencies. However, they were not engaging in postmaterialist behaviour;

they were seeking precisely to advance the capacity of their groups to pursue material security interests.

## The 1950 Senate Special Committee on Human Rights and Fundamental Freedoms

### Social Esteem and Security: Jewish Canadians, Japanese Canadians, and Communists

The 1950 Senate Special Committee on Human Rights and Fundamental Freedoms was a direct Canadian response to the 1948 UN Declaration, whose goals signatory nations had pledged to promote within the scope of their respective sovereign capacities. In Canada's case, this proved a contentious undertaking. A preparatory inquiry conducted by the 1947 Special Joint Committee on Human Rights and Fundamental Freedoms, which consulted only government officials and experts, concluded that any attempt to entrench a domestic version of the Declaration would cause "a considerable provincial rights controversy."[6]

Nevertheless, international commitments made in an atmosphere of postwar moral reckoning dictated that the 1950 Senate Special Committee would proceed. Its public hearings offered witnesses the opportunity to express their views on the desirability of entrenching a justiciable Canadian bill of rights based on the thirty articles of the UN Declaration.[7] Although the provincial rights objection would remain decisive until the landmark "kitchen accord" agreement on the 1982 Charter of Rights and Freedoms, the 1950 hearings provided an entry point for actors and concerns which up to that point had been almost entirely unheard in the Canadian civic arena.

The Canadian Jewish Congress (CJC) was among the most enthusiastic of the committee's witnesses to argue in support of a domestic bill of rights. Yet despite its enthusiasm, the CJC did not buttress its case for a charter by discussing the Holocaust, mentioning Canada's "none is too many" policy on wartime Jewish refugees, or even emphasizing the more routine instances of domestic anti-Semitism.[8] Instead, the CJC argued that a more energetic respect for human dignity would help achieve peace and security for the world as a whole. Congress Vice-President Monroe Abbey began by reminding his audience that the focus on the "common denominator of our humanity" in the "Universal Declaration ... bespeaks the urgent desire to find the way to lasting peace." The "very force of its moral implications," he continued, "imposes upon the signatory the necessity of extending its provisions in the realm over which that sovereignty has power."[9]

The CJC's silence on anti-Semitism eventually prompted the committee's Senator Kinley to ask forthrightly: "Is there any discrimination in this country that can be especially complained of, or do you regard it as an absolutely free country where you have the same privileges as everyone else?"[10] In response, CJC National Director Saul Hayes mentioned the problems of employment discrimination and restrictive covenants (which aimed to prevent the sale of designated properties to Jews), as well as the exclusion of Jews from various commercially operated entertainment and recreation facilities. Yet Hayes then hedged these examples: "By and large the record of Canada is particularly excellent." As he explained: "These are unfortunate situations. Where they are unimportant we don't feel, as a minority group, that it is worthwhile starting a terrific fight about them."[11]

Sociologist Yaacov Glickman reports that this "quiet diplomacy" approach reflected the cautious pessimism of an organization surrounded by "anti-Jewish and antiethnic sentiments."[12] Instead of provoking its audience with aggressive complaints of Canadian wrongs, the CJC chose to tailor its presentation to the majority's self-interest. As Hayes stoically put it, although discrimination "hurts ... the person discriminated against, we accept that as a penalty." More important was "the effect on the total community ... when you allow one pattern of citizenship to be imposed on one group and another upon another group."[13]

This strategy of quiet diplomacy distinguished carefully between advocating formal equality and impugning the prejudices of dominant groups. The CJC allowed repeatedly that "the Jewish community do not pretend to have all the virtues," that "in given cases Jewish people are [not] without fault," that "people are entitled to their likes and dislikes," and that "there can be no law of the land which says that people must like each other."[14] By insisting that it was seeking only a formally equal citizenship and that it would refrain from targeting the "likes and dislikes" of others, the CJC was making it clear that it was not proposing a direct challenge to Canada's existing distribution of social esteem.

Yet even this attempt to discuss human rights at the highest possible and thus least controversial level of generality appeared to spark the resentment that dominant majorities often reserve for "special interests." For instance, Kinley objected that racial discrimination in Canada was not "altogether a matter of indignity to one element"; he had even "heard of farmers who put up the notice 'No Englishmen need apply.'"[15] Hayes refrained from suggesting that anti-Semitism was perhaps the more pervasive form of discrimination, and professed to be "as much against that."[16]

Kinley seemed won over by this approach. He praised Hayes as "a very intelligent man" and wondered "why [discrimination] should exist with regard to such well-educated people."[17] But this praise reflected nothing if not the prevailing conviction that it was understandable to discriminate against minorities of less agreeable pedigree or comportment. At the same time, the problem of Canadian anti-Semitism – which the CJC, "as a minority group," did not want to start "a terrific fight about" – remained largely unconfronted.[18]

Like the CJC, the National Japanese Canadian Citizens' Association (NJCCA) represented a community traumatized – albeit on a less intensely overwhelming scale – by recent experiences of racist oppression. It also strongly supported the idea of a Canadian charter of rights. Yet unlike the CJC, the NJCCA saw Canada's new focus on human rights as a propitious signal that victimized minorities should begin demanding increased respect.

Executive Secretary George Tanaka commenced his remarks by praising Canada's "growing awareness" and by observing that he was addressing "a body that has, in effect, already shown much sympathy toward the question of human rights."[19] A similar optimism informed the NJCCA's decision to frame the internment experience as a source of moral authority – a stance reflecting its anticipatory judgment that its audience was not a gathering of unrepentant racists. Emphasizing the importance of learning about the "individual experiences" of those who "know the harmful ... effect discrimination has worked upon them," Tanaka suggested that "some aspects of the past experiences of Canadian citizens of Japanese ancestry merit consideration."[20]

The NJCCA's optimism about the new political context was tempered by a sense that the dominant society would require considerable instruction in the new principles of human rights. This understanding shaped the NJCCA's orientation toward the notion of a charter, which it viewed in primarily symbolic terms. Tanaka argued that a bill of rights would be of "tremendous educational significance"; it would serve as a "constant teacher," "promote the idea of the dignity of the human person constantly," and "constitute a powerful force to foster, in the minds of the people, the conviction that discrimination is wrong."[21] That "the minds of the people" were of the sort to require a "constant teacher" was an insinuation that the CJC had been careful to avoid.

Most controversial was the NJCCA's attempt to establish a new consensus on the internment. Tanaka pointed out that "despite their Canadian citizenship status," Japanese Canadians had been deprived "of civil, political, social, and economic human rights on racial grounds."[22] As he explained at some length, the advocates of this treatment had appeared indifferent to the virtues and contributions of the internees: "Canadian Pioneers" of "undivided loyalty," who had "courageously ... determined to build for the future as citizens of Canada," yet whose "half-century's advance toward economic security and success" had been brought to a "drastic and disruptive end."[23]

Committee members responded indignantly to what they viewed as presumptuous effrontery. For example, Kinley noted that it was "always said that the Japanese had two loyalties, that they never became quite separate from their home obligations." Even the committee's avuncular chairman, the dedicated civil libertarian Arthur Roebuck, appeared to second Kinley's slur: "What do you say to that, witness?"[24] The remainder of the NJCCA question period consisted of the committee's extended collective warning – which took the form of a series of rhetorical questions – to be grateful that Canadian law now tolerated a Japanese-Canadian presence: "What remains now?"; "Were you pretty well satisfied up to the time of the war?"; "But that is all cured now?"; "Is that not private? Is that not the attitude of the private employer?"; "The Japanese are allowed now to go back to Vancouver, are they?"; "They are allowed now, are they?"; "Can ... a man of Japanese origin ... engage in the fishing industry now?"; "He can own a boat now?"; "So there is not that objection today?"[25]

Despite the postwar liberal emphasis on inalienable rights as the corollary of our innate human dignity, the view that minorities should not exercise those rights vigorously remained strong. A powerful example of minority political criticism in its own right, the NJCCA's presentation was also an attempt to defuse the specific prejudices behind the belief that Japanese Canadians lacked the informal right to offer political criticism. As Tanaka so poignantly put it: "All our lives we have been forced to bear this taunt ... the suspicion that we were Japs and not loyal to Canada ... I feel very strongly as a Canadian citizen ... I would venture to say without hesitation that if we were permitted to volunteer in the armed forces in 1942 we would have had a large number [of Japanese Canadians] in the Canadian Armed Forces, and I think that in itself would have wiped away a great deal of the fear that was created by Pearl Harbor."[26] By emphasizing this imagery of loyal dedication to Canada and insisting on the unjust nature of the internment, the NJCCA was seeking recognition for Japanese Canadians as legitimate civic participants. As we have seen, the Senate Human Rights Committee responded by rehearsing racist suspicions and by insisting that Japanese

Canadians had no right to criticize the dominant society or its political authorities.

Ann Gomer Sunahara notes that community activists had greeted the conclusion of the Second World War internment operations by insisting that it was "time ... to [force] the Canadian government to acknowledge the injustice," for otherwise "the wartime myths of Japanese Canadian disloyalty would continue."[27] The NJJCA must therefore have found it dispiriting to find so little sympathy from a parliamentary body charged with advancing the cause of human rights; its Senate Committee appearance would be virtually the last organized Japanese-Canadian political intervention until the first stirrings of the internment redress movement in the late 1970s.[28]

The NJCCA had made a direct bid for increased respect, and the CJC had opted for quiet diplomacy; by contrast, Canadian communists took an approach to human rights advocacy that was downright surreptitious. Still operating under the name it had taken in response to the wartime ban on communism, the Labour-Progressive Party, the Canadian Communist Party (CP) established the League for Democratic Rights (LDR) in 1950 as a front organization in order to combat a renewed anticommunist offensive without having to suffer the liabilities of an increasingly disreputable banner.[29] The tone for the Senate Committee's reception of the LDR was set immediately by Senator David, who demanded to know "who are the members of the board."[30] Despite Marx's insistence that "communists should openly, in the face of the whole world, publish their aims, their tendencies," the LDR representative avoided the senator's question.[31]

Instead, spokeswoman Margaret Spaulding emphasized the LDR's enthusiasm for the idea of a bill of rights. "Canada is at the crossroads," she declared; the world's nations were debating the question of human rights, and it was time to lead the way.[32] Citing the UN's assistant secretary-general, she suggested that domestic actions would help determine whether the Universal Declaration of Human Rights was going to be "powerful and far-reaching" in its impact or a "limited, weak, mild ... disaster." For this reason of international contribution alone, she explained, "a Canadian Bill of Rights is sorely needed."[33]

The remainder of the LDR's presentation focused on various domestic injustices in order to illustrate the need for a Canadian charter. Conveying the new, socially progressive commitments of Canada's postwar communist left, Spaulding complained about "discrimination against Negro citizens," condemned the fact that "Indians and Eskimos are segregated in their own schools, given no opportunity for employment, and denied the right to vote," and demanded that "Canadian women ... be placed in a position of complete equality with men."[34]

But the Cold War atmosphere of the early 1950s determined the real thrust of the LDR's presentation. Insisting that "no Canadian should be discriminated against, or refused employment, or penalized in any way because of his or her political beliefs," Spaulding offered an extensive account of anticommunist persecution in Canada.[35] Although some dispute among anglophone and francophone members arose when Spaulding mentioned Quebec's Padlock Act, the committee had no difficulty agreeing that avowed communists were undeserving of human rights protection.[36]

Senators were incredulous at the suggestion that equal rights and liberties should be granted to people who deserved their reputation as treasonous servants of an enemy power. David declared that a communist "could not take the oath of allegiance," while the chairman, Roebuck, argued that in one of the LDR's cited cases, "the victim owed his allegiance to Russia rather than to Canada."[37] "We know," David added, "that a man took the oath of allegiance not to be a traitor to England, and got work on a government project, and was a traitor from the first month he was there." He concluded: "It is a well known fact that a communist would take allegiance to any country, and remain loyal to Russia."[38] The LDR's front-organization strategy prevented Spaulding from rising to communism's defence when confronted with these and similar interventions. She was confined instead to reiterating principle: "We used the cases, sir, to illustrate the lack of protection [for] freedom of expression, which is one of the articles before this committee."[39]

Marx's famous attack on liberal rights posits that anti-discrimination charters encourage political passivity and egoistic individualism by framing politics as a matter of coping with conflicting private interests rather than of realizing human emancipation through collective action.[40] Thus, communism's tremendous unpopularity in Cold War Canada placed the LDR in the paradoxical position of seeking refuge in the liberalism that Marx sought to reject. In at least one key respect, this approach can be regarded as an extreme version of the CJC's quiet diplomacy. Both groups opted for the discourse of legal universalism rather than the rhetoric of virtue and merit, and both saw a charter of rights as potential shelter from the impact of disesteem.

### Retrenching Maternal Virtue: The National Council of Women

Postwar universalism was in some respects a source of encouragement for the National Council of Women (NCW). By 1950, for instance, it had responded to the new international focus by convening two major conferences on women's rights.[41] Universalism also provided the language and the basic impetus for the NCW's main proposal to the Senate Special Committee: "We ... believe that it is of the utmost importance that our Constitution explicitly affirm that [the] fundamental rights [in the UN Declaration] are the equal possession of every citizen without discrimination because of race, religion, language, or sex."[42]

Enthusiasm for the postwar rights agenda also informed the new NCW position that "the principles set forth" in the UN Declaration would require significant federal intervention in support of "social and economic rights." NCW Vice-President Mrs. Robert Dorman emphasized the following rights in particular: "the right to employment and [the going] rate for the job, regardless of sex, race, or marital status; social security and health services ... education [and] ... an adequate standard of living."[43]

Perhaps most strikingly, the NCW reacted to the new political climate by abandoning its traditional practice of invoking maternal virtue to justify a greater political role for women. Dorman instead took the more modern position that "since women are about 50 per cent of the adult population, we regard it as our right that we should have women on the Boards that control and direct many public services." Similarly, she argued that "more women [should] be appointed to the Senate, seeing that about half the population of Canada is female."[44]

But this is not to say that an emboldened NCW believed that questions of virtue were now politically irrelevant. When Dorman turned to explain the NCW's two main proposals for addressing women's economic security needs, the emphasis on maternalism returned. The first proposal urged federal action to guarantee "the wife's right to one-half of the earnings of her husband." Dorman justified this measure by reminding her audience that women's "contribution to the family and the State in bearing and raising children is foremost in the building of any nation."[45] The NCW framed its other economic security plank as a reward for maternal virtue as well. This proposal sought a federal law that would exempt widows from having to pay succession duties. Using language almost identical to Dorman's, the chair of the NCW's Standing Committee on Economics and Taxation, Mrs. Clark Hamilton, pressed Ottawa to honour the widow's "contribution to the building of the estate and her contribution to the state in the bearing and raising of children."[46]

Thus, while the NCW argued for both a charter of rights and political representation in the language of universalism, it framed its measures for advancing women's economic security in terms of maternal virtue. This approach allowed the NCW to temper its emphasis on human rights with a conspicuous embrace of the gender regime that had been partially dislodged by war.[47] As Dorman explained: "In peacetime [women's] contribution is made in many ways. For good homes and well brought-up children, the contribution of women is at least equal to that of men."[48]

Despite the NCW's reassuring emphasis on domesticity, the Senate Human Rights Committee responded with a ritualistically obsessive series of injunctions to observe the established boundaries of gender. For instance, Senator Reid greeted the NCW women's arrival by observing that "these delegations get better looking all the time."[49] This greeting heralded a subsequent question period in which not one senator seriously discussed the NCW's stated views on women's equality rights, economic and social rights, or representation in federal institutions. The following sample of sometimes bizarre digressions captures the tone of the committee's reception: "Children must be brought up right"; "[In] the country from which I came ... if a young man was escorting a young lady and she discovered that there was tuberculosis in his family, the marriage would be called off"; "I suppose you agree that proper discipline is an element of freedom?"; "If a woman had a sizable income and the husband did not, should she share that equally with her husband?"; "[If] we set ourselves forward to saying that we believe in the preservation of the Sabbath, we might be doing something useful."[50]

Unable to engage the senators in meaningful dialogue or debate, Dorman elected to signal the NCW's retreat, stating with sudden finality: "Our contribution has been a short one."[51] As had also been true for Japanese Canadians in particular, a group hoping to use the participation rights of Canada's ostensibly equal framework of postwar citizenship found it exceedingly difficult to do so in a climate of profound disrespect.

## Trade Unions and the Power of the Strike
By 1950, eight Canadian provinces had passed collective bargaining legislation following Justice Ivan Rand's landmark 1946 ruling protecting the mandatory payroll check-off for collecting union dues.[52] Canadian labour had thus secured the major elements of T.H. Marshall's "industrial citizenship": a set of civil rights "parallel with and supplementary to political citizenship" that aims to diminish the vast power differential between owners and workers.[53] This achievement was a significant victory for the vision and methods of industrial unionism, whose craft counterpart soon retreated to its British stronghold. The final de-

velopment came in 1956, when the Trades and Labour Congress (TLC) merged with the Canadian Congress of Labour (CCL) to form today's Canadian Labour Congress (CLC). By leading directly to formal affiliation with the CCF-NDP, this merger signalled the demise of the posture of non-partisan respectability associated with the old TLC.[54]

However, continuity with the interwar past was also to be found: Canadian labour appeared before the 1950 Special Senate Committee hearings as an enthusiastic proponent of a national bill of rights. The CCL declared that a charter was vital to "our very existence as a free society," while the TLC demanded "an immediate avenue for the enactment of ... human rights and fundamental freedoms into the law of Canada."[55] Indeed, much like the traditional left at the Rowell-Sirois hearings, the CCL's excitement about the topic shaded into enthusiasm for constitutional politics itself. As the CCL Director of Research Eugene Forsey explained: "The work of this Committee is ... of the highest importance to Labour and to all Canadian citizens. Indeed, it seems to us so urgent that we feel the Committee should ... arrange to hold hearings in various parts of the country [to] secure invaluable evidence both of the necessity for a Bill of Rights and other protection of fundamental rights and freedoms and of the wide-spread and growing public opinion in favour of such action."[56]

A further point of continuity was labour's relative indifference to federalism. While neither group seemed worried about the impact of a charter on provincial rights, Forsey's CCL was particularly bold. Noting that even the most robust bill of rights could not keep "disastrous invasions of fundamental freedoms" from slipping "through the meshes of the legal nets," Forsey urged Ottawa to rehabilitate the powers of reservation and disallowance as a way of keeping wayward provinces in line: "These powers are important and should be used to protect fundamental rights and freedoms whenever necessary."[57]

Although antecedents exist, Canadian labour's new strong stand against racism suggests that the postwar human rights agenda was having an important effect on the movement; the CCL and TLC took pains to advertise their respective leadership roles in the antiracist struggle.[58] Forsey pointed out that the CCL's National Committee for Racial Tolerance (established in 1946) had undertaken a "careful survey" of the existence of "racial and religious discrimination ... in Canada."[59] Not to be outdone, TLC Research Director and Ontario CCF MPP Leslie Wismer announced that his own organization's Standing Committee to Combat Racial Discrimination (also established in 1946) had offices in the "main trade union and industrial centres." He explained: "As their work has progressed, a better feeling as between members of diverse racial and religious groups has become evident."[60]

Thus, it seems that the emerging postwar consensus linking racism to international violence and insecurity was helping antiracism become a potential basis of domestic prestige. Yet it also appears that the new emphasis on human rights did not include women; neither trade union group saw fit to even mention gender equality, let alone trumpet any actual pro-feminist achievements or commitments.

On the question of which groups might find inclusion in the postwar rights agenda, trade unions were not without problems of their own. When CCL and TLC spokesmen demanded that Canadian authorities refrain from using court injunctions and police intervention to vitiate the new collective bargaining rights, committee members responded by suggesting that special limitations on rights were necessary for a movement notorious for its troublemaking and turbulence.[61] Senator Kinley took issue with the "opinion that labour unions are pure and undefiled," while Senator Baird dismissed Forsey's defence of "entirely peaceful picketing" as disingenuous: "Why do you want picketing if it has to be peaceful?" Kinley, who considered that picketing did not merit protection because it was so often "carried on forcibly," contended that "it rather shocks people in Canada to see the extent to which these things are carried on." Senator David supported Kinley's short speech on the subject by adding that picketing "is more fists than anything, I think."[62]

Given the committee's reliance on negative stereotypes to justify restrictions on trade union freedoms, it is interesting to note that unionists did not envisage using the hoped-for statement of fundamental rights as a tool for undermining prejudices about workers. Perhaps most tellingly, neither the CCL nor the TLC showed an interest in the UN Declaration's proscriptive reference to discrimination on the basis of "social origin, property, birth, or other status" as a source of symbolic capital. This indifference stood in contrast not only to the enthusiasm of Japanese Canadians for the political education function of a charter, but also to labour's own view of the political dynamics of racism. While trade union leaders believed that by "promoting education ... racial and religious prejudice ... [could] be reduced and finally eradicated," they contemplated no similar solution for the manifold injuries of class.[63]

Instead, a preference for the strike weapon as a tool for eliciting respect shaped the orientation of both the TLC and the CCL toward the notion of a bill of rights. For example, the CCL spent seven pages of its presentation arguing for a charter that would be capable of protecting the new collective bargaining rights from diminution. This led one committee member to predict that "the matter of picketing is going to be a very prominent feature in the Bill of Rights."[64] Above all, trade unionists saw a bill of rights as a tool for securing the freedoms and liberties they had "worked all their life to build" and which they would not "give ... up without a struggle."[65]

## The 1960 House of Commons Special Committee on Human Rights and Fundamental Freedoms

### Labour and the Canadian Jewish Congress: Strikes and Exhortations

The prospect of a domestic charter as the basis for a new civic identity, which would become such an important constitutional theme in the Trudeau years, did not seem to have occurred to the King or St. Laurent governments. Yet the notion of forging new bases of Canadian identity was in fact a significant preoccupation for Ottawa in a postwar setting defined by America's rise to economic and cultural hegemony and Britain's fall from global prestige.[66] Several early postwar initiatives reflected the new focus. Measures such as the Canadian Citizenship Act of 1946, the abolition of JCPC appeals in 1949, and the appointment of the Royal Commission on National Development in the Arts, Letters, and Sciences in the same year were all animated by the hope that Canadians might come to see themselves first and foremost as citizens of one politically sovereign and culturally distinct nation.

By 1960, Prime Minister John Diefenbaker had revived the idea of a domestic bill of rights, and in a way that linked the notion of such a bill directly to an identity agenda. While Louis St. Laurent had quietly abandoned the nationalist citizenship focus in the face of growing Quebec opposition, Diefenbaker was a different figure.[67] The German-Canadian Prairie outsider's disdain for Quebec nationalism broke entirely with the sensitivities of his Liberal predecessors. Keen to undermine the priority accorded to French-English dualism, Diefenbaker sought a new national symbol that, in Leslie Pal's words, could stand as an authoritative "rejection of 'second-class citizenship' grounded in the particularisms of race or ethnicity."[68]

Animated by a charter vision that was primarily symbolic rather than legal, Diefenbaker's Progressive Conservatives found it unnecessary to explore the possibility of constitutionally entrenching the 1960 Canadian Bill of Rights.[69] They were certainly not interested in helping disappointed would-be citizen litigants attack the shortcomings of a hortatory statement that would have only the force of an ordinary statute. An almost furtive series of procedural moves forced prospective witnesses to prepare their briefs on the proposed bill with less than a week's notice.[70] As a consequence, only six groups appeared before the 1960 House of Commons Special Committee on Human Rights and Fundamental Freedoms, and only two of these – the Canadian Jewish Congress and the Canadian Labour Congress – represented equality-seeking social movements.

The distinction between the minimal legal potency of the Diefenbaker Bill and its appeal as a manifesto of equal citizenship was paralleled by two contrasting reactions from social movements. Although the CJC regretted the bill's weaknesses, it embraced Diefenbaker's emphasis on "recognizing the sacredness of the human personality [with a] Bill of Rights."[71] But the CLC, which was more interested in establishing a constitutional bulwark against union-busting provincial governments, saw Diefenbaker's approach as a woefully insufficient response to labour's traditional civil rights objectives.

CLC President Claude Jodoin began the CLC presentation by observing that since the labour movement had "consistently pressed for a bill of rights," workers might "be expected [to] welcome this bill unreservedly."[72] However, trade union leaders were appalled by the bill's almost certain uselessness against "flagrant violations of fundamental rights and freedoms," of which Jodoin cited police harassment of union organizers and Newfoundland's labour laws as glaring instances.[73] The Diefenbaker Bill would "not provide any protection against violation of rights or freedoms by a future parliament." Nor would it "provide even momentary protection against ... provincial outrages on freedom." Jodoin concluded: "That is why the congress cannot accept it as ... anywhere near adequate."[74]

The trade union presentation reflected the continued influence of Forsey, who joined Jodoin in appearing before the House Special Committee. In his similar capacity with the CCL in 1950, Forsey had proposed cross-country parliamentary hearings on the notion of a Canadian bill of rights as a way of confronting the idea's provincial rights critics with evidence "of the wide-spread and growing public opinion in favour of such action."[75] This strategy, which future Prime Minister Pierre Trudeau would deploy successfully in 1980-82 using the slogan "people versus powers," was also a key recommendation of the CLC in 1960. Urging the Diefenbaker government to abandon its timid approach in favour of efforts to shame recalcitrant provinces into relinquishing their jurisdictional preoccupations, Jodoin declared: "Let us find out which province might be opposed to such a bill of rights. Maybe it would be a good idea to have a nice debate on the matter. I would like to know which province would be opposed to such a bill of rights."[76]

The CJC's view of the Diefenbaker bill contrasted with that of the CLC, yet it would be a mistake to interpret the venerable Jewish organization's support as an indication of quiescence. The 1950 CJC had avoided making remarks that even hinted at activism; its 1960 counterpart was a changed organization. CJC Executive Vice-President Saul Hayes described his organization as "prime movers in this field" and as "pioneers in this matter [of] human rights" who were even "a little too much in advance of our time."[77] In a similar shift from the quiet diplomacy of the past, Hayes emphasized the history of discrimination endured by Canadian Jews as a means of underscoring the CJC's stature as an authority on human rights. To this end, he told the committee the story of Zachary Hart, a man who despite having been twice elected to the old Lower Canadian parliament had been barred by British law from taking his seat. By learning about such experiences, Hayes observed, the House Committee might better understand why "the Jewish community ... have been alive to the issue of human rights and fundamental freedoms with a certain sensitivity that may not be true of other groups."[78]

The CJC's support was influenced by an awareness of the bill's status as the latest in a series of Diefenbaker initiatives symbolizing Canada's growing official openness to ethnocultural minorities. These initiatives included the unprecedented ethnic diversity of Diefenbaker's Cabinet, the milestone appointment of an ethnic-minority senator, and – as Hayes acknowledged appreciatively – Ottawa's decision to recognize "that this year the Canadian Jewish community is observing its 200th anniversary of settlement in Canada."[79] For Canadian Jews, and probably for other minorities as well, these sorts of actions served as cues that the civic arena was becoming more hospitable to their participation and involvement. As Hayes put it, referencing the earlier parliamentary discussions on the question of a domestic charter, "the climate is different in 1960 from what it was in 1950."[80]

This focus on political symbols of recognition and respect led the CJC to "highly commend the government for having introduced" the Canadian Bill of Rights. Concerned to see Canada adopt "some form of legislation which would conform to the spirit of the universal declaration," the CJC approached Diefenbaker's bill not from the standpoint of a prospective litigant but as a marginalized group seeking a "declaration of citizenship."[81]

## The Royal Commission on Bilingualism and Biculturalism: Hearings and Briefs, 1963-65

### Cosmopolitan Virtue: Ethnic Minority Organizations and the B&B Commission

The formation of the Royal Commission on Bilingualism and Biculturalism (the B&B Commission) in 1963, three months after Lester Pearson's minority victory in the April election, sparked the emergence of a new, loosely organized coalition of ethnic minorities. Dedicated to challenging the civic primacy accorded to what the commission's mandate unabashedly referred to as the "two founding races," this coalition dubbed itself Canada's "third force."[82] Although representatives of ethnic minorities had been advocating anti-discrimination principles since at least the end of the Second World War, it is with only mild exaggeration that analysts would later describe the third-force intervention as the "first stirrings of protest" from groups "politicized ... by the Royal Commission."[83]

Initiating a public challenge can be a wrenching experience. In Erving Goffman's sociology of human interaction, deference tends to reflect a fear that breaking with the given "definition" of a particular situation will cause one to "lose face" for disrupting what would have otherwise been a smooth encounter.[84] Although the fear of losing face undoubtedly helped promote minority quiescence at a time when Canada's self-definition was of almost completely British- and, to a lesser extent, French-Canadian authorship, traditional definitions were precisely what the postwar trajectory of constitutional reform had been calling into question. The commission's emphasis on "two founding races" was assailed by critics as a sudden and unwelcome departure from the postwar emphasis on human rights and universalism, which had been manifested most recently in the 1960 Bill of Rights.[85] By illuminating its divergence from the broader tenor of postwar constitutionalism, minority representatives argued that the B&B Commission – and not its citizen critics – was the party guilty of causing an out-of-place disruption.

The official mandate of the B&B Commission was to "recommend what steps should be taken to develop the Canadian Confederation on the basis of an equal partnership between the two founding races, taking into account the contribution made by other ethnic groups to the enrichment of Canada and the measures that should be taken to safeguard that contribution."[86] In its early days the commission interpreted this mandate as a directive to educate English-speaking Canadians about the necessity and virtues of a renewed binational partnership.[87] Shock at seeing this conception come under fire may help explain a striking feature of the commission's public hearings. Rather than engaging critics in debate, the commissioners tended to sit silently while witnesses denounced the basic assumption on which the deliberations were predicated. And in what was perhaps a reflection of their status as last-minute "afterthought" additions, the commission's ethnic minority members, Jaroslav Rudnyckyj and Paul Wyczynski, proved as reticent as their colleagues.[88]

Both in their written briefs and in their presentations to the commission's public hearings, ethnic minority organizations condemned the B&B's mandate with a vehemence that had once been the almost exclusive hallmark of the traditional left. A "disturb[ed]" Ukrainian Canadian Committee (UCC) criticized the "retrograde and discriminatory ... division of Canadian citizens into ... first and second class Canadians"; a "seriously disturbed" Canadian Polish Congress (CPC) rejected the "discriminatory ... assertion" that its members were "second class citizens"; and a "most unhappy" CJC urged that "this loose document be so amended [so] that [the] reference to races [or] ethnic groups be eliminated altogether."[89]

Although the CJC expressed support for linguistic and cultural dualism, it was appalled by a document that spoke of "founding races." The CJC saw this terminology as evidence that Canadian authorities had failed to absorb a key lesson of the Second World War: "Race ... is a very dangerous word ... [that has] caused a great deal of trouble throughout the world ... It is a word not to be used."[90] With an astute twist on the colony-to-nation theme, an angrier UCC argued that the B&B's mandate was "inconsistent with the existing concept of Canadian citizenship." Because Canada had "evolved from the status of a subordinate British colonial dependency to an independent and self-governing democratic nation ... any principle which would tend ... to imply the superiority of one group ... over another" was tantamount to a "return to a colonial status from which it has taken so long to emerge."[91]

The CPC stated flatly that the B&B's mandate constituted "discrimination against the remaining ethnic groups and a violation of the Bill of Rights."[92] According to the CPC, any notion of dualism beyond bilingualism would make "the statement ... that all Canadians are first class citizens ... a platitude and a negation of the truth." To underline its point that the commission's mandate was "contrary to ... the Canadian Bill of Rights ... and the Preamble" of the UN Declaration, the CPC appended passages from both documents to its written brief.[93]

Third-force participants did not simply demand formal equality in the name of universalism. Strongly concerned to combat the negative judgments associated with their past mistreatment and exclusion, they supplemented the language of universalism with a discourse of virtuous citizenship. Emphasizing the quintessential virtue of citizen loyalty, the Communist Party of Canada (CP) declared its "devotion to Canada," its "concern for ... unity," and its desire "to serve this country in the common interest of all its citizens."[94] Similarly, the UCC highlighted the military contribution of Ukrainian Canadians, pointing out that "seven [Ukrainian] Canadian Legion Branches" testified to the fact that their members had "given Canada good service, including comrades departed." "In two world wars," declared the UCC, "Canada's soldiers were better, stronger, braver, and more plentiful because of the added direct positive contribution of the Ukrainian language and culture."[95]

Third-force representatives also conveyed their respective communities' contributions to Canada by emphasizing the virtues of cultural and linguistic cosmopolitanism. This imagery of refinement was certainly a means of defusing the anticipated charge that the B&B Commission's critics were insufficiently sophisticated to appreciate linguistic and cultural dualism. At the same time, it helped counter the dominant society's view of ethnic minorities as uneducated farmers and labourers – a view that third-force spokesmen clearly associated with their subordinate status. Thus, Dr. I. Hlynka began the UCC presentation by pointing out that "I have with me two colleagues, one is bilingual Ukrainian-English, and the other is bilingual, Ukrainian-French. I also am bilingual, Ukrainian-English, and I do have a reasonable knowledge of French and German."[96] The CPC's Dr. J.A. Wojciehowski began with a similar emphasis. Dissenting from the proposition that "teaching a child a second language is wrong or is lost," he informed the commission that "I know from my experience and my family experience that the knowledge of ... several languages is not only possible but feasible."[97]

The CPC's written brief made this cosmopolitan self-positioning more explicit. It introduced the reader to Polish-Canadian history by characterizing the community's early immigrants as "penniless, uneducated ... farmers ... [who] filled the ranks of Canadian unskilled labour."[98] Now "even among this oldest group ... there were some exceptional cases of outstanding individuals or families who were able to play an important part in Canadian politics, science, or jurisprudence." But most impressive were the more recent arrivals, whose "initiative and ingenuity" enabled them to achieve "a relatively high standard of living." Although "we still find ... blue collar workers," the brief continued, "there are increasing numbers of clergymen, engineers, architects, doctors, lawyers, teachers, professors, scientists, journalists, merchants, industrialists, civil servants, etc. There is no lack among them of prominent and especially gifted individuals who have ... [rendered] this country valuable services." The CPC's brief concluded by declaring that "the Polish ethnic group is now entitled to full participation in all the various fields of public life in Canada."

The claim that class advancement "entitled" Polish Canadians to "full participation" amounted to a symbolic eviction of those unfortunate "blue-collar workers" who remained. The UCC's emphasis on martial virtue was slightly more inclusive because it evoked achievements for which working-class community members – albeit predominantly male ones – could also take credit. Yet the latter group's cosmopolitan emphasis, which depicted the "multilingual" Ukrainian-Canadian community as a source of "experts" who could serve their country internationally as "trusted and efficient world servants," reflected the same calculation made by its Polish-Canadian counterpart: that stereotypically bourgeois and professional attributes would be the most politically useful of all.[99]

### The CLC, the Communist Party, and the B&B Commission: Divergent Constitutional Directions

It is interesting to contrast the responses to the B&B Commission, from the trade unions and the Communist Party, which reflected disagreement among progressive forces about how to address the Quiet Revolution then under way in Quebec. For its part, Canada's national trade union umbrella organization, the CLC, introduced an approach to the new Quebec nationalism that would become an enduring staple on the mainstream English-speaking left: defensive avoidance.

The CLC's written brief was driven less by actual anti-Quebec feeling than by fears that Canada's new constitutional focus would work to labour's disadvantage. Accordingly, it proposed to reframe the debate over national unity. This approach reflected the CLC's apparent fear that the commission's emphasis on cultural policy as the basis for a renovated citizenship would serve to marginalize working-class concerns. Unlike third-force representatives, who responded to the commission by deploying a rhetoric of cosmopolitanism and class ascent, the CLC decried a putative understanding of "culture ... as the private property of the upper income classes."[100] The CLC preferred T.H. Marshall's emphasis on industrial citizenship and social rights as a means for integrating workers into a common national culture.[101] Arguing that trade unions "have a contribution to make not only to the economic well-being of [their] members but [to] their cultural benefit as well," the CLC trumpeted the labour movement's role in bringing "leisure to working people through the shorter working day and work-week, paid vacations, and statutory holidays." These victories, the brief noted, had "made it possible for workers ... to participate in the cultural heritage ... which was in large measure denied to them."[102]

The CLC said remarkably little on the topic of Quebec's role in Confederation, although it did observe that "the breeding ground for nationalism in its more extreme forms is exploitation, social and economic inequality, ignorance, and insularity."[103] Accordingly, the brief suggested that the root causes of nationalist dissatisfaction be addressed by applying the redistributive solutions of the social democratic left. In the CLC's words, Ottawa could foster "successful bilingualism and biculturalism" by initiating a sharp reduction in "marked differences of income and other economic impediments" and through a "vast expansion in educational opportunity."[104] This rather improbable argument ignored both the vehement jurisdictional objections of Quebec nationalists and the difficulties of applying Marshall's vision of integration in a context where a national minority's determination to develop its own welfare state was precisely the issue.

In contrast, the CP contended that centralism was untenable in the era of the Quiet Revolution. Its brief proposed a restructuring of the Canadian federation with a "new confederal pact" that would see Quebec representatives vacate the federal Parliament for a National Assembly armed with quasi-sovereign powers.[105] The two-nations position reflected delight at the ideological transformation of a nationalism that the CP's Depression-era counterpart had denounced for "landlordism and feudalism."[106] As the CP explained, Quebec seemed poised to "choose a course of development which involves ... extensive measures of nationalization moving in the direction of socialism rather more quickly than the people of English Canada will be prepared to move."[107]

The CP thus celebrated developments that the CLC seemed determined to ignore. While the CP was certainly innovative in proposing what must surely count as one of English-speaking Canada's first grassroots calls for asymmetrical federalism, it must be noted that Cold War ignominy had given the party a freedom of manoeuvre that its social democratic counterparts lacked. The CP's dwindling support base meant that its leaders could adopt virtually any position short of direct defiance of Moscow; by contrast, the CLC faced the paralysing task of devising a response to demands that were guaranteed to cause significant internal conflict.

**Defending (Anglophone) Diversity and Universalism:**
**The National Council of Women**

The civic-minded National Council of Women (NCW) found it quite easy to accept the new constitutional focus. In a short presentation that made no mention of women's rights, NCW President Mrs. Saul Hayes embraced the unity issue as paramount.[108] Invoking the council's long service "to the betterment of the family and the State," she declared that her organization was "no 'Johnny-come-lately' to the whole problem of biculturalism, bilingualism, and Canadianism."[109]

However, though the NCW accepted the emphasis on unity and bilingualism, it rejected the commission's "most unfortunate" terms of reference, which Hayes criticized for dividing "Canada into a primary group of First Citizens and a secondary group of citizens who may qualify as Canadians, under certain conditions."[110] It is difficult to tell precisely why the traditionally deferential council was now taking a more politically challenging position. Perhaps Hayes, as a Jewish woman whose husband was a CJC stalwart, was more attuned than her predecessors to problems of racism. However, Hayes pre-empted this as an explanation when she informed the commission: "I am not here [simply] as an individual ... We do not operate that way."[111]

Indeed, the NCW's historic decision to choose a non-Anglo-Saxon leader was consistent with the more sweeping changes it was embracing as an organization.[112] Hayes made this point clear when she described the council as a mirror of Canada's multicultural mosaic, "including – and I say including – ethnic groups such as the North American Indian, Polish, Italian, Jewish, Chinese, Negro, Ukrainian, and Greek."[113] At the same time, this same membership structure – which involved no links with francophone Quebec, where women belonged to a separate confessional organization – militated against a two-nations stance.[114]

Because it rested on an appeal to universalism, the NCW's attack on the notion of two founding races also constituted an indirect attempt to defend a constitutional language of potential utility for Canadian feminists. It is certainly difficult to imagine that when Hayes denounced the idea of a country with "two-thirds first class citizens and one third on probation" – a view she amplified by reciting Lincoln's dictum that "a nation cannot be half slave and half free" – women's civic status was entirely absent from her mind.[115]

**Early Postwar Constitutionalism and the New Politics of Respect**

Although they certainly expressed their frustration and dissent, Canada's social movements demonstrated continued enthusiasm for constitutional politics during the early postwar years. Their excitement was perhaps most evident when discussion turned to Canada's domestic obligations under the UN's Universal Declaration of Human Rights.

As the trade-union CCL noted in 1950 when it asked Ottawa to hold roving public hearings on human rights, parliamentarians charged with evaluating the desirability of a domestic charter were required to consider "evidence ... of the necessity for a Bill of Rights."[116] Given the relatively meagre possibilities offered by the day's more routine political forums, such evidence was something that marginalized groups were extremely eager to provide. The NCW used the 1950 Senate Committee hearings as a forum to call attention to discrimination against women in employment and political representation, while the NJCCA condemned the internment as a violation of "civil, political, social, and economic human rights."[117] For its part, the LDR criticized such Canadian McCarthyisms as the Quebec Padlock Act and the admission requirements of the British Columbia bar.

At their most optimistic, social movement representatives approached the 1950 and 1960 hearings as political "worlds in reverse" – as venues where the ordinarily disrespected became valued experts from whom elites had to learn. In their view, who better to explain the need for a charter than the groups most unhappily familiar with repression and tyranny? Thus, the CJC told the Diefenbaker committee that it was "alive to the issue of human rights and fundamental freedoms with a certain sensitivity that may not be true of other groups," while the NJCCA urged the 1950 Senate Committee to hear those who "know the harmful ... effect discrimination has worked upon them." Not to be outdone, in 1960 the CLC argued that workers had "suffered more from the deprivation of human rights and fundamental freedoms than any other section of the community."[118] These remarks reflected a shared view that charter discussions were opportunities to attach a symbolic capital of human rights expertise to the oppressed.

This dynamic seemed to startle parliamentarians. Angry senators enjoined women to embrace the "more useful" work of ensuring that "children [are] brought up right" and "upholding the preservation of the Sabbath." They insisted that "the Japanese" should be grateful for being allowed to return to British Columbia while suspicions of "two loyalties" remained, and they rebuked Jewish representatives for treating discrimination as a "matter of indignity to one element."[119] Confronted with a human rights mandate that threatened to erode the behavioural certainties of "politics as usual," authorities responded by attempting to silence voices that they were unaccustomed to hearing.

Even when witnesses disagreed bitterly with the proposals at hand – which was certainly the case for critics of the B&B Commission – an underlying enthusiasm for constitutional politics remained. Official discussions on unity and identity provided a forum where ethnic minorities could explain their visions of citizenship and seek recognition for their neglected Canadian histories and contributions. Representatives of Canada's Ukrainian, Polish, and Jewish communities were quick to seize this opportunity, thereby turning the commission into a platform for a multiculturalism discourse that authorities found increasingly difficult to ignore.[120]

While third-force representatives promoted multilingual sophistication as a resource for Canada on the world stage – anticipating the neoliberal practice that Yasmeen Abu-Laban and Christina Gabriel call "selling diversity" – labour expressed unease with the new constitutional focus.[121] That an emphasis on identity had the potential to overshadow trade unions' concerns had already been demonstrated at the 1960 hearings of the House Special Committee on Human Rights. Labour's demand for a charter that could provide meaningful protection for trade union activities went unheeded; instead, Diefenbaker's Bill of Rights came into existence as a hortatory device for according recognition to ethnocultural minorities.

New Politics theorists argue that the postwar context of unprecedented economic security and personal safety provided a perfect environment for the identity emphasis to flourish. Citing an impressive array of opinion data, New Politics scholars explain how a long-term climate of peace and prosperity helped create societal audiences less obsessed with economic and defence issues and more comfortable with dissent and minority appeals.[122] However, the more specific adequacy of the postmaterialism concept as an interpretation of the social movement emphasis on esteem and belonging is a different question. The evidence presented in this chapter suggests that it is incorrect to characterize feminist and minority participants in Canada's early postwar constitutional debates as actors who had "moved up the needs hierarchy ... surpass[ing] concern for material security."[123]

Feminist and minority groups prioritized safety and security goals. Indeed, it is impossible to make sense of the constitutional participation of Jewish and Japanese Canadians without accounting for the profoundly material impetus provided by the traumas of Holocaust and internment. At the same time, minority representatives were also concerned about the more everyday injustices of a racist social order, such as discrimination in housing, property transactions, and employment.

Feminists, too, focused on problems of material security, including discrimination in employment, women's economic vulnerability in male-breadwinner families, and gendered disadvantage under Canadian divorce and tax law. The NCW supplemented this emphasis with a call for social security and social rights.

Yet a still more important point remains: social movements saw the aforementioned obstacles to security as manifestations of broader underlying problems of esteem and belonging. For instance, the CJC objected to the "founding races" notion because "the suffering of the smaller groups" seemed to follow "whenever this word is emphasized." Similarly, the NJCCA linked internment to the prejudice "that we were Japs and not loyal to Canada," while the NCW protested the economic consequences of disrespecting women's "contribution to the family and the State in bearing and raising children."[124] The fears and aspirations behind these remarks suggest that it is inaccurate to interpret their common focus on social esteem as an expression of postmaterialism.

It is perhaps more plausible to discuss the constitutional interventions of the relatively secure Ukrainian and Polish Canadian communities in terms of postmaterialism. These groups approached the B&B Commission with a symbolic capital of cosmopolitan sophistication that emphasized their economic success and demonstrated their increasing concern with questions of civic symbolism and respect. Armed with strong group memories of a proletarianized past, the CPC and UCC brandished the badges of class ascent and demanded acknowledgment as "full particip[ants] in all the various fields of public life in Canada."[125]

However, the view of participation informing this emphasis calls attention to a crucial point that New Politics theory does not discuss: the role of social esteem as a basis for successful claims making. While it may be true that Polish and Ukrainian Canadians pursued social esteem in ways not directly connected to material goals, their presentations to the B&B Commission expressed a powerful awareness of their status as civic outsiders, which third-force representatives equated with being sidelined, ignored, and unheard. To the extent that the CPC and UCC were silent on questions of material disadvantage, their focus on esteem and belonging may have been oriented primarily toward what New Politics theory calls the "aesthetic and intellectual needs."[126] But as this chapter has shown in the cases of women and Japanese Canadians, in particular, disesteem also raised a tall barrier to groups struggling for security and safety.

This point can be amplified by noting the tendency of some stigmatized groups to deploy universalism as a second-best strategy for confronting disrespect. At the 1950 Senate hearings, Jewish Canadians and Communists attempted to capitalize on the elevated postwar role of universalism as a substitute for having to confront the negative perceptions of others. But this appeal was incapable of vanquishing the problems of disesteem that underpinned political marginality and insecurity in the first place.

For instance, when the LDR used the discourse of equal rights as a means of avoiding the charge that Communists were likely to use their citizenship rights disloyally, they were tacitly admitting that Communists were disloyal. And when the CJC insisted that other Canadians were "entitled to their likes and dislikes," it seemed to be conceding the legitimacy, or perhaps the tolerability, of anti-Semitic bigotry.[127] In short, although universalism undoubtedly represented a great advance over putatively virtue-based patterns of rights allocation, reversing societal judgments of disrespect remained the greater prize – and, for marginalized groups struggling against disadvantage, an object of considerable material significance.

It would be remiss to argue for the materialist character of the postwar social movement emphasis on social esteem without noting the distinctiveness of the approach taken by the mainstream trade unions; they stood aloof from the new emphasis on civic recognition and belonging. Interestingly, this stance was a departure from what previous chapters have identified as the strong concern of the interwar traditional left with the public image of its constituency.

The earlier working-class emphasis on social esteem was not solely a phenomenon of the craft unions. Starting in the interwar years and continuing through the Second World War, the modern industrial unions placed a heavy emphasis on working-class identity, public education, and civic outreach. A key factor behind labour's postwar change of stance was the impact of the new collective-bargaining rights. As Janine Brodie and Jane Jenson suggest, wartime victories soon led to complacency: "Unions were confident that they had carved a legitimate place for themselves in the Canadian social fabric."[128] At the same time, an increasingly professionalized cadre of union leaders became absorbed in working the new collective-bargaining machinery. In the process, industrial unionism gave way to what the American labour expert Kim Moody calls "business unionism," an orientation that sees "members primarily as consumers ... negotiating the price of labour."[129]

The point is not to argue that the sheer presence of collective-bargaining rights doomed labour to the narrow economism that business unionism's critics condemn. Rather, it is that labour's capacity to wield the strike weapon stood in dramatic contrast to the political footing of feminist and ethnocultural minority movements – groups whose major bases of organization did not allow them to exert strategic power over the processes of economic production. As the following chapter will show in more detail, although this contrast would grow sharper as some marginalized groups came to strengthen their focus on the politics of respect, it is not adequately grasped by the distinction between materialism and postmaterialism.

# 5
# Charter Politics as Materialist Politics

In the mid-1960s, while the B&B Commission's deliberations were ongoing, Prime Minister Lester B. Pearson's government sought provincial agreement on a domestic constitutional amending formula, which the BNA Act lacked. Since 1945 a series of federal administrations had been pursuing such an agreement – albeit with fluctuating levels of commitment – as part of a broader effort to replace Canada's quasi-colonial identity with the symbols of sovereign maturity. However, soon after Premier Jean Lesage rejected the proposed Fulton-Favreau amending formula as an insufficient response to the basic Quiet Revolution premise of expanded powers for the Quebec state, the scope of the constitutional debate began to broaden significantly.[1]

Crucial ingredients in this expansion were Pierre Elliott Trudeau's 1967 appointment as federal justice minister and his election as prime minister the following year. Trudeau rejected the view that Quebec nationalism was simply a fact to be accommodated, and set out to launch an attack of his own. As classic essays by Alan Cairns and Peter Russell explain, Trudeau challenged the new Quebec nationalism as well as Western regionalism with a vision of pan-Canadian belonging in which subnational identities and provincial autonomy would be subordinate to national citizenship and individual rights.[2] Although this vision would not find direct constitutional expression until the 1982 Charter of Rights, Trudeau introduced its core elements to the Canadian public in early 1968. In a manifesto titled *A Canadian Charter of Human Rights,* Trudeau proposed an entrenched bill of rights as a vital instrument for recognizing the "basic human values of all Canadians" and for "establish[ing] that all Canadians, in every part of Canada, have equal rights."[3]

The prime minister who promised a "just society" and who initiated the 1971 multiculturalism policy hoped to build a new civic pride by transforming Canada's image on the world stage.[4] What amounted to a concerted exercise of national rebranding under Trudeau's leadership was shaped considerably by postwar international human rights discourse. As the previous chapter observed, this discourse enjoined decent nations to contribute to world peace by serving the values enshrined in the Universal Declaration of Human Rights.[5] Accordingly, when Trudeau unveiled his official Charter proposals in 1968 – the UN's International Year of Human Rights – he reminded Canadians of "the hopeful expectation of the General Assembly that in 1968 an aroused awareness by all peoples will result in government action everywhere." "Canada," he declared, "has the opportunity to take a lead in this respect."[6]

The Machiavellian dedication with which Trudeau pursued his unity vision during his nearly two decades as prime minister was a boon for many equality-seeking movements. As Leslie Pal has explained so well, Trudeau's governments provided funding, as well as opportunities to participate, to groups whose focus on pan-Canadian inclusion made them valuable allies in the prime minister's serial battles with his constitutional rivals.[7] At the same time, Trudeau's attempt to promote national unity and civic pride by framing Canada as a multicultural country dedicated to human rights meant unprecedented official attention for movements employing discourses of equality and social justice.

This chapter explores the role played by social movements in these unity battles by focusing on two key episodes in Canadian constitutional development: the public hearings of the 1970-72 Special Joint Committee of the Senate and of the House of Commons on the Constitution of Canada; and the more well-known 1980-81 proceedings of the Special Joint Committee of the same name.

Co-chaired by MP Mark MacGuigan and Senator Gildas Molgat, the 1970-72 Special Joint Committee on the Constitution solicited citizen input on a set of proposals that led to a short-lived 1971 intergovernmental agreement known as the Victoria Charter. The Molgat-MacGuigan hearings proved irrelevant to the Victoria Charter's fate; the deal collapsed when Quebec Premier Robert Bourassa withdrew after nationalists criticized him over the alleged tokenism of its social policy provisions. However, equality seekers made good use of two years of roving public hearings in forty-seven cities presided over by a committee that had declared itself open to "expanding the traditional procedures of ... decision-making."[8]

In response to pressure from ethnic minorities, the Molgat-MacGuigan Committee played a key role in convincing Trudeau to adopt Canada's landmark official multiculturalism policy.[9] Furthermore, social movement witnesses persuaded the committee to recommend the reintroduction of Trudeau's original 1968 Charter proposals, which the intergovernmental bargaining in Victoria had significantly weakened.[10] Thus, by demonstrating vocal public support for a pan-Canadian vision framed in terms of equality and inclusion – a vision whose social justice credentials their own participation served to burnish – social movements confirmed the presence of a significant activist constituency for Trudeau's unity approach.

Although the Victoria Charter's failure and the Liberals' near defeat in the 1972 elections resulted in temporary silence on the constitutional front, Trudeau soon responded to the sovereignty movement's growing momentum by seeking intergovernmental agreement on an amending formula and bill of rights. Once again, parliamentary hearings revolving around official charter proposals attracted groups eager to seize the opportunity that Trudeau's unity strategy presented. What had changed was the relative importance of intergovernmental negotiation and citizen participation in Trudeau's approach to entrenchment. Buoyed by his surprise return to office in 1980, by Ottawa's subsequent victory in Quebec's sovereignty-association referendum, and by the boisterous advocacy of equality-seeking movements, Trudeau used public opinion as a cudgel for intimidating reluctant premiers, most of whom saw the charter vision as a threat to parliamentary sovereignty and provincial rights.

Co-chaired by Senator Harry Hays and MP Serge Joyal, the proceedings of the 1980-81 Special Joint Committee on the Constitution were broadcast on national television. With evening newscasts featuring powerful clips of activists demanding a charter by recounting past instances of Canadian discrimination and oppression, the Hays-Joyal hearings became what Russell calls the "crucial instrument in the process of building legitimacy for the federal initiative."[11] At the same time, federal officials blasted proponents of provincial autonomy for placing government interests ahead of popular rights. In Cairns' words: "The federal government brilliantly employed a 'people versus powers' antithesis to contrast what it sought – a Charter of Rights for the people – with the jurisdictional goals of provincial governments, which were portrayed as selfish aggrandizement."[12]

Following a remarkable series of developments, Ottawa and all the provinces except Quebec reached agreement on the set of proposed amendments that paved the way for The Constitution Act, 1982. Controversy over the circumstances and propriety of Quebec's exclusion remains.[13] However, the role of the Hays-Joyal hearings in shaping the future Charter is clearer. Robert Sheppard and Michael Valpy report that committee members "fell over each other" in their eagerness to side with the supporters of citizen rights.[14] Responding chiefly to complaints from social movements, the Hays-Joyal Committee recommended 123 amendments to Trudeau's charter proposals, more than half of which were accepted by a government forced to honour its own constitutional rhetoric.[15]

As will be seen, English-speaking feminist and ethnocultural minority organizations were particularly successful in exploiting the political opportunity offered by Trudeau's vision. These equality seekers achieved specific revisions that reflected some of their key immediate concerns. Furthermore, armed with narratives and understandings borne of decades-long struggles against marginalization and disrespect, they provided Canada's new constitution with much of its political meaning and valence. To these battles and accomplishments we now turn.

## The 1970-72 Special Joint Committee of the Senate and of the House of Commons on the Constitution of Canada

### Asymmetry and Identity: The Traditional Left

For almost thirty years the mainstream labour movement was Canada's leading civil society exponent of a constitutional charter of rights and an interventionist central government. It was thus a significant break with tradition that the Canadian Labour Congress (CLC) failed to participate in the parliamentary hearings occasioned by Trudeau's charter proposals. The CLC's absence reflected a difficult dispute with its main francophone affiliate, the Fédération des travailleurs du Québec (FTQ), which had begun demanding the functional equivalent of a sovereignty-association relationship with its pan-Canadian counterpart.[16] At the same time, in labour organizing as in constitutional matters, the CLC's English-speaking membership continued to prefer the classic CCF-NDP vision of a single national community under the guiding direction of an activist centre.[17] This unity standoff would keep the CLC on Canada's constitutional sidelines well into the late 1980s.

With its vanguard structure and subservience to Moscow, an increasingly irrelevant Canadian Communist Party (CP) faced none of the membership pressures that made post-Duplessis constitutional politics so difficult for the CLC.[18] Nevertheless, the CP's appearance before the Molgat-MacGuigan Committee – its last in the Canadian constitutional arena – remains useful as a guide to the reasoning that would eventually force even the CLC to accept asymmetrical federalism. Thoroughly disabused of its old premise that Quebec workers needed Canada's protection from a reactionary provincial elite, the CP recommended a new confederal arrangement, one that would exempt Quebec from what would otherwise remain a pan-Canadian social program regime while providing the province cum nation with explicit constitutional self-determination rights and special powers.[19]

Although many on the committee rejected the emphasis on self-determination as "words for the pleasure of words," the CP offered a logical program for reordering the constitutional underpinnings of Canadianness.[20] It preferred a Quebec-only exemption from Canada's shared-cost program regime because it feared the decentralizing implications of Pearson's earlier decision to make available the social policy "opt-out" – which Quebec alone had demanded – on the basis of provincial equality.[21] According to CP Secretary General William Kashtan, the premise that whatever is given "to one people ... you must give to all ... provinces" would lead to "the balkanization [of] Canada."[22]

Above all, the CP feared that accommodating Quebec nationalism and Western regionalism within a framework of provincial equality would reinforce territorial identities at the expense of class consciousness and thus harm the future prospects for Canadian socialism. Regionalism was therefore to be countered by eliminating the opt-out device that threatened to nourish it, while Quebec nationalism was to be managed by transforming an "oppressed nation" into a coequal partner armed with extensive political autonomy and explicit self-determination rights.[23] In this way, the CP hoped to defuse a dynamic that was sapping the "unity of the working class" and making "the struggle against their common enemy ineffective."[24]

### The Prestige Dilemma of Feminism

With the National Action Committee on the Status of Women (NAC) engaged in the business of its 1971-72 founding, the role of arguing for women's equality at the Molgat-MacGuigan hearings remained with the National Council of Women (NCW).[25] Appearing just one month before the Victoria Charter's June 1971 collapse, the NCW devoted its presentation to protesting the deletion of Trudeau's 1968 anti-discrimination rights from the tentative intergovernmental agreement of February 1971. Above all, the NCW wanted to do what Diefenbaker's Bill of Rights had not: force governments to amend or abolish existing laws that discriminated against women. Drawing on the milestone 1970 report of the Royal Commission on the Status of Women, the NCW cited the Canada Pension Plan, the Public Service Employment Act, the Canada Labour Code, and the Fair Employment Practices Act as examples of discriminatory statutes that it expected a sufficiently robust charter to reach.[26] The NCW was thus pursuing a bill of rights as a tool for redressing women's economic disadvantage in employment, promotion, remuneration, and social benefits.

However, an evident sense of the futility of attempting to sway unsympathetic audiences led the NCW to say remarkably little about sex discrimination. For example, although the NCW's legal advisor, Ann Booth, described the absence of anti-discrimination rights in the Victoria Charter as "disappointing," "unsatisfactory," and "disturbing," she did not apply these adjectives to the specific case of women. She instead spoke generically of "any person who for one reason or another might be discriminated against."[27] "There is nothing," she continued, "about racial or ethnic origin, nor religion, none of these things." The intergovernmental agreement was "unsatisfactory from the point of view of lack of protection against discrimination of any kind, not just that against women."[28]

This universalist appeal reflected the council's realist awareness of the conventional human rights agenda, which male exponents often managed to espouse while simultaneously ignoring or even supporting discrimination against women. For instance, when Prime Minister Diefenbaker sold the 1960 Bill of Rights as an instrument for assuring "equality to every Canadian, whatever his race, his colour, or his religion," it seemed, incorrectly, as if the bill did not mention women's equality at all.[29] Tory Justice Minister Davie Fulton went further when he reassured traditionalists that the bill's reference to sex was inconsequential. The Bill of Rights, Fulton promised, "would not be interpreted by the courts so as to say we are making men and women equal, because men and women are not equal: they are different."[30]

Fulton's emphasis on women's "natural ... difference" highlighted a crucial political dilemma faced by mainstream Canadian feminists.[31] This dilemma was that the prestige that accrued to women as wives and mothers – two key roles in which the difference Fulton alluded to was prized by men – garnered them virtually no respect in the political arena.

We have just seen that the NCW tried to sidestep this dilemma by using antiracist rather than feminist language in pressing for the restoration of the 1968 Trudeau charter. At the same time, the council held out the longer-term hope that men could be persuaded that women were sufficiently responsible to deserve equal citizenship. In a novel tactic that departed from its past emphasis on maternal virtue, the council emphasized its willingness to seek civic acceptance in men's own evaluative terms. Criticizing those provinces which either excluded women from jury duty or allowed them to avoid service without having to submit reasons, Booth stressed that her organization's view of equality was "not a completely one-sided thing." She accepted the proposition that "if women are to assume their rights and their proper place in society it is absolutely essential for them as well to assume the duties of a citizen."[32] Here, Booth was using the case of jury service, with its classic connotations of citizenship and duty, to telegraph the council's eagerness to embrace "the corresponding responsibilities and challenges that go with the rights that we are demanding."[33]

Whatever frustration was involved in acknowledging that women needed to prove themselves before being treated as civic equals must have been compounded by how some men on the committee responded to the argument about jury duty. For example, Mr. Hogarth suggested that women's contributions were valued in other areas: "I know no male married member of Parliament who is not married to a woman." In any event, he did not believe that women were appropriate candidates for the equal-rights-and-responsibilities approach that the NCW was advancing. "For instance," he threatened, "take the provincial legislation concerned with deserted wives. Should husbands be responsible to support their wives when they desert them or should there be complete equality?"[34] For his part, Mr. Prud'homme discussed "mixed juries" with a jocularity that indicated women's difficulty in gaining respect as civic participants. "I would like to be a member of that jury," Prud'homme quipped. "If it is a mixed jury, it might take a long time."[35]

The committee was not entirely frivolous or disrespectful in its response. For instance, Liberal Senator Muriel Fergusson congratulated the NCW on its "very well documented brief," although she seemed less certain about the merits of a charter itself.[36] Of perhaps greater future significance was the reaction of Trudeau stalwart and soon-to-be federal cabinet minister Warren Allmand. While adding little of substance to the debate on women's rights, Allmand's remarks highlighted the growing reliance of Trudeau's constitutional vision on support from social movements: "What I would suggest to your Council and to other groups is that they write the provincial attorneys general and premiers and tell them that you do not find the [existing intergovernmental] agreement on entrenched civil liberties ... satisfactory, and that you want something along the lines of the original [1968 charter] proposal ... That would help the federal government and help us and help everybody who believes in an entrenched Bill of Rights."[37]

### Ethnic Minorities at the Molgat-MacGuigan Hearings:
### Multicultural Prestige

The Molgat-MacGuigan Committee's main presenters representing ethnic minorities, the Canadian Polish Congress (CPC) and three separate regional sections of the Ukrainian Canadian Committee (UCC), appeared roughly six months before Trudeau's October 1971 multiculturalism announcement.[38] Although they supported an entrenched charter, the CPC and UCC focused their remarks on two themes that would inform the multiculturalism policy. First, third-force representatives argued that "ethnic minorities [should] be duly recognized as a presence" with a constitutional statement celebrating Canada as "a complex ethnocultural country."[39] The 1971 multiculturalism declaration offered an important preliminary response to these demands by calling ethnocultural minorities "essential elements in Canada."[40] Second, the UCC and the CPC appealed for "encouragement and support" for "cultural communities" and "funds for ... study of all Canadian languages"; these calls were heeded by the policy's emphasis on "government assistance [for] various cultures and ethnic groups."[41]

In his insightful account of official multiculturalism as a reconstruction of Canada's symbolic order, Raymond Breton argues that Trudeau's coast-to-coast bilingualism policy generated among third-force minorities "a status anxiety ... [a] fear of being defined as second-class citizens, marginal to the identity system being established."[42] Status anxiety permeated the UCC and CPC presentations. Convinced that the assimilation of their communities was the unstated corollary hope of Ottawa's emphasis on protecting minority francophone communities, the CPC and UCC saw heritage funding not only as a practical matter but also as a symbol of respect. The CPC wanted official acknowledgment that "the preservation and influence of all the great values that can be found in the tradition of ethnic groups is no less precious to all Canadians than the British and French traditions."[43] As the UCC's Bohdan Zarowsky argued, an unalloyed policy of bilingualism depicted minorities as people "to be kicked around." "We are not apes," Zarowsky declared. "We have backgrounds and we are proud of them."[44]

Much like at the B&B hearings, this emphasis on respect reflected a particular frustration with the presumed tendency of dominant groups to associate East European ethnicity with working-class status. Suggesting that their "ancestors were just as good, or better, than some of the most distinguished people here," UCC and CPC spokesmen invoked such stereotypically professional accomplishments as "23 years ... teaching ... at McGill University" and a "knowledge of ... seven modern languages."[45]

However, ethnic minority organizations were less likely to emphasize the individual achievements of group members than in the past.
They instead proffered a more generalized discourse that highlighted
the benefits of diversity itself. Framing multiculturalism as a potential
hallmark of Canadian cosmopolitanism, this discourse translated minority bids for respect into a more politically saleable form. Third-force
representatives insisted that a drab colonial dualism was inimical to
forward-looking development; Canada could not "afford in the age of
conquest of space to adhere rigidly and inflexibly" to past ways. Rather
than stay "fossilized as it was ... 100 years ago," the country needed to
embrace its identity as "a constantly changing thing" and recognize
itself as a "multicultural nation." Doing so would provide a "creative
contribution to the community of nations," prove that Canada knew
"better than other nations how to preserve unity in diversity," and confer an international "advantage in business."[46]

In their book *Selling Diversity,* Yasmeen Abu-Laban and Christina
Gabriel argue persuasively that neoliberal governments in the 1990s
began to turn Ottawa's original multiculturalism policy, which was at
least partly informed by an emphasis "on respect and recognition," into
a propaganda exercise for promoting the interests of Canadian business.[47] It is therefore interesting to note that third-force participants
themselves employed a business-friendly language that saw multiculturalism as a branding tool, which they used in turn to "sell" their
bids for recognition and respect.

This is not to say that the entrepreneurial theme was picked up by
policy makers in the early 1970s. Instead, Ottawa's more characteristic
early interest in multicultural prestige was expressed by the committee's Mr. Ryan, who responded to the Toronto UCC's "excellent" brief
by suggesting that the "encouragement of multiculturalism" would help
Canada "continue [as] an independent country" by differentiating it
"from the United States."[48] Thus, a re-examination of the B&B and
Molgat-MacGuigan hearings suggests that early Canadian multiculturalism discourse was forged in part from a process of de facto political
exchange between third-force groups seeking symbolic capital and the
civic rebranding agenda of Trudeau-era nationalism.

### The 1980-81 Special Joint Committee of the Senate
### and of the House of Commons on the Constitution of Canada

The national unity drama of the late 1970s and early 1980s, which
revolved around Trudeau's daring, last-ditch bid for entrenchment, is
well-studied elsewhere.[49] Suffice it to say that the 1976 election of a

sovereigntist government in Quebec, Trudeau's surprise return to office in February 1980, the May 1980 Parti Québécois referendum loss, a pivotal Supreme Court reference, and an edgy Western regionalism all played important parts. The following analysis of the 1980-81 hearings of the Special Joint Committee on the Constitution focuses on the role of social movements. As will be shown, synergy between Trudeau's people-versus-powers framing and the Hays-Joyal context of televised parliamentary hearings provided an immense political opportunity for movements seeking pan-Canadian citizenship inclusion.

In terms of formal revisions to the final entrenchment package, social movement actors achieved the significantly tightened Section 1 "reasonable limits" clause, the thoroughly strengthened Section 15(1) and (2) equality rights and affirmative action provisions, the long-sought Section 27 multiculturalism reference, and the dramatic last-minute addition of the overriding Section 28 statement on women's equality.[50] These results were not gifts from above. On the contrary – as James Kelly argues, the consistent tendency of previous intergovernmental bargaining sessions to produce ineffectual draft charters deferring to the concerns of provincial governments indicates that the organizing premises of Canadian constitutionalism "shifted in 1980-81 during the [Hays-Joyal] proceedings ... through citizen participation."[51]

As Kelly's analysis suggests, the social movement victory was not simply legal. Addressing not only parliamentarians but also wider societal audiences, feminist, ethnic minority, and antiracist groups denounced the discriminatory practices and disrespectful assumptions under which their constituencies suffered. This advocacy explained both the long-run symbolic significance and the immediate concrete importance of innovations such as multiculturalism and a charter of rights. Thus, equality seekers injected Canadian constitutionalism with a striking new aura of purpose. In doing so, they helped create a fund of symbolic capital for social movements, in the form of constitutional clauses that conveyed not only legal force but also political lessons and memories – authoritative reminders of the historic campaigns that forced Canada to officially renounce its past commitments to patriarchy and white supremacy.

### Labour (not) at the Hays-Joyal Hearings

The trade union movement was Canada's most long-standing civil society proponent of a charter, yet the Canadian Labour Congress (CLC) was nowhere to be found in the Hays-Joyal debates. This irony would prove costly for the labour movement, which failed to garner any of the heightened profile enjoyed by movements more immediately associated with the charter's creation.

Yet even the basic repertoire of intergovernmental manoeuvres and political rhetoric that Trudeau deployed in pursuit of the charter idea had been recommended years earlier by the trade union movement. Beginning at the Rowell-Sirois hearings, trade unions fighting hostile provincial governments had argued that explicit constitutional protection for civil liberties was a transcendent matter of national importance. This was also the position of the CCF-NDP academic and civil libertarian F.R. Scott, Trudeau's former teacher and an ardent defender of federal power, who had been calling for a Canadian bill of rights since at least 1949.[52] Trudeau himself was close to the labour movement through his involvement in the famous miners' strike at Asbestos, Quebec, his years as a labour lawyer and teacher at labour schools, and his friendships with key union personnel.[53] The similarities between Trudeau's entrenchment tactics and labour's charter advocacy under the tenure of his friend Eugene Forsey are particularly striking. While serving as research director and constitutional advisor for the Canadian Congress of Labour from 1943 to 1956, and then in the same capacity for the CLC until the early 1960s, it was Forsey who had made the original case for placing the charter's provincial rights critics on the defensive.

When protests from the premiers torpedoed the federal government's admittedly tepid interest in an entrenched bill of rights during the late 1940s, Forsey urged Ottawa to respond by "hold[ing] hearings in various parts of the country." Such an approach, he argued, could help change the course of the debate; an expanded menu of hearings would provide "invaluable evidence both of the necessity for a Bill of Rights ... and of the wide-spread and growing public opinion in favour of such action."[54] The emphasis on publicity was above all a shaming tactic. As a frustrated Claude Jodoin demanded in 1960, with Forsey sitting at his side: "Let us find out which province might be opposed to such a bill of rights. Maybe it would be a good idea to have a nice debate on the matter. I would like to know which province would be opposed to such a bill of rights."[55] Indeed, it was Forsey who pioneered the people-versus-powers rhetoric that dominated the intergovernmental battles of the 1980s. Labour's in-house constitutional expert proclaimed in 1950 that a charter would "subtract from the sovereignty of the legislative bodies to add to the sovereignty of the citizens."[56]

The uncompromising tone of this charter advocacy suggests that for decades the labour movement's Quebec affiliates were either insufficiently powerful or insufficiently determined in their nationalism to sway their pan-Canadian parent. It is therefore a reflection of the Quiet Revolution's impact that in 1980-81 the CLC missed the opportunity that its predecessors had been seeking for decades. The Fédération des travailleurs du Québec (FTQ), which had become the CLC's second-largest member organization, forced the national congress to abstain from the Hays-Joyal debates. As Leo Panitch and Donald Swartz explain, the FTQ "was determined that labour not get involved in improving the Constitution in case this strengthened the federalist case among Quebec workers."[57] The only exception to this position of official abstention was a brief written statement that the CLC sent to the Hays-Joyal Committee in support of Aboriginal rights.[58]

It is important not to exaggerate the Charter's potential to staunch what Panitch and Swartz call the *Assault on Trade Union Freedoms*.[59] Nevertheless, the CLC's absence from the Hays-Joyal hearings was certainly a mistake. During the 267 hours of televised hearings that turned "the concept of an entrenched Charter into a motherhood issue," trade unions' concerns received only desultory attention.[60] As a result, labour failed to secure constitutional protection for such core union activities as picketing, collective bargaining, and striking – objectives for which it had argued in detail at the 1950 parliamentary hearings and in more abbreviated form at the Rowell-Sirois Commission and 1960 Diefenbaker hearings. Furthermore, the movement would be excluded from a new constitutionalism and civic symbolism in which other equality seekers managed more readily to find space.[61]

**Expert Witnesses: Ethnic and Racialized Minorities**
Although they supported a charter, representatives of ethnic minorities did not arrive at the Hays-Joyal hearings in a celebratory mood. Instead, they launched bitter attacks on constitutional proposals that focused extensively on official bilingualism but made no mention of multiculturalism. For example, the Canadian Polish Congress (CPC) protested the "insult to Canada's smaller ethnic groups," arguing that their "partnership in this country is of legally equivalent validity."[62] The Ukrainian Canadian Committee (UCC) also complained about Ottawa's neglect, and demanded a "new constitutional house [to] enter ... through the front door together."[63] As Rita Desantis of the National Congress of Italian Canadians (NCIC) put it, minorities were sick of hearing "about the English and French forever ... I am a Canadian and I belong in that constitution."[64]

Minority advocates continued to pursue constitutional recognition by promoting multiculturalism as an emblem of civic distinction. The

UCC called multiculturalism "what makes us different, wonderfully different," while the CPC described its own contribution to "Canada's mosaic" as "vibrant and colourful."[65] At its most enthusiastic, this view was expressed by the Council of National Ethnocultural Organizations, a new national umbrella for Canadian minority groups. Citing Toronto's metamorphosis from the "cold wasp city [of] 30 years ago," and describing that city as a microcosm of Canada's postwar transformation, the council sought "recognition [for] the multicultural reality of this country" – "alive, vibrant, beautiful, cosmopolitan ... rich in the diversities of its people ... enhanced by the cultures and languages of scores of communities."[66]

The message underlying this advocacy was that Ottawa's constitutional drafters were about to depreciate a key source of symbolic capital for the country as a whole. As the CPC put it, multiculturalism "is a way of life in Canada": "Book Four [of the B&B Commission] affirmed this," "the Prime Minister tabled it as ... official policy," and "all parties accepted it." The alternative to recognizing multiculturalism was to "stop beating around the bush and admit that there is only room for two chartered ethnic groups in this country and that it is official policy, by carrot and stick, to induce all other groups to assimilate into one of these two."[67]

This group shaming prompted Liberal committee member Bryce Mackasey to pledge his support for recognizing "officially ... that this is indeed a multicultural country."[68] And when Justice Minister Jean Chrétien closed the Hays-Joyal hearings in January 1981 by tabling a list of amendments to Ottawa's original proposals, he included the future Section 27 guarantee that "this Charter shall be interpreted in a manner consistent with the preservation and enhancement of the multicultural heritage of Canadians."[69]

With the important exception of Japanese Canadians, national organizations representing racialized or "visible" minorities had not participated in official Canadian constitutional discussions before. Many commentators have noted a difference between this more recent advocacy and the older third-force emphasis on multiculturalism and heritage preservation.[70] Visible minorities certainly brought to the Hays-Joyal hearings a distinctive focus on the relationship between racism and economic insecurity. For example, Sebastian Alakatusery, chair of the Afro-Asian Foundation of Canada (AAFC), complained that non-whites faced the threat of "discrimination in employment, job promotion, [and] housing ... every minute of our life." Similarly, Wilson Head, president of the National Black Coalition of Canada (NBCC), who spoke of his upbringing in "segregated housing" and "black ghettos" in the United States, sought constitutional protection for affirmative action programs on the grounds that even if "one simply opens up equality of opportunity ... it would take another 100 years before we were able to make up for ... past discrimination."[71]

The leaders of visible minority groups also spoke about the fear of racist violence that affected their communities. Head, president of the NBCC, pointed to the phenomenon of toll-free telephone numbers relaying "hate messages ... in favour of the destruction of black people"; he worried that Canada was "ripe for the evolution of a group like the KKK."[72] Similarly, spokespeople for the AAFC decried the "aggression and violence" perpetrated "by groups whose stated objective is to promote hatred and racism." This hatred was generating a "sense of insecurity" that the "haphazard nature of provincial human rights legislation" and "unequal protection by law enforcement agencies" did little to ease.[73] Thus, visible minorities sought an entrenched charter that would offer meaningful anti-discrimination rights and that would not impede the government's capacity to fight hate speech and provide effective affirmative action programs.

But antiracists did not pursue this materialist focus on economic and physical security as an alternative or in opposition to a more symbolic focus on recognition and respect. The AAFC valued the potential symbolism of a charter, which it saw as a lever for overturning the "false perceptions" – the "hatred and disdain for that which is different" – that seemed to create the need for anti-discrimination rights in the first place.[74] As the NBCC explained, a charter would signal "that the protection of human rights is a very important consideration in Canadian society today"; entrenchment itself would help make "the people ... aware that ... certain types of behaviour ... [are] not acceptable here." Certainly, the fact that bills of rights in other countries had "not been lived up to fully" meant that entrenchment might "merely be symbolical." "But," Head concluded, "I think in this case the symbolical act is important."[75]

This focus on fighting racism with symbols of equality and respect also led visible minorities to join their third-force counterparts in seeking constitutional recognition for multiculturalism. On behalf of the "stereotyped, ostracized, victimized, and ghettoized," Alakatusery of the AAFC argued that "the two nation concept" ignored "the significant contributions of non-white Canadians" and "relegate[d] nonwhites to a peripheral position in our society." Thus, he defended official multiculturalism as a way to help build "a truly Canadian identity," to promote awareness of "the many significant contributions that have been made by Afro-Asian Canadians," and to erase the "impression that those of Asian and African descent are all newcomers."[76]

The NBCC made a similar argument. Observing that "a great number of Canadians seem to feel that most black people who are in Canada now are recent immigrants," Head stressed that "black people ... have contributed greatly to the growth and development of Canada ... including fighting in the wars that Canada has been involved in." Since "we tend to lose sight" of such facts, concluded NBCC Executive Secretary J.A. Mercury, "the policy of multiculturalism must be ... entrenched in our constitution."[77]

Decades earlier, Japanese Canadians had affronted parliamentarians by asking the 1950 Senate Committee on Human Rights to hear those who knew "the harmful ... effect discrimination has worked upon them."[78] As the previous chapter observed, this plea attracted racist hectoring rather than respectful attention. In contrast, an identical social movement emphasis was a well-received theme – indeed, a definitive one – of the Hays-Joyal hearings.

Although its presentation to the B&B Commission had been silent on such matters, the UCC emphasized that it did "not wish ever to see the experience of World War I repeated, when over 8,000 Ukrainian Canadians were interned by the Canadian government as enemy aliens." Similarly, while the CPC's B&B brief had focused on the economic achievements of Polish Canadians rather than on their past oppression, its Hays-Joyal presentation noted a "time [when] persons of central European origin were prohibited from the use of their languages."[79] The Canadian Jewish Congress (CJC) offered a group-memory perspective on entrenchment as well, reminding Canadians that its members had been "victims of human rights violations" and that there were areas "where the Jewish interest happens to be ... very sensitive."[80]

This focus on past oppression as a basis of moral authority was most prominent in the remarks of the National Association of Japanese Canadians (NAJC). The NAJC representatives spoke of facing "locked doors in practically every line of pursuit," of "having to pay taxes for 70 years without even the right to vote," of seeing Ottawa "confiscate homes and sell them without the owner's consent," and, finally, of being "uprooted and dispossessed" when more than 22,000 Japanese Canadians were unjustly interned during the Second World War. "Surely," concluded the NAJC's Roger Obata, a "Charter of Rights entrenched in the constitution to prevent what we have gone through is the least that Canada can do to ... ensure that such injustices will never be repeated."[81]

The new power of this emphasis was demonstrated strikingly by the committee's response. The NDP's Svend Robinson welcomed the NAJC's "very moving presentation," praised Ken Adachi's "very fine book" on internment, and condemned Ottawa's "embarrassing" draft charter as a document "which would permit exactly the same kind of shameful history ... which happened to your people." Bryce Mackasey expressed a "latent feeling of guilt ... about the grave injustice," declared that the NAJC had "eliminated any doubt" in his mind about the need for a charter, and promised to take the group's written brief back to his riding to be "circulated in the schools of the Niagara Peninsula." Not to be outdone, Vancouver-area Progressive Conservative MP John Fraser informed the NAJC and the committee's television audience that his own childhood had been marked by "fights ... because [he] was born in Japan" and that his father had even "spoke out against the internment."[82]

While somewhat more fervent, the committee's treatment of the NAJC delegation was indicative of how it received other suggestions that the victims of racism were the true experts on Canada's need for a charter.[83] Thus, its reaction to the NAJC provides a useful window on the broader role of minority activists in helping dissolve the provincial opposition to entrenchment. Fraser's solicitude was particularly revealing. As the most significant federal ally of the eight provincial governments that opposed the charter, Fraser's Tories hoped to use the Hays-Joyal hearings to derail the entrenchment initiative.[84] Yet Fraser wound up seeking the NAJC's help in strengthening the Charter: "Can you give us any guidance as to what ought to be done? ... Do you think that you ought to be able to view [a redrafted resolution] to consider whether in fact it has met your objections?"[85]

### Constitutional Ambivalence: The National Action Committee on the Status of Women

For Canadian feminism, the years between the Molgat-MacGuigan hearings and the early 1980s entrenchment battles were marked by an organizational transformation: the National Action Committee on the Status of Women (NAC) replaced the National Council of Women (NCW) as Canada's pre-eminent women's organization. Indeed, NAC was an important participant in the Hays-Joyal debates, whereas the NCW failed to appear at all. Generational changes hastened NAC's ascent. As historian N.E.S. Griffiths notes, while younger women showed an increasing interest in NAC, the NCW entered a period of decline.[86]

Yet NAC's emergence as Canada's "parliament of women" also required intergenerational consensus.[87] Most notably, for example, two figures from the pre-baby boom generation, Laura Sabia and Thérèse Casgrain, played key roles in persuading the federal government to establish the 1968-70 Royal Commission on the Status of Women, whose recommendations both informed the NCW's Molgat-MacGuigan presentation and prompted the formation of NAC.[88] With their emphasis on formal equality in law and social policies to help women in housework, pregnancy, and child-rearing, these recommendations reflected long-standing NCW positions.[89] As rallying platforms for traditional women's organizations, younger feminist groups, and trade union women, they also furnished a basis of initial unity that was critical to NAC's success.[90] According to Jill Vickers, Pauline Rankin, and Christine Appelle, this work of "generational bridging ... proved to be one of NAC's greatest strengths."[91]

Intergenerational continuity also informed NAC's Hays-Joyal presentation. In particular, NAC criticized Section 15(1) of Ottawa's draft charter for failing to advance the NCW's perennial concern: economic security for women. The proposed Section 15(1) mirrored the Diefenbaker Bill of Rights in speaking of the citizen's "right to equality before the law and to the equal protection of the law without discrimination."[92] As NAC President Lynn McDonald explained, the courts had already used this wording to discriminate against women. Judges had read the phrases "equality before the law" and "equal protection of the law" simply to mean that "laws, once passed, will be equally applied to all individuals in the category concerned." Accordingly, NAC, which supported entrenchment "in principle," argued that a more adequate charter would require "equality in the laws themselves."[93]

To make the point concrete, NAC representatives offered several instances of discrimination that the Bill of Rights had failed to catch, including the denial of Unemployment Insurance benefits to pregnant women, the failure of court-ordered divorce settlements to address women's economic contributions, and discrimination against Aboriginal women in eligibility for band-status benefits.[94] These examples reflected NAC's strong economic focus. McDonald also registered more general notes of economic complaint, pointing out that women earned only "60 per cent of what men do," that conservatives continued to believe "that women do not have a right to jobs on the same basis [as] men," and that several international conventions contained references to "economic equality ... much more positive that what we have in the present charter."[95]

NAC's focus contrasted with the more emotionally engaged advocacy of minority groups, which tended to describe charter rights as symbols of recognition and respect. Not once did NAC speak of changing societal attitudes, of bringing women more fully into the polity, or of gaining recognition for unappreciated contributions. Even its initial words of address to the committee were spartan. While groups such as the AAFC and the NAJC prefaced their remarks by noting the "historic event" or "momentous occasion," McDonald simply said: "Thank you, Mr. Chairman. We will first of all give our written brief, all three of us will be speaking, and I will make some remarks and then we will be available for questioning."[96]

Beneath this utilitarian approach lay simmering disagreement among NAC members over the desirability of a pan-Canadian charter. One line of division mirrored labour's ongoing anglophone-francophone constitutional standoff. Important objections also arose from NAC's "radical grass roots," women who believed that "the basic unit of feminist politics ought to be the small primary group" rather than the "official political system."[97]

Although these divisions militated against enthusiasm, even many charter critics believed that it was important to press Ottawa for improvements. Their fear was that "women could be worse off if the proposed charter of rights and freedoms is entrenched."[98] McDonald's own suspicion of the courts placed her among the critics. As she explained, the "sorry record of the courts" made sceptics "very nervous" about future "ludicrous decision[s]" from a judiciary known for its "terrific inability ... to understand inequality against women."[99] Thus, the consensus position within NAC was to press for additional wording that might more adequately constrain a judiciary whose future policy-making role many feminists viewed with alarm. McDonald expressed this consensus by saying: "I do not think we can leave this one to chance."[100] Nevertheless, four months after NAC's Hays-Joyal appearance, the Fédération des femmes du Québec withdrew from the organization in protest against even this rather lukewarm endorsement of entrenchment.[101]

In a different context, NAC's attacks on the Canadian judiciary, coupled with its use of phrases like "reproductive freedom" and its demand for a "representative number of women on the bench," would have sparked parliamentary outrage.[102] Yet the committee's questions were invariably respectful. Perhaps aware that the customary male-chauvinist scolding would fit poorly with the dominant people-versus-powers framing, the committee's three political parties used only female representatives to question NAC witnesses. The wisdom of their choice appeared to be confirmed when Senator Harry Hays, the committee's joint chairman, offered the following words of leave taking: "We appreciate you coming and as a matter of fact we are honoured. However, your time is up and I was just wondering why we do not have a section in here [in the charter] for babies and children. All you girls are going to be working and we are not going to have anybody to look after them."[103]

It is easy to understand why a traditionalist like Hays might have felt overwhelmed. A host of enthusiastic charter proponents, including the Advisory Council on the Status of Women, the Native Women's Association of Canada, the Canadian Congress of Learning Opportunities for Women, and the National Association of Women and the Law, were pressing with energy and skill for many of the same revisions urged more cautiously by NAC.[104] This concerted advocacy was rewarded two months after NAC's November 1980 appearance, when Ottawa amended its entrenchment resolution to include the future Charter guarantees to equality "under the law" and to the "equal benefit of the law."[105]

Women pursued additional revisions as well. Worried that other charter rights might be used to undercut the equality provisions, a coalition called the Ad Hoc Committee of Canadian Women on the Constitution mounted a successful campaign to entrench a separate, overriding constitutional statement of women's equality.[106] Employing a combination of mass protest and elite lobbying that relied significantly on NAC connections and resources, the Ad Hoc women persuaded the federal Justice Department to add a new provision to the entrenchment package on 23 April 1981.[107] This provision, which became Section 28 of the Charter of Rights and Freedoms, stated: "Notwithstanding anything in this Charter, the rights and freedoms referred to in it are guaranteed equally to male and female persons."

Yet shocked activists soon found themselves engaged in a third phase of mobilization. The 5 November 1981 intergovernmental "kitchen accord" made a number of concessions to the provinces, including a legislative override that would allow governments to declare designated pieces of legislation immune from Charter challenge for successive five-year periods.[108] The Ad Hoc Committee responded to the "notwithstanding clause" by initiating a lobby of federal and provincial officials the intensity of which Cairns has called "without parallel in Canadian history."[109] On 24 November the Ad Hoc women succeeded in exempting the special Section 28 statement of women's equality from the Section 33 override. The campaign that Penney Kome calls the "taking of twenty-eight" was complete.[110]

Although NAC's initial approach to the charter was reserved and sceptical, a different view slowly took hold. Emboldened by their victories, the forces within NAC that favoured participation in the official political system began to celebrate the new equality provisions as an "outstanding achievement in the face of incredible odds."[111] Thus, as Naomi Black suggests, and as the next chapter will show in detail, "the Charter ... retroactively ... developed into a source of pride and solidarity among federalist feminists in Canada."[112]

### The Charter and the Politics of Respect

While disappointing from a traditional unity-and-federalism perspective, the results of Canada's postwar crisis of rival nationalisms and intergovernmental conflict were remarkable from the standpoint of social movements.[113] Marginalized groups transformed Canadian constitutionalism between the years 1980 and 1982 by infusing it with some of their own aspirations and concerns. The key initial fruits of their activism – the Section 15 equality rights and affirmative action provisions, the Section 27 statement on multiculturalism, and the Section 28 declaration of women's equality – became authoritative tributes to movements struggling for security and respect.

Trudeau's "just society" unity project reflected the shaping influence of the international human rights agenda and the "government generation" belief that the state's role is to defend people against power.[114] Steeped in a similar milieu, movements were well placed to capitalize on the opportunity that Trudeau's project presented – and thus to influence significantly the character of Canadian constitutionalism and citizenship. A more participatory ethos in constitutional matters, a new symbolism emphasizing multiculturalism and difference, a novel attentiveness to the historical experiences of victims, reinterpretations of equality and rights – as transitory or contradictory as these innovations may have been or may ultimately prove to be, they were forward strides reflecting key aspirations of social movements.[115]

The social movement role in Canada's most profound set of constitutional changes since Confederation has attracted considerable scholarly attention. Alexandra Dobrowolsky has shown how English-speaking women forged multiple, creative, and overlapping routes to representation in an arena hostile to feminist involvement.[116] James Kelly has identified the Hays-Joyal hearings as a pivotal moment when social movements pushed the locus of Canadian sovereignty toward the citizenry.[117] Most famously, Alan Cairns has explained how a "citizens' constitution" emphasizing non-territorial identities and claims came both to complement the "governments' constitution" of parliamentary sovereignty and federalism and to jostle for primacy with it.[118] In their own unique ways, all these authors illuminate core aspects of Canada's civic transformation by attending to the citizen campaigns involved.

Social movement studies were relatively underdeveloped in Canadian political science prior to entrenchment; as a consequence, scholars seeking a broader view of the aspirations that helped reshape Canadian constitutionalism have turned to the New Politics approach. That school's major empirical contribution has been survey evidence indicating that more secure and better educated publics became increasingly receptive to feminist and minority appeals in the five decades following the Second World War.[119] This focus on the intergenerational effects of postwar prosperity sheds light on a key transformation noted in this chapter. Parliamentarians in previous decades resorted to tactics of avoidance, trivialization, and bullying when women or minorities failed to "mind their place"; their counterparts at the Hays-Joyal hearings responded with sympathy and respect. As New Politics theory would suggest, this openness to alternative political appeals and identities would have been unthinkable in eras when life's more evident precariousness led to a comparatively rigid insistence on traditional relations and roles.[120]

More contentious is the New Politics interpretation of the politics of recognition as a postmaterialist departure from concerns about economic security and personal safety. I have argued that this interpretation misconstrues the constitutional participation of equality-seeking movements in Canada. Groups seeking recognition and respect in the Canadian constitutional arena have tended to do so not in abstraction from or in opposition to material needs but rather in order to address their problems of economic security and personal safety more effectively.

A widespread view of "Charter politics as postmaterialist politics" paints a different picture of Canada's constitutional transformation.[121] Three features of the entrenchment debates would appear to support the New Politics view. The first is labour's general absence from constitutional politics after the Quiet Revolution. F.L. Morton and Rainer Knopff emphasize this point, arguing that "the postmaterialist analysis explains one of the most distinctive characteristics of Charter politics: the division of the Canadian left" on the question of a charter.[122] Yet Communists and trade unionists were in fact the first Canadian social movement actors to propose a national bill of rights. Indeed, the CLC only ceased its long-standing charter quest when Quebec nationalists' objections threatened to tear the organization apart. Moreover, the CLC's absence from the Molgat-MacGuigan and Hays-Joyal debates demonstrated that Québécois and English-Canadian workers placed an importance on the "postmaterialist" questions dividing them, such as national identity and group recognition, that outweighed their consensus on traditional trade union issues.[123] Thus, the postmaterialist analysis fails to explain the CLC's constitutional behaviour between 1968 and 1982.

Second, Morton and Knopff cite the feminist role in "shaping the Charter's content" as a classic instance of how "postmaterialism ... provided the political buoyancy that breathed life and energy into the Charter."[124] Emphasizing the shared origins of feminist and judicial elites in the "postmaterialist 'chattering classes,'" Morton and Knopff argue that the anglophone women's movement saw "the courts ... as a favoured vehicle for achieving its policy ends."[125] But as we have seen, NAC withstood radical feminist and Quebec nationalist objections to participating in the Hays-Joyal debates not because it welcomed, but rather because it feared the enhanced role in future policy making of the judiciary, which had already shown a tremendous failure "to understand inequality against women."[126] Furthermore, the policy ends with which NAC was most concerned – greater economic equality, affirmative action, the equitable disposition of family assets in divorce, and equality in social program benefits and employment opportunities – were not postmaterialist objectives.

The third aspect of the entrenchment debates that might support a New Politics view is the specific nature of the constitutional advocacy of ethnic minorities. After all, third-force representatives said little about material insecurity; instead, they appeared to value constitutional recognition for expressive and psychological reasons.[127] It would therefore not seem unreasonable to describe them as postmaterialists pursuing status concerns rather than security needs. However, visible minority organizations also pursued esteem, symbolism, and respect; and they did so with an animating purpose that suggests the potential error of treating these priorities as expressions of postmaterialism.

Like their third-force counterparts, non-white minorities strongly emphasized the symbolic value of constitutionally recognizing multiculturalism and entrenching a charter of rights. But they also stressed problems of hate crime, inadequate police and human rights protection, and discrimination in housing and employment – problems they linked to broader questions of misrecognition and disrespect. Visible minority leaders argued that a new framework of supportive civic symbolism would help undermine the "hatred and disdain" that had presented their communities with such significant economic security and personal safety concerns in the first place.[128] Thus, the New Politics view, which categorizes esteem and belonging a priori as expressive or postmaterialist aspirations, and which seems to ignore the instrumental uses to which esteem and belonging can be put, fails to capture the constitutional participation of racialized minorities.

This focus on the diverse potential uses of esteem and belonging provides a different perspective on constitutional politics after the Quiet Revolution. Rather than constituting the founding moment of Canada's postmaterialist transformation, the entrenchment debates were a key historical juncture when social movements increased their capacity to voice material complaints that dominant groups preferred not to hear. Movements sought favourable constitutional symbolism not for psychological reasons or as an end in itself, but in order to confront more effectively "hate messages ... in favour of the destruction of black people"; "an immigration policy ... [that] sought to maintain Canada as a [Northern European] refuge ... the segregation of blacks"; and "discrimination in employment, job promotion, [and] housing."[129]

When it comes to the proposition that equality-seeking movements pursued favourable civic symbolism in order to defend material interests, NAC stands as the exception that proves the rule. Although it certainly prioritized material concerns, NAC did not approach the Charter debates as an opportunity for garnering esteem and belonging. That organization's aloofness reflected the unique nature of women's civic marginalization; although men routinely trumpeted women's importance as wives and mothers, they tended to pay them remarkably little respect in the civic arena. This is one reason why the radical feminists of the 1970s and 1980s made a point of shunning the male-dominated institutions of Canadian officialdom.

But the abstentionist position lost adherents after the unexpected victory of 1980-82 turned the Charter "into a source of pride and solidarity among federalist feminists in Canada."[130] As symbols of the time when the "Mothers of Confederation ... rose up angry ... [and] proved themselves a formidable national political force," the Section 15 and Section 28 anti-discrimination and women's equality provisions became valued instruments for underscoring the illegitimacy of women's civic exclusion, and thus for increasing women's capacity to defend the material interests that drove NAC's Hays-Joyal presentation.[131] In summary, therefore, the chapter's argument about racialized minorities holds for anglophone feminists as well; the Charter debates were a crystallizing moment for traditionally disrespected groups pursuing materialist aspirations and concerns.

# From Meech Lake to Charlottetown: Symbolic Power and Visions of Political Community

From the Rowell-Sirois Commission to Trudeau's quest for a charter, Canadian constitutional politics reflected a left-liberal consensus that favoured, however cautiously or partially, increasing the polity's responsiveness to marginalized groups. This pattern was shattered by the Meech Lake and Charlottetown initiatives of the late 1980s and early 1990s, which exhibited a neoliberal focus on diminishing the social role of the state. This historic shift forced equality-seeking movements to prioritize defensive constitutional goals.

The new footing was not entirely unprecedented. As chapter 4 observed, the B&B Commission aroused a defensive reaction from third-force minorities, who argued that the proposed "founding races" partnership was an affront to the UN Declaration and the Diefenbaker Bill of Rights. What distinguished the new debates, aside from their neoliberal context, was the more variegated constitutional setting, wider array of participating interests, and broader menu of proposals for change. Accordingly, this chapter examines an expanded cast of players seeking multiple defensive goals in a multifaceted, post-Charter order subject to unprecedentedly ambitious schemes of reform. While officialdom pursued an aggressive agenda of free trade, privatization, and decentralist constitutional change, trade unions fought to save the welfare state; anglophone feminists emphasized the welfare state and women's rights; visible minorities defended racial equality rights and multiculturalism; and ethnic minorities focused on multiculturalism and minority rights in Quebec.

From the standpoint of social movements, two core features of post-Charter constitutional politics demand particular attention. The first is the function of Charter recognition as a basis of political voice for traditionally marginalized groups. As the emphasis on "authorization" in Pierre Bourdieu's concept of symbolic capital suggests, actors who can speak an institutionally sanctioned discourse are situated differently in relation to power than those whose claims are more readily dismissed as idiosyncratic.[1] Drawing on Bourdieu's concept and also on the work of Alan Cairns, this chapter shows how the Charter's role in conferring symbolic capital increased the capacity of recognized movements to resist unwelcome constitutional change – a development that prompted consternation on the political right.[2] At the same time, the seeming fragility of Charter recognition in turbulent times made Charter-identifying movements intensely protective of gains achieved in the past.

Canada's unity crisis also placed mounting pressure on equality seekers to articulate broader visions of the country's constitutional future. The second major theme in this chapter is the emergence of two divergent responses by social movements to these pressures. One response favoured "asymmetrical federalism," or special constitutional powers for Quebec, the other a more traditional, pan-Canadian approach. Suspicious of any proposal hinting at the anathema concept of "founding races," ethnic and racialized minorities insisted on the primacy of the Charter in a country defined by multicultural pluralism. Asymmetrical federalism was not on their list of priorities. By contrast, in a historic reversal, which began hesitantly with the Canadian Labour Congress in 1987 and became more pronounced with the robust advocacy of the National Action Committee on the Status of Women in 1991-92, Canadian feminist and labour movements embraced the emphasis on special status that they had previously resisted.

As will be seen, the emergence of a clear split between movements over two constitutional visions – asymmetrical versus equal-provinces federalism – was not an arbitrary or chance phenomenon. Rather, it reflected contrasting judgments about group security made by actors shaped by prior histories of constitutional engagement in a context of national division. Because the two visions are likely to divide English-Canadian social movements if a new unity crisis places constitutional change on the agenda in the future, this chapter places particular emphasis on explaining their respective motivations and concerns. Before taking up the task, a brief synopsis of the Meech-to-Charlottetown saga is in order.

## From Meech to Charlottetown

The 1987 Meech Lake Accord was a unanimous intergovernmental bargain designed to elicit Quebec's formal assent to the 1982 constitution, whose "bloody Charter" sovereigntists refused to accept.[3] But the Meech Lake deal collapsed in 1990. Following sustained attack from

First Nations, distinct society opponents, and pan-Canadian social movements, the provinces of Manitoba and Newfoundland – whose electorates had since returned governments markedly cool to the Accord – failed to ratify the package within the three-year window required by the 1982 amending formula.[4]

Although Progressive Conservative Prime Minister Brian Mulroney stressed the importance of constitutional reconciliation upon taking office in 1984, the real genesis of the Meech Lake agreement lay in the 1985 election of a federalist government in Quebec. Liberal Premier Robert Bourassa announced that he would sign the 1982 Constitution Act if Mulroney and the other first ministers would accept certain conditions. The amendment package that resulted from this opening extended to all provinces the gains demanded by Quebec. However, there were two exceptions to the provincialization of Quebec's conditions. The major one was a requirement instructing judges to interpret the Canadian constitution "in a manner consistent with ... the recognition that Quebec constitutes within Canada a distinct society."[5] The second exception, a provision declaring linguistic duality "a fundamental characteristic of Canada" that Ottawa and the provinces were required "to preserve," sought to protect official-minority language rights in a post-Meech environment. At the same time, and in a somewhat more activist vein, the Accord affirmed the National Assembly's mandate to "preserve and promote the distinct identity of Quebec."

The four key remaining provisions reflected the decentralizing dynamic that tends to characterize multiparty intergovernmental negotiations when only one delegation speaks for the whole.[6] Provinces were to be awarded a key role in determining immigration criteria; future senators and Supreme Court judges would be selected from provincial lists; and the unanimity principle was to be extended to amendment areas formerly subject to the provision requiring federal consent along with seven provinces with 50 percent of the population. Finally, the Accord proposed to restrict the federal spending power by offering full compensation to any province choosing to opt out of a future shared-cost program in an area of provincial jurisdiction. These proposals attracted vehement opposition from social movements.

Critics were also angered by the secrecy of the intergovernmental process and by Ottawa's refusal to contemplate alterations to the amendment package. Although authorities seemed unmoved at first, the evident failure of the Meech Lake entrenchment approach – Cairns describes it as "a military manoeuvre by governments to keep the citizens at bay" – shaped Ottawa's response to the Accord's June 1990 collapse.[7] Mulroney brought a chastened demeanour to the new imperative of staving off a sovereignty referendum with a last-ditch attempt to address Quebec's unresolved grievances in a manner acceptable to the whole country.[8] As Patrick Monahan recounts: "Promising that 'you will not be able to get me to ever cut off debate on a constitutional resolution,' Mulroney said that, in future, the Constitution would be taken to the people: 'They can go on for as long as they want, years. I want to hear everybody.'"[9]

In November 1990 Mulroney named long-time civil servant Keith Spicer to chair the Citizens' Forum on Canada's Future, a constitutional tribunal for individual – or, to use the parlance of the day, "ordinary" – Canadians. At the same time, a Special Joint Committee on the Process for Amending the Constitution began exploring the possibility of a constituent assembly or national constitutional referendum.[10] The new participatory emphasis also informed six televised "mini constituent assemblies" on constitutional reform, convened by Ottawa in early 1992.[11]

However, the major constitutional venue of the period was the more traditionally pitched Special Joint Committee on a Renewed Canada. This committee's mandate was to solicit citizens' and experts' input on Ottawa's official proposals for resolving the constitutional crisis. These proposals had been released in September 1991 under the title *Shaping Canada's Future Together*.[12] Throughout the winter of 1991-92 the committee heard boisterous, extensive, and in many cases well-informed presentations, particularly from equality-seeking social movements.

The Renewed Canada hearings were a qualified success. After considering presentations from seven hundred witnesses, the committee recommended significant changes to the federal government's original proposals. This parliamentary initiative paved the way for a new round of intergovernmental bargaining, which culminated in the sprawling, controversial agreement known as the Charlottetown Accord. The Accord itself was rejected by voters in a majority of the provinces in a precedent-setting national referendum on 26 October 1992. Quebec nationalists rejected the Accord's weak asymmetry as an insufficient response to their traditional demands; voters in the rest of Canada seemed unprepared to accept even the mildest notion of special status.[13]

Nevertheless, the Renewed Canada hearings merit consideration even today as the best available guide to the constitutional thinking of pan-Canadian social movements after three decades of national debate. Our analysis starts with the historic Meech Lake battles, which confirmed the heightened importance of equality-seeking movements as constitutional players and thereby inaugurated Canada's fractious post-Charter era.

## Meech Lake: The Special Joint Committee on the 1987 Constitutional Accord

### Symbolic Capital and Unsettling Contrasts

The public hearings of the Special Joint Committee on the 1987 Constitutional Accord, co-chaired by Senator Arthur Tremblay and MP Chris Speyer, demonstrated the Mulroney government's failure to grasp the sense of constitutional ownership among the movements recognized in the new Charter.[14] With its hopelessly paternalistic mandate of "explor[ing] the implications of [Meech Lake] so it is well understood by everyone," the committee became a fresh provocation for groups already angered by the Accord.[15]

Representatives of social movement groups wanted the Tremblay-Speyer Committee to persuade Ottawa to reconsider the decision to constitutionally elevate the "distinct society" reference over Charter equality rights. For non-francophone feminists, subjecting sex equality to a clause mandating special consideration of Quebec's uniqueness meant defining "women's rights ... as second class rights."[16] Visible minority leaders launched an analogous defence of ethnic and racial equality rights.[17] And although Section 16 of the Meech Lake Accord expressly exempted multiculturalism from the purview of the distinct society and linguistic duality clauses – thus angering feminist groups, who noted the absence of a parallel provision for women's rights – minority groups denounced "the outdated and discredited concept of two founding nations" and insisted that "the concepts of multiculturalism and bilingualism [be made] equal."[18] Thus, feminist and minority witnesses viewed Charter recognition as the basis of a valued new civic status and saw distinct society's intended constitutional supremacy as a partial repudiation of their still vulnerable gains.

Attachment to the Charter as a source of symbolic capital drove the movements' attacks on the Meech Lake Accord. A key dimension of this attachment was the Charter's discursive role in providing invocable representative criteria that the old "governments' constitution" of federalism and parliamentary sovereignty could not provide.[19] The Ukrainian Canadian Committee (UCC) denounced Meech Lake for violating "the letter and spirit of the Charter," complaining that the deal's focus on provincial representation in the Senate and the Supreme Court was unaccompanied by any consideration of minority under-representation in the same institutions.[20] The Chinese Canadian National Council (CCNC) also invoked the Charter as Canada's yardstick of adequacy in constitutional reform. Because the Charter was "in place to protect the rights and freedoms of all Canadians regardless of their race or origin ... every facet [of Meech would have to be] examined to make sure that ... Canadians [were] not overlooked in any way."[21]

Social movement witnesses were thus defending the Charter as an authoritative signal to respect traditionally marginalized groups as equal civic participants. Indeed, the National Action Committee on the Status of Women (NAC) was so impressed by this new constitutional function that its former ambivalence about participating in the official political system seemed to have vanished.[22] NAC's previous approach to the idea of a charter was sceptical; now, President Louise Dulude proclaimed the "very strong symbolic significance" of the Section 28 statement on gender equality for the "women who fought to get it there."[23] And whereas Lynn McDonald had introduced NAC prosaically to the Hays-Joyal Committee as a "voluntary organization working to improve the status of women," Dulude called the group "the defender of women's rights in Canada."[24] This transformed sense of organizational mission reflected the availability of a feminist symbolic capital that the land's highest law directed the country to recognize.

However, constitutional recognition did not translate into easy confidence for equality-seeking movements; problems of material insecurity and political marginalization fuelled a pronounced sense of unease among feminists and racialized minorities in particular. One source of concern was women's vulnerability in times of neoliberal change. NAC member Wendy Williams criticized the Accord's proposal to allow provinces to opt out of national shared-cost programs with full compensation, arguing that this constraint on the federal spending power would "weaken ... the ability of the federal government to initiate progressive ... social policies," "encourage privatization and ... decrease accessibility and the control of quality." Keenly aware that "women [were] disproportionately represented among the poor," NAC sought the certainty and protection of "national standards and objectives."[25]

Non-white minorities also opposed the Accord's plans to decentralize federal powers. Citing the "misinformation, racism, and prejudice" faced historically by Chinese immigrants in British Columbia, the CCNC criticized the Accord's focus on increasing the provincial role in immigration policy and resettlement. The CCNC knew that the constitution already recognized immigration as an area of shared federal and provincial authority, but as a "minority community in Canada that has had unpleasant experiences," it viewed "national standards as our safe refuge."[26] The National Association of Canadians of Origins in India (NACOI) feared similarly that decentralization would empower intolerant local majorities. "Disturbed at the general trend on the part of the federal government to abdicate its responsibility and author- ity," the NACOI saw Meech Lake as a "prelude to the Balkanization of Canada."[27]

This nervous insistence on central power and national standards also shaped how feminists and minority organizations viewed Meech Lake's impact on the Charter. Critics worried that the distinct society provi- sion could allow a future Quebec government to "prohibit the use of a specific language [to prevent] ... a dilution of ... [Quebec's] distinctive identity," or to implement "pro-family measures ... encouraging [francophone] women to have children."[28] Insisting that past wrongs militated against future confidence, witnesses reminded the committee that "equality is a very fragile thing"; that reflecting on "history [makes one] realize that yes, it can happen"; and that "the past has not been glorious with respect to the treatment of minorities in Canada."[29]

The committee majority's response was twofold. First, members from the government side cited "a distinguished group of constitutional ex- perts" who had concluded that Meech threatened "no derogation of the rights in the Charter." Second, they warned that reopening the Accord would unleash a "potential unravelling effect"; the concerns of femi- nists and ethnocultural minorities would have to wait until a "second ... round of negotiations."[30] In summary, marginalized groups valued the Charter as a symbol of inclusion and respect, while the committee's indifference to the new constitutional setting produced an unsettling contrast. The persistence of business as usual in the post-Charter era engendered a renewed, even intensified sense among women's and mi- nority groups that they were "forgotten people," an "afterthought" rel- egated "again to the lower class of people in this country."[31]

### Charter Canadians and Political Exchange

Yet supporters of the Charter from social movements wielded consider- able clout in the broader Canadian debates over the Accord. One indi- cator of their influence was a backlash from right-wing commentators, who despite their own tendency to oppose the distinct society clause used phrases such as "constitutional machismo" to characterize the "spe- cial interests" that were instrumental in Meech's defeat.[32]

The mobilization against Meech Lake began in earnest following the Conservative majority's refusal to countenance amendments in the Sep- tember 1987 Tremblay-Speyer report. Manitoba Native leader and NDP MLA Elijah Harper perhaps struck the decisive blow two-and-a-half years later when he used a procedural rule to prevent his legislature from meeting the ratification deadline. Yet it was growing public anger in English-speaking Canada that paved the way for Harper's opportunity in the first place. In 1988 and 1989, governments chary of the Accord were elected in New Brunswick, Manitoba, and Newfoundland. These victories led in turn to the creation of legislative committees and other official platforms that kept a parade of anti-Meech complaints before the media. Combined with opposition in the federal Liberal Party and an outcry over Quebec's December 1988 decision to shield its sign law with the notwithstanding clause, these developments slowed the ratification process to a halt, ultimately killing the deal.

The core theme in this assault was Trudeau's vision of a shared civic nationhood based on equal citizenship rights. To understand how defenders of the Trudeau vision articulated their opposition, it is useful to explore Cairns' "Charter Canadians" concept.[33] As Cairns explains, this label targets both the generalized allegiance to the Charter of Trudeau nationalists and the more oppositional attachment to the Charter of movements mobilized around the document's equality, anti-discrimination, and multiculturalism provisions.[34] To push the distinction further, it is useful to differentiate between what we can call the Trudeauite and the social movement Charter Canadians: the former valued Charter rights as part of a generalized commitment to pan-Canadian unity and citizenship; the latter were mobilized supporters of particular activist projects. Highlighting this distinction delineates more clearly the role of equality-seeking movements in the defeat of Meech Lake.

Although the Trudeauite perspective was primarily nationalist rather than activist, that camp's rhetoric placed the social movement Charter Canadians front and centre. For example, Deborah Coyne, then a key advisor to Newfoundland's anti-Meech Liberal premier, Clyde Wells, argued that "the most significant lesson" of the controversy was the "firm belief in the equality of all citizens" voiced by the "new popular coalitions."[35] According to Coyne, this activist commitment to equality was shared by Canadian nationalists as a whole; it reflected "fundamental values that are common to all of us and that define ourselves, our concept of the Canadian federation, and our commitment to a fairer, more compassionate society."[36]

Social movements' equality concerns featured with particular prominence when the Trudeauite critics attacked the notion that the Charter might be applied differently in Quebec. For instance, Liberal MP and Meech opponent Donald Johnston declared: "If you believe that ... sexual equality rights should be protected against the collective rights of a distinct society, you must reject Meech Lake."[37] New Brunswick's Liberal

Premier Frank McKenna voiced similar unease that "women's equality rights, hard fought for and achieved in 1981-82, [were] threatened by [the] Accord." Asked McKenna: "Are you the person who is going to say ... to heck with the rights the women have achieved? Is that going to be your position? It is not mine."[38]

The Manitoba Task Force on Meech Lake, which Progressive Conservative Premier Gary Filmon initiated in response to Quebec's December 1988 invocation of the notwithstanding clause, also enlisted the social movement Charter Canadians when it issued its final report recommending against the Meech bargain.[39] The creation of the task force reflected the Filmon government's desultory commitment to the Accord. The public hearings themselves manifested a "significant degree of anti-Quebec feeling."[40] Yet the final report skirted the Quebec issue; it emphasized a different set of "doubts and uncertainties," which feminist and ethnocultural minority witnesses had outlined in their "persuasive" and "truly impressive" briefs. These briefs "made it clear," the report concluded, "that Canadians cherish their rights and freedoms and will not tolerate any real or perceived threats to those rights."[41]

The point is not that concerns about equality rights were wheeled in cynically to mask francophobia. It is that social movement Charter supporters, in their new role as "Canadians [who] cherish their rights and freedoms," conferred valuable credibility on the Trudeauites' insistence that Meech Lake violated a "Canadian spirit" of "justice and freedom and equality and mutual respect."[42]

The Trudeauian position informed New Brunswick's willingness to contemplate amendments to the Accord, Newfoundland's insistence on the Charter's inviolability, the decision of Manitoba's task force to oppose the Accord, and of course the influential interventions of the former prime minister himself. But on its own, the mantra of Canada as "a model of tolerance and a demonstration to all the nations that unity can be formed out of diversity" lacked a certain depth. It became more convincing when linked to the movements seeking the "justice" and "equality" of which the Trudeauites so proudly spoke.[43] Thus, in mounting a pro-Charter campaign that shaded into a defence of the existing constitutional order, equality-seeking activists supplied vital authenticating support for the Trudeauite forces, whose closer access to the levers of power helped amplify social movements' concerns. Put differently, the Accord's defeat reflected what some scholars would call an exchange relationship between the defensive appeals of the social movement Charter Canadians and the legitimation needs of their Trudeauite counterparts.[44]

**Conflicted Communities: Feminism and Trade Unionism**
Almost from the moment of Trudeau's first election, Quebec's increasingly sovereigntist trade union leaders anticipated an exchange relationship between social movements and Trudeauites when it came to supporting a charter. They understood the Charter's potential to orient emancipatory projects toward the existing Canadian framework, and they had no intention of "strengthening the federalist case among Quebec workers." The Canadian Labour Congress (CLC) responded to these potentially explosive concerns by abstaining from the early 1980s Charter debates.[45]

From the standpoint of intra-group unity, the CLC's move was understandable. Even NAC's ambivalent initial stance of Charter support prompted the Fédération des femmes du Québec (FFQ) to depart from the pan-Canadian organization in 1982.[46] Although the FFQ rejoined in 1984, the nationalist breach widened during the Meech Lake debates. NAC claimed that the FFQ supported its call to insulate women's equality rights from the distinct society clause; however, the FFQ's presentation to the Tremblay-Speyer Committee did not mention this point. Instead, the FFQ suggested that NAC's concerns reflected the more regressive conditions prevalent in the rest of Canada; while anglophone feminists were "much more distrustful of their provincial authorities than we are," in Quebec the "respect of women's rights [was] more and more becoming part of the political culture."[47] The denouement came in 1989, when the FFQ responded to NAC's persistent anti-Meech campaign by quitting the organization for good.[48]

This rivalry between the country's competing nationalisms forced pan-Canadian feminist and labour groups to make hard choices with often unsatisfactory outcomes. By deferring to its Quebec affiliates in 1980-82, the CLC lost the opportunity to entrench collective-bargaining, picketing, and strike rights in the Charter. English-Canadian labour then watched from the sidelines while Charter-recognized movements became high-profile defenders of their constitutionally sanctioned symbolic capital. For its part, although NAC was initially ambivalent, it rejected the CLC's cautious approach; soon after assuming its mantle as the "defender of women's rights in Canada," NAC lost a key partner organization for failing "to comprehend ... the aspirations of francophone women in Quebec."[49]

Canadian labour hoped to avoid this nationalist dilemma in its approach to the Meech Lake Accord. On the one hand, the trade union movement broke with the abstentionism of the early 1980s to resume its historical role as an advocate for the left-centralist views of its majority

English-speaking membership. In its presentation to the Tremblay-Speyer Committee the CLC demanded amendments that might mitigate the Accord's potential threats to social programs and equality rights. It also launched a blistering attack on executive federalism as an amendment approach, complaining that "the people of Canada had been effectively excluded" by an "authoritarian ... process."[50] The National Union of Provincial Government Employees (NUPGE) seconded the point when it denounced the "power-brokers and the jurisdiction traders" for their "incredibly arrogant" authorship of a deal "negotiated in secret."[51] Besides supporting these positions, two other CLC member organizations – the United Electrical, Radio, and Machine Workers and the Public Service Alliance of Canada – also argued for adding collective-bargaining, picketing, and strike rights to a revised Charter.[52]

Yet the CLC did more than restate familiar positions from the past. It broke new ground by addressing frankly its inability to speak for the country's working population as a whole. Citing its "recent convention ... resolution on Quebec," it proclaimed the full autonomy of Quebec affiliates in matters of constitutional politics and public policy. As Executive Vice-President Nancy Riche explained, Quebec unionists were now free to express – and indeed, were likely to express – "completely different arguments from those we are raising."[53]

Thus, the CLC resumed its long-standing emphasis on human rights, civil liberties, democratic participation, and national social programs – which the 1980-82 crisis had significantly muted – by using the two-nations principle to reorder its internal affairs.[54] The CLC was edging closer to the position discovered by the Communists during the Quiet Revolution: the only way to defend left-wing constitutional objectives for English Canada without having simultaneously to battle progressive forces in Quebec was to accept asymmetrical federalism. In 1991-92, with the Canadian welfare state under increasing pressure and sovereigntist resolve strengthening markedly, the CLC would embrace this conclusion wholeheartedly.

### Charlottetown: The Special Joint Committee on a Renewed Canada
The failure of the Meech Lake Accord in June 1990 was received by many francophone Quebecers as a final demonstration of English Canada's congenital inability to respond to their needs. A growing sense that the "soft nationalist" project of constitutional renewal had run its course led Premier Bourassa to announce that a sovereignty referendum would be held on 26 October 1992 in the absence of new federalist proposals.

Yet a desperate bid to satisfy Quebec's constitutional grievances could scarcely have been more out of tune with the mood in the rest of the country. The failed national discussions around Meech Lake had already been billed as a "Quebec round," only to be condemned as a "provincial-izing round."[55] Furthermore, what David Milne calls "public exaspera-tion with elite manipulation of the constitutional process" was quickly eroding the legitimacy of executive federalism as an approach to amend-ing the Constitution.[56] Thus – and during a significant economic reces-sion, no less – first ministers faced the nearly impossible task of addressing Quebec's frustrated constitutional ambitions, mollifying Meech Lake's critics, and combining elite accommodation with new experiments in citizen involvement. The latter included the 1990 Spicer Commission, the six "mini constituent assemblies" of early 1992, and, ultimately, the Charlottetown referendum of 26 October of the same year.[57]

Ottawa responded to these diverse pressures by framing the process leading up to the August 1992 Charlottetown Accord as the "Canada round." In terms of substance, the winter 1991-92 hearings of the Spe-cial Joint Committee on a Renewed Canada, co-chaired by Senator Gérald Beaudoin and MP Dorothy Dobbie, considered an official federal pack-age of twenty-eight amendment proposals, many of them targeted at constituencies angered by Meech Lake. The proposals were grouped around eight subject areas: a "Canada clause" of fundamental national characteristics to guide constitutional interpretation; a watered-down distinct society clause; entrenched property rights and a tightened not-withstanding clause; Aboriginal self-government; Senate reform; the Meech Lake Supreme Court proposals; an "economic union" of internal free trade and harmonized fiscal and monetary policies; and, finally, the decentralization of federal powers, including an even more restric-tive approach to the spending power than that seen in Meech. As Russell notes, the new motto appeared to be "Something for everyone."[58]

Yet Ottawa had constitutional aims of its own. As Stephen McBride and John Shields argue, the governing Progressive Conservatives sought to further the revolutionary aims of the 1988 Canada-US Free Trade Agreement. The Renewed Canada proposals on decentralization, en-trenched property rights, and nationwide fiscal and monetary harmo-nization aimed to constitutionalize elements of neoliberalism – that is, to cement durable long-term limitations on government that would help "downsize the state and liberate market forces from the state's regu-latory constraints."[59] On the procedural front, this neoliberal thrust was complemented by a rhetorical assault on the social movements that had made equality rights and welfare programs key issues in the debates over Meech. Responding to the new constitutional prominence of oppositional voices, federal officials drew repeated contrasts between a baleful coterie of "special interest groups," whose activist focus was characterized as unpatriotic and divisive, and the more wholesome input of "ordinary Canadians."[60]

Despite these attacks, social movements waged moderately successful campaigns strengthened by a novel combination of inter- and intra-movement networking.[61] Drawing support from like-minded opposition MPs, other activist organizations, and three NDP provincial governments, equality seekers forced the Beaudoin-Dobbie Committee to table significant changes to the original Renewed Canada proposals. Thus, the property rights proposal was eliminated; the economic union segment was weakened; a "social charter" was inserted in order to shield social welfare standards from the economic union and decentralization provisions; and the decentralization proposals were modified, particularly by altering wording that would have virtually abolished the spending power.[62] These recommendations then formed the basis for the summer 1992 intergovernmental bargaining that produced the Charlottetown Accord.

Because the era's expanded constitutional agenda strains this chapter's requirements of space, the following analysis is necessarily selective. It addresses only the social movement contributions to the public hearings of the Special Joint Committee on a Renewed Canada. Most notably, therefore, it neglects the historic referendum campaign of fall 1992. It is enough to point out the following: a negative verdict from the electorate defeated the Charlottetown Accord; the precedent set by a national referendum on constitutional change appeared to delegitimize executive federalism as a framework for similar efforts; and the seeming fruitlessness of three decades of "megaconstitutional politics" cast severe doubts on the viability of formal constitutional change as a national unity solution for the future.[63]

**Constitutional Visions: Asymmetrical versus Equal-Provinces Federalism**
Cairns notes that Bourassa's post-Meech sovereignty threat stimulated the "development of a separate, incipiently nationalist self-consciousness in the ROC [rest of Canada]." But Cairns also points out that their ongoing attachment to a "federal constitutional order that defines Canadians in the traditional terms of province and country" made most anglophones strong supporters of the status quo.[64] Thus, a novel willingness to accept asymmetry positioned NAC and the labour movement as constitutional pioneers – English Canada's leading advocates of a new

federal contract between Québécois, Aboriginal, and English-speaking nations.

Left-leaning feminists and trade unionists readily supported Aboriginal self-government; taking a stance on the Quebec question was more complex. The conversion of NAC and the CLC into advocates of special status was a laborious process, one that both groups resisted until they finally concluded that the insistence on equal-provinces pan-Canadianism had become a threat to their own constitutional interests and priorities. As NAC President Judy Rebick told the Renewed Canada Committee, a "long discussion ... on Meech Lake" had convinced her organization that "women [cannot] get what [they] need from the Constitution unless we break this log-jam ... between Quebec and the rest of Canada." Canadians needed to "recognize that Quebec is a distinct society and that this has implications."[65] The CLC agreed: Riche described the new autonomy of her organization's Quebec affiliates as "a model" for the whole country. "We're saying ... clearly by our actions," she declared, "that we support ... different powers for Quebec than for the rest of Canada."[66]

Minority organizations upheld a more traditional perspective. While institutional links to Québécois labour and feminist groups helped push NAC and the CLC toward asymmetry, ethnocultural minority organizations – whose anglophone Quebec wings cleaved strongly to a singular conception of Canadian citizenship – encountered the opposite effect.[67] The Canadian Jewish Congress (CJC), the National Congress of Italian Canadians (NCIC), and the Hellenic Canadian Congress (HCC) underlined the point by sending a joint delegation to the Renewed Canada hearings that was led by a group of anglophone and allophone leaders from Quebec. Stressing a "vision of Canada" as a "society based upon diversity, but, at the same time, unity," the group insisted on subordinating distinct society to the "importance of preserving and promoting pluralism in Quebec."[68]

Similarly, the Canadian Ethnocultural Council (CEC) emphasized "one Canada" and demanded that distinct society be subjected to the overriding "responsibility of governments" to uphold "the fundamental values upon which Canadian society is built."[69] The National Association of Japanese Canadians (NAJC), the National Black Coalition of Canada (NBCC), and the Canadian Association of Visible Minorities (CAVM) also advocated a singular conception of Canada as a "multicultural society."[70] The NBCC took no position on distinct society, while the CAVM would accept such a reference, "provided of course that [it] does not derogate from the equality provisions" of the Charter. For its part, although the NAJC professed to accept distinct society, the shallowness of its commitment was exposed by its reference to "people of French background [as] part of multiculturalism."[71]

The fundamental conservatism of this perspective is striking. The CJC et al. aimed to salvage whatever they could of the pan-Canadian status quo, whereas most of the other ethnocultural minority participants, who skirted Quebec's insistence that its claim to nationhood be addressed, carried on as if the Meech Lake fiasco had never happened. By no means was this conservatism peculiar to ethnocultural minorities. As Cairns observes more generally, a solid majority of ROC citizens seemed to prefer "the inertial world of the status quo."[72] Thus, the decision of NAC and the trade unions to endorse asymmetry suggests the influence of considerations that weighed less heavily on other participants.

These considerations were primarily economic. As the leading roles of NAC and the CLC in the 1988 coalition against the Canada-US Free Trade Agreement suggest, the era's neoliberal turn had rallied feminist and labour activists around a common set of social democratic objectives.[73] In the constitutional arena, these objectives centred on the federal government's capacity to maintain and develop social programs for the ROC. Accordingly, NAC and the trade unions pressed the same conclusion at the Renewed Canada hearings that the Communist Party had urged the Molgat-MacGuigan Committee to adopt in 1971: Canada's major constitutional problem was its tendency to respond to Quebec's aspirations with proposals for across-the-board decentralization. The main fear was that decentralization would trigger a "race to the bottom," with individual provinces competing against one another for investment with policies of social program retrenchment and tax cuts.[74]

Thus, the new ideological and constitutional conjuncture led NAC and the trade unions to embrace the unfamiliar. Fearing that decentralization would "weaken the federal government's ability to ... develop national programs" while "pitting province against province," the CLC proposed "asymmetrical federalism": "a strong central government for outside of Quebec and different powers for Quebec."[75] A joint delegation of the Public Service Alliance of Canada (PSAC) and the National Union of Provincial Government Employees (NUPGE) made the same point more informally. These groups advocated "generosity towards Quebec" while pleading, "for God's sake don't decentralize things in the rest of Canada."[76] NAC also condemned the notion of parcelling out "piece by piece, province by province," powers best given to Quebec alone. Insisting that "women in the rest of Canada ... want a strong federal government to deliver social programs," Rebick defended asymmetry as the "way people in the rest of Canada can get what they want and people in Quebec can get what they want."[77]

By the same token, the opposition of ethnocultural minorities to asymmetrical federalism was accompanied by a relative indifference to the welfare state concerns that preoccupied NAC and the labour movement. For example, this contrast structured the different group reactions to Ottawa's call for a constitutional ban on interprovincial trade barriers and the creation of new federal powers to ensure the economic union's "efficient functioning."[78] The CLC saw a "corporate agenda [for] ... constitutionalizing ... a free market economy," while NAC perceived a blueprint for a "market-driven capitalism in which the government doesn't have very much to say."[79] But the Canadian Ethnocultural Council (CEC) praised the economic union proposals as a welcome symbol that "we are all of one Canada."[80] Similarly, the CEC ignored the economic and social policy implications of the decentralization provisions, requesting only "guarantees" to protect "multiculturalism" and "minority rights."[81]

One exception to this contrast bears notice: welfare state themes were a strong secondary focus in the CAVM's presentation. Much like NAC's Judy Rebick, who saw "social programs [as] absolutely critical for women [because] [w]omen are the majority of the poor," Reverend Ogueri Ohanaka of the CAVM noted that many racialized people were "smothering in airtight cages of poverty."[82] Accordingly, the CAVM supported the NDP's call for a constitutional "social charter," finding its focus on national welfare standards "very pertinent." Reverend Ohanaka also made a broader point about racism and economic insecurity when he implored the committee to consider those parents "who find their tongues twisted and their speech stammering as they seek to explain to their children ... why they are denied access to opportunities."[83]

It would also be a mistake to equate the relative silence of the other ethnocultural minority organizations on social programs with indifference to questions of security. Rather, the priority they placed on a distinctive set of group security concerns militated against accepting the asymmetrical solution that NAC and the labour movement saw as the welfare state's best hope. Influenced by strong group memories of past Canadian racism, minority groups opposed any form of constitutional experimentation that might privilege local majorities. "As to the impact of including the distinct society clause in the Constitution," observed Max Bernard of the Quebec CJC, "it would be fair to say that Quebec, as well as the rest of Canada, has seen some troubling moments with regard to the treatment afforded to minorities."[84]

Fears about a French-centred vision of Quebec had a corollary apprehension: that any move toward asymmetry would precipitate an explicitly majoritarian refashioning of the ROC's identity as well. Thus, while NAC and the CLC optimistically described the ROC in terms of its putative commitment to social democracy – the CLC stressed English Canada's "unequivocal ... support for a strong central government," for instance – minority groups sounded a note of alarm.[85] As the NBCC explained: "We notice in western Canada particularly, a majority of Canadians ... embracing right wing parties with right wing philosophies and, mind you, racist policies like the ... Reform Party." For its part, the CEC cited the growing emphasis on "free votes, recall of MPs, and referenda" as an example of a new ROC populism that could "work against the interest of minorities."[86]

In short, ethnocultural minority participants were averse to Philip Resnick's "Thinking English Canada" project.[87] Viewing asymmetrical federalism as a spur to intolerant populism rather than social democracy's saviour, minority leaders subordinated economic questions to what they saw as more pressing security concerns. These concerns, which reflected both historical experiences and the basic uncertainties of minority status, are almost certain to resurface if asymmetry receives serious consideration in future.

**Trade Unions and Women's Groups: The Economic and the Symbolic**
Trade unions had their own concerns about constitutionalism and civic identity. Reeling from plant closures, the assault on trade union freedoms, and an overall climate of state retrenchment, labour was politically weaker and more symbolically marginal than at any time since the red-baiting 1950s.[88] The movement's sense of declining economic clout was aggravated by an awareness that workers were losing their political voice at precisely the moment that Charter recognition was helping amplify feminist and minority struggles. For example, NUPGE President James Clancy noted that "labour did not participate in the repatriation of the Constitution in 1981. Many of us have felt very strongly about that and indeed very bitter about that, that labour officially did not involve itself in the debate in those early years." PSAC President Daryl Bean was similarly "upset that the labour movement did not get involved in 1981. I thought it was a mistake then and I still believe it was a mistake."[89]

Suggesting that this lack of constitutional recognition had left "working people ... feel[ing] disenfranchised," Clancy underscored the social charter's importance for labour: workers had come to "see the social charter as their connection with this round of constitutional change."[90]

While other activists promoted the social charter as a tool for confronting neoliberal governments in the courts, trade union representatives viewed the idea in a more symbolic light. When asked by a sceptical committee member how a social charter would "create more jobs, provide better housing, or do all the good things you see forthcoming from it," Clancy shrugged that it would "not solve all the ills of the world tomorrow," and that there were "difficulties [with] the whole question of enforceability and so forth."[91]

These questions were secondary for a movement whose civic distinctiveness had come to be defined negatively via its lack of constitutionally sanctioned symbolic capital. Impressed by the gains made by enumerated movements, and in contrast to the largely practical thrust of its bill-of-rights advocacy in industrial unionism's heyday, labour sought a tool of recognition with which to amplify working-class concerns. As Clancy put it, working people "need a connection to the Constitution. For many people in this country that idea of a social charter represents the connection." Bean of the PSAC also promoted the social charter as "an important connection for millions of Canadians when it comes to the Constitution."[92]

This emphasis by the trade unions on constitutional symbolism and civic connection is interesting in light of NAC's role as a key voice against neoliberalism in the Canada round debates. As preceding chapters have shown, although Canadian women's movements focused consistently on redistributive questions, pervasive disrespect for women as civic actors often kept this focus from view. The more noticeable feminist economic advocacy of the late 1980s and early 1990s contrasted strongly with this earlier position of coerced invisibility. Noting the contrast, Jill Vickers and her co-authors say the following about NAC's participation in the historic free trade debates of the 1980s: "[Women] had achieved a significant framework of rights, and they were now exploring them. They were increasingly coming to see themselves as equal partners in the process of making choices about Canada's future."[93]

Though the "framework of rights" to which Vickers and her co-authors refer is the framework provided by the Charter, the statement highlights the broader importance of anglophone feminism's increased stock of symbolic capital. By achieving a new status as constitutionally authorized participants with recognized civic interests, pan-Canadian women's groups increased their capacity to resist both direct political exclusion and the more subtle forms of silencing that had compromised their participation in the past. This is not to portray Charter rights as a panacea, and neither is it to present symbolic gains as a meaningful sub-

stitute for organization in the workplace – but it *is* to say that entrenchment redrew the Canadian polity's lines of esteem and belonging. Wom-
en's increased presence in the economic, social policy, and constitutional
battles of the late 1980s and early 1990s was one significant result.

### Meech Lake and the Canada Round: Constitutionalism Reshaped

The bitter struggles over the failed Meech Lake and Charlottetown constitutional amendment packages were frustrating for all involved. Five
years of political warfare appeared to have solved little, beyond yielding
the rather punishing demonstration that reaching a consensus on constitutional change would probably require the stimulus of a truly extraordinary crisis. In a more optimistic vein, however, Simone Chambers
cites the relative inclusiveness and wide-ranging character of the debates
as hopeful evidence of an ongoing constitutional conversation open to
new voices and claims.[94] And if this is insufficient comfort, researchers
can take solace in Cairns' reminder: "A constitutional process dealing
with issues of nationhood, survival, identity, and community at a time
of crisis shakes the inertia and ongoingness characteristic of society in
normal times. When the dust has settled on such existential episodes,
they should receive intense academic scrutiny for the light they may
throw on what normality conceals."[95]

This chapter has scrutinized the Meech Lake and Canada round debates as a crucial historical juncture when equality-seeking movements
managed significantly to expand Canadian debates about rights and recognition. The circumstances were not propitious: corporations, governments, and right-wing think tanks had united around a nation-changing
agenda of decentralization, deregulation, and state retrenchment. Yet
traditionally marginalized groups found some success in using new bases
of civic voice to resist unwelcome change, and to impress their aspirations and presence on the broader political community in the process.

Social movements played important roles in blocking two subsequent
attempts at constitutional reform – attempts backed almost unanimously
by Canada's state and business elite. Certainly, key elements of the
neoliberal agenda would resurface, most notably in the sweeping program changes in the historic 1995 federal budget. Yet Ottawa's formal
powers were left untouched, Charter rights survived unscathed, and the
constitutional stakeholdership of equality-seeking movements – which
the authors of Meech Lake had sought so aggressively to ignore – was
strikingly affirmed. These results elicited concern from right-wing observers, who argued that constitutionalism had been hijacked by the
forces of "postmaterialism" and "political correctness."[96]

From a different critical perspective, Gerald Kernerman argues provocatively that it was rather the forces of nationalism that wound up hijacking equality-seeking movements.[97] While not denying the perils for marginalized groups of entering an arena ringing with the claims of rival nationalisms, my own assessment is somewhat more positive. Drawing on Cairns, I have argued that the profile of equality-seeking groups was boosted significantly by a de facto exchange relationship between the groups I have called the social movement and the Trudeauite Charter Canadians: the former primarily concerned with defending particular symbolic capitals, and the latter with pan-Canadian unity.

Trudeau nationalism developed within a postwar international metric that measured nations in terms of their fidelity to the values enshrined in the UN Universal Declaration of Human Rights. In this context, the original "just society" idea and multiculturalism policy were simultaneously national-rebranding and national unity moves: they sought to build civic attachment by developing Canadian citizenship as a badge of international prestige, as "a model of tolerance and a demonstration to all the nations that unity can be formed out of diversity."[98] But the project-oriented, progressive character of this nationalism required continuing acts of verification, which, in the context of the Meech Lake and Charlottetown debates, only close attention to traditionally disadvantaged groups could provide. Thus, the Trudeau camp wound up devoting much of its considerable political clout to amplifying the concerns of social movement Charter supporters, whose role as "Canadians [who] cherish their rights and freedoms" furnished a vital source of legitimating prestige.[99]

The exchange relationship certainly brought pitfalls and challenges for social movements. As pan-Canadian feminist and labour organizations discovered, Québécois member groups resented stances of aggressive Charter support and rejected Ottawa as the necessary guarantor and supervisor of national programs. At the same time, an emergent new status as recognized constitutional actors with authorized civic interests drew many movements deeper into the constitutional arena, prompting an array of citizens' organizations to articulate their own visions of Canada's future. These contributions reflected increased political responsibility stemming from increased political voice.

NAC and the labour movement broke with tradition and supported asymmetrical federalism. In doing so, they hoped to neutralize the combined impact of Québécois aspirations for autonomy, regionalist ambitions in English-speaking Canada, and the corporate world's emphasis on state retrenchment. But ethnocultural minority organizations rejected the proposed move toward a differentiated citizenship for Quebecers, insisting instead on a singular overarching framework of multicultural pluralism. Thus, while left-wing advocates saw asymmetry as the best way to shore up social democracy, ethnic and racialized minorities feared that any constitutional distinction between Québécois and English-Canadian nations would "work against the interest of minorities" and, at the potential extreme, make "tyranny of the majority an everyday feature of life."[100]

This chapter has explained the divergent constitutional visions by observing that two groups of social movement participants viewed the same proposals through the distinctive prisms of economics and culture. While NAC and the labour movement worried primarily about the future of the welfare state, minority organizations emphasizing what Ronald Inglehart would call "cultural or 'ideal' politics" showed relative indifference to economic fears and concerns.[101]

The apparent similarity between this contrast in movement positions and Inglehart's materialism-postmaterialism distinction is important to consider. Indeed, many analysts treat the broader role of social movements in post-Charter constitutional politics in precisely these New Politics terms. Highlighting such themes as the new constitutional focus on recognizing particular citizen identities, the vigilance and constitutional proprietorship of Charter-recognized groups, and the heightened prominence of movements emphasizing esteem and belonging, scholars influenced by the New Politics perspective use the postmaterialism concept to identify and describe the major structural changes and citizen aspirations involved.[102] They see these themes as reflections of the political arrival of a new, relatively privileged set of actors, shaped by a postwar environment of prosperity and peace, and therefore "less preoccupied with satisfying material wants or with security [than with] 'higher order,' postmaterial needs."[103]

Interestingly enough, this chapter has found that in Canada's post-Charter debates, the key social movement cleavage – asymmetrical versus equal-provinces federalism – reflected a prior distinction between movements emphasizing economics and movements prioritizing culture. This is precisely what New Politics would lead us to expect. Yet the materialism-postmaterialism distinction actually fails to illuminate the key visions and concerns at stake. Most obviously, feminists were central players in the "materialist" or pro-welfare state coalition – a role difficult to square with the postmaterialist characterization of the women's movement in the New Politics literature.[104] The fundamental insecurity and constitutional conservatism expressed by feminist and antiracist participants is also at odds with a New Politics view. Feminists and minorities did not bring postmaterialist dispositions – which Inglehart describes as confident attitudes of flexible experimentalism reflecting formative experiences of security – to the prospect of change. Instead they reacted as quintessential materialists: they preferred central control over local authority, sought "rigid, predictable rules," and expressed considerable "anxiety [about] what [was] going to happen."[105]

Understanding post-Charter constitutional politics requires attending to the basic character of equality-seeking movements as reactions to hardship and exclusion. For example, NAC's emphasis on welfare-state defence was a response to gendered economic disadvantage, a problem that had made Canadian women's groups consistent advocates of egalitarian intervention since at least the Great Depression. Similarly, group histories of discrimination and oppression made ethnocultural minority organizations suspicious of any changes that seemed likely to empower local majorities or to facilitate populist political expression. This point also applies to the cleavage among social movements on the question of asymmetrical versus equal-provinces federalism; although one vision prioritized culture while the other emphasized economics, both reflected an overarching focus on group security interests. The postmaterialist label obscures the common character of all these constitutional interventions as responses to problems of economic and personal insecurity.

More generally, to enjoy security in human society, people must also enjoy a measure of respect. When members of disrespected groups interact with more powerful groups, they tend to experience problems of political voice that make them exceedingly vulnerable to the decisions and inclinations of others. Histories of long-term engagement with this problem shaped the participation of equality-seeking movements in the Meech Lake and Charlottetown rounds. Feminist and minority groups defended their new capitals of constitutional symbols with a vehemence that took observers and authorities by surprise, while trade unions sought through the social charter campaign some comparable mechanism for their own constituencies. Rather than the lamentable result of a novel, postmaterialist fixation with the "merely" symbolic, these were serious political struggles that treated security as a matter of voice. Their result was a reshaped Canadian constitutionalism with more room for traditionally neglected, but still quintessentially materialist, concerns of inclusion and respect.

# 7
# Conclusion: Misrecognized Materialists in Canadian Constitutional Politics

Canada's constitutional battles arouse little nostalgia. Accounts of the Meech Lake and Charlottetown rounds describe a "complete disaster" brought on by "dangerous meddling."[1] But focusing historically on the participation of social movements paints constitutional politics in a different light. Equality-seeking movements approached Canadian constitutional debates as spaces in which to pursue far-reaching questions of civic inclusion that regular politics tended to exclude.

This approach began with the public hearings of the Rowell-Sirois Commission. Like the subsequent reconstruction debates, the commission offered a forum for civic discussion in which working-class criticisms of laissez-faire could no longer be brushed aside with the easy jurisdictional formalism of business-as-usual. Excited by the new opening, the Trades and Labour Congress (TLC) proposed a scheme of regular periodic inquiries that would "give all sections of the public a hearing on ... constitutional questions."[2]

The proposal almost became reality, first with the mid-century focus on reconstruction and the welfare state, and then with the growing preoccupation with national identity and the constitutional status of Quebec. Although Canadians sometimes resented this preoccupation, the ensuing debates helped marginalized groups direct civic attention toward their neglected contributions·and concerns. For instance, the third-force mobilization against the B&B Commission culminated in an official multiculturalism discourse that, whatever its limitations, gave "leverage to prod and provoke."[3] And most famously, Trudeau's unity focus made human rights a topic of significantly increased official concern. In short, the postwar constitutional context was congenial to movements raising questions of inclusion and respect.

Cairns illuminates the basic dynamic at play. As he explains, the tendency of constitutional politics to ask "who are we as a people" exposed the country's "informal constitutional culture of meanings and assumptions" as a matter for questioning and debate.[4] This dynamic was crucial for marginalized groups. Disadvantaged by dominant meanings and assumptions, they used the constitutional focus to highlight aspirations that a country not engaged in querying the conditions of its togetherness might have found easier to ignore. Thus, constitutionalism became increasingly an arena for the politics of recognition and respect.

This book has criticized the postmaterialism thesis as an interpretation of the role played by social movements in Canada's constitutional struggles. The conceptual problem at issue is the reliance of the postmaterialism thesis on an imagery of sequencing and opposition to characterize two dimensions of social life that are coexistent and interdependent.[5] The first dimension is that of economic security and personal safety; the second lies in the realm of social interaction and communication – in the "postmaterial" world of esteem and belonging. These dimensions are coexistent and interdependent because security and safety are socially produced conditions. They depend on our interaction with others, and pursuing and safeguarding them tends to require recognition and voice.

Political philosophers Charles Taylor and Axel Honneth both emphasize the importance of recognition for individuals and groups. In Honneth's account, the "intersubjective structure of personal identity" makes healthy relations to self and others depend on respectful relations of mutual recognition.[6] Similarly, Taylor holds that "nonrecognition or misrecognition can inflict harm ... imprisoning someone in a false, distorted, and reduced mode of being."[7] Without disputing the importance of this culturalist emphasis on self-esteem and authenticity, I have taken a more materialist view.[8] This view is influenced by the sociologist William J. Goode, who observes that "all people share the universal need to gain the respect or esteem of others, since without it they can not as easily elicit the help of others."[9] A similar understanding informs Erving Goffman's dramaturgical approach to sociology, which sees social interaction as a series of performances hinging on "symbolically conveyed appraisals of social worth."[10]

In highlighting the quintessentially material significance of recognition for equality-seeking movements, I have also been guided by the words of Pierre Bourdieu: "Only an inconsistent ... materialism can fail to see that strategies whose object is to conserve or increase the honour of the group ... are dictated by interests no less vital than are ... practices directed towards the maximizing of [economic] profit."[11] This message is a useful corrective for the New Politics approach to recognition politics, which leaves the material dimension of recognition untouched.

Yet there is a sense in which chronicling the diminished material importance of social esteem was what early social science was all about. The original scientific analysts of modernity charted the ways in which capitalism and bureaucracy had attenuated the former role of esteem as a basis of social and political power. For Marx, there remained "no other nexus between man and man than ... callous cash payment," while Weber described a transition from the enchantment of charisma and tradition to a rational domination based on "the legality of enacted rules and the right of those elevated to authority under such rules to issue commands."[12] As recently as the early 1970s, the sociologist Peter Berger characterized modernity in terms of the "obsolescence of honor."[13]

Thus, the increased prominence of movements emphasizing what can fairly be described as questions of honour has presented social theory with a paradox. This paradox is that the move from the politics of particularism to the politics of universalism – the fabled transition from status to contract and enchantment to reason – has been accompanied by a renewed rather than a decreased emphasis on the premodern problematic of honour and virtue. In many respects, this is the paradox to which New Politics applies itself: the postmaterialism thesis maintains that prosperity and peace led movements to pursue goals, such as belonging and esteem, that the modernist obsession with economic security and growth precluded.

Focusing on the Canadian constitutional arena, I have suggested that this resolution tends to misconstrue the recognition struggles of traditionally stigmatized groups. Stigmatization, which informs not only oppressive societal practices but also the treatment of those who seek politically to change the practices, is a powerful basis of insecurity: a pivotal moment in a mutually reinforcing dynamic of oppression, exclusion, and silencing. This book has explored constitutional politics as an arena for confronting this cluster of problems: it has shown how social movement organizations used constitutional politics as a venue in which to seek respect for traditionally disrespected constituencies; and it has argued that they did so in order to pursue more effectively the safety and security concerns that dominant groups preferred to ignore. In short, it has argued that their participation was motivated by stakes that the postmaterialism thesis fails to consider.

In the years after the Second World War, Canadian social movements often battled discrimination and exclusion on straightforwardly universalist grounds. But they also rebelled against being treated as unimportant afterthoughts whose newfound inclusion was significant primarily as a reflection of the enlightened nature of the dominant society. The harsh reality behind the unreflective postwar nationalist position was exposed when the 1950 Senate Human Rights Committee attacked Japanese Canadians for having the gall to raise actual human rights complaints. Similar problems confronted feminist groups, who time and again found women's alleged "natural difference" trumping putative commitments to human rights.[14]

Groups responded by exploiting a symbolic capital implicit in the new international discourse of human rights; the victims of oppression capitalized on the postwar "never again" motto as a basis of political voice and moral authority. Minority leaders enjoined those "running ... this country" to heed "the knowledge and experience" of citizens "subjected to internment or imprisonment as aliens and even enemies."[15] They insisted that others learn from those who "know the harmful ... effect discrimination has worked upon them."[16] And in the case of women, they urged men to "learn to see these things the way we see them, by listening to us, and by recognizing that we have valid expertise ... informed and coloured by being on the receiving end of a substantial amount of inequality."[17]

The ensuing advocacy was more than just talk. By amplifying the voices of social movements, it helped inject into the citizenship arena a host of previously unutterable concerns, the list of which is remarkable: gendered discrimination in wages and hiring practices; women's unequal access to social programs, such as the Canada Pension Plan and Unemployment Insurance; income security for widows and divorced women; discrimination in allocating assets in divorce; racial discrimination in hiring, promotion, housing, and property transactions; laws excluding minorities from particular professions; instances of internment, deportation, and the confiscation of property; racist violence and hate crime; biases in law enforcement protection; the feminization of poverty; and the gendered impact of free trade and state retrenchment. Structural changes in immigration patterns, a transformed workforce, increased access to postsecondary education, and a more secure citizenry better able to expand its sympathies were undoubtedly important. But it is inconceivable that social movements could have achieved such a dramatic broadening of the polity's menu of acknowledged security concerns without undertaking a "postmaterialist" focus on recognition and respect.

Movement participants in constitutional politics placed particular value on what I have described as the authorizing dimension of constitutional recognition. Whereas pre-Charter political elites were almost serene in dismissing social movements' interventions as irrelevant and out of place, actors bearing explicit constitutional identities, and therefore authorized constitutional interests, were more difficult to dispense with. As the Ad Hoc Committee of Women on the Constitution proclaimed during the Meech Lake debates: "We have our rights in our own country to protect ... and we will do what needs to be done."[18] This striking transformation prompted one disgruntled parliamentarian to complain that women's concerns were taking "more time ... [than] all the other issues put together."[19]

More easily missed is the function that recognizing traditionally marginalized groups has sometimes fulfilled for political authorities and the dominant society. Uneasy about the diminished viability of the British connection, postwar federal governments began to recast Canada's identity in terms of new commitments to diversity and human rights. The most skilful and energetic proponent of this shift was Prime Minister Pierre Trudeau, who unveiled the charter idea during the International Year of Human Rights as Canada's "opportunity to take a lead" in a grand international endeavour.[20] Drawing on Cairns' "Charter Canadians" concept, I have suggested that the new approach fostered an exchange relationship between social movement Charter Canadians and Trudeauite Charter Canadians. This relationship peaked during the Meech Lake debates, when the Trudeauite foes of dualism and provincialism spoke repeatedly in defence of those Charter-recognized actors whose status was threatened by the Accord. The evident transformation of the latter groups into "Canadians [who] cherish their rights and freedoms" was a repeated theme for Meech Lake's Trudeauite critics.[21] Little wonder: the Trudeau unity project was founded in part on a concerted attempt to develop a prestigious international image for Canada as "a fairer, more compassionate society."[22]

Angered by this "politically correct" solicitude, the political right attacked the new power of the Charter-claiming "special interests."[23] From a different vantage point, the exchange relationship raised the spectre of co-optation; it threatened to subordinate marginalized voices to the priorities and assumptions of the hegemonic nationalism.[24] But actors speaking an authorized discourse of constitutional recognition had gone some distance toward using prestige considerations – which once worked so consistently against them – as bases of civic voice.

The exchange relationship now seems largely over. Ottawa's postwar focus on enlisting equality seekers as national unity allies, whose institutional and fiscal dimensions are compellingly charted in Leslie Pal's *Interests of State,* is a thing of the past.[25] The Canadian Advisory Council on the Status of Women has been scrapped, and a somewhat Orwellian makeover has transformed the former multiculturalism ministry into the Ministry of Canadian Heritage.[26] The idea of negotiating reparations for historical injustices, which Prime Minister Brian Mulroney pursued with willingness if not consistency, has been for the most part replaced by boutique programs of "acknowledgment" and assorted empty gestures.[27] New funding regimes are striving to turn social movement organizations into depoliticized service providers.[28] More generally, the post-Charlottetown preference for quiet, "non-constitutional renewal" over open constitutional debate has returned discussions over the country's future to the closed and quintessentially backstage world of executive federalism.[29] As the broader argument of this book would suggest, the result is a national political life with a diminished array of voices and less space for materialist concerns.

# Notes

## Chapter 1: Constitutional Politics and the Politics of Respect

1 Patrick Boyer, "'Whose Constitution Is It, Anyway?' Democratic Participation and the Canadian Constitution," in *Challenges to Canadian Federalism*, ed. Martin Westmacott and Hugh Mellon (Scarborough, ON: Prentice-Hall, 1998), 83; Peter H. Russell, *Constitutional Odyssey: Can Canadians Become a Sovereign People?* 3rd ed. (Toronto: University of Toronto Press, 1992), 93.

2 For example, see Alexandra Dobrowolsky, *The Politics of Pragmatism: Women, Representation, and Constitutional Reform* (Don Mills, ON: Oxford University Press, 2000); and Gerald Kernerman, *Multicultural Nationalism: Civilizing Difference, Constituting Community* (Vancouver: UBC Press, 2005).

3 Russell, *Constitutional Odyssey*.

4 Harvey Lazar, "Non-Constitutional Renewal: Toward a New Equilibrium in the Federation," in *Canada: The State of the Federation 1997 – Non-Constitutional Renewal*, ed. Harvey Lazar (Kingston, ON: Queen's University Institute of Intergovernmental Relations, 1998).

5 Alan C. Cairns, *Reconfigurations: Canadian Citizenship and Constitutional Change*, ed. Douglas E. Williams (Toronto: McClelland and Stewart, 1995), 9.

6 Boyer, "Whose Constitution," 85; Mr. Breau, quoted in Canada, Special Joint Committee of the Senate and of the House of Commons on the Constitution of Canada, *Minutes of Proceedings and Evidence*, No. 81, 27 May 1971, 15.

7 Canadian Association of Lesbians and Gay Men, Presentation to the Special Joint Committee of the Senate and of the House of Commons on the Constitution of Canada, *Minutes of Proceedings and Evidence*, No. 24, 11 December 1980.

8 For example, see Charles Taylor, "The Politics of Recognition," in *Multiculturalism: Examining the Politics of Recognition*, ed. Charles Taylor and Amy Gutmann, 2nd ed. (Princeton: Princeton University Press, 1994).

9 See Pierre Bourdieu, "The Forms of Capital," in *Handbook of Theory and Research for the Sociology of Education*, ed. John G. Richardson (New York: Greenwood Press, 1986); Bourdieu, *Outline of a Theory of Practice*, trans. Richard Nice (Cambridge: Cambridge University Press, 1977); and Bourdieu, "Social Space and Symbolic Power," *Sociological Theory* 7 (1989): 14-25.

10 Robert D. Putnam, *Bowling Alone: The Collapse and Revival of American Community* (New York: Simon and Schuster, 2000).

11 Bourdieu, "Forms of Capital," 245.

12  Ibid., 242; Bourdieu, *Outline of a Theory,* 176-77.
13  John B. Thompson, *Studies in the Theory of Ideology* (Cambridge: Polity Press, 1984), 48.
14  Cairns, *Disruptions: Constitutional Struggles, from the Charter to Meech Lake,* ed. Douglas E. Williams (Toronto: McClelland and Stewart, 1991), 131, 118.
15  Ibid., 133.
16  Cairns, *Reconfigurations,* 127.
17  Guy Laforest, *Trudeau and the End of a Canadian Dream,* trans. Paul Leduc Browne and Michelle Weinroth (Montreal and Kingston: McGill-Queen's University Press, 1995), 137; Allan Tupper, "English-Canadian Scholars and the Meech Lake Accord," *International Journal of Canadian Studies* 7-8 (1993): 352.
18  Yasmeen Abu-Laban and Tim Nieguth, "Reconsidering the Constitution, Minorities, and Politics in Canada," *Canadian Journal of Political Science* 33 (2000): 465-98; Dobrowolsky, *Politics of Pragmatism;* Miriam Smith, *Lesbian and Gay Rights in Canada: Social Movements and Equality-Seeking, 1971-1995* (Toronto: University of Toronto Press, 1999); and Linda Trimble, "'Good Enough Citizens': Canadian Women and Representation in Constitutional Deliberations," *International Journal of Canadian Studies* 17 (1998): 131-56.
19  Ronald Inglehart, *Modernization and Postmodernization: Cultural, Economic, and Political Change in 43 Societies* (Princeton: Princeton University Press, 1997).
20  Ronald Inglehart, *Culture Shift in Advanced Industrial Society* (Princeton: Princeton University Press, 1990).
21  Ronald Inglehart, "Post-Materialism in an Environment of Insecurity," *The American Political Science Review* 75 (1981): 880-900.
22  F.L. Morton and Rainer Knopff, *The Charter Revolution and the Court Party* (Peterborough, ON: Broadview Press, 2000); Neil Nevitte, "New Politics, the Charter, and Political Participation," in *Representation, Integration, and Political Parties in Canada,* ed. Herman Bakvis (Toronto: Dundurn Press, 1992); and Ian Brodie and Neil Nevitte, "Evaluating the Citizens' Constitution Theory," *Canadian Journal of Political Science* 26 (1993): 234-59.
23  Neil Nevitte, *The Decline of Deference: Canadian Value Change in Cross-National Perspective* (Peterborough, ON: Broadview Press, 1996).
24  Morton and Knopff, *Charter Revolution.*
25  Inglehart, *Modernization and Postmodernization,* 33.
26  Inglehart, *Culture Shift,* 336.
27  A.H. Maslow, *Motivation and Personality,* 2nd ed. (New York: Harper, 1954).
28  Inglehart, "Post-Materialism."
29  Inglehart, *Culture Shift,* chap. 11, "New Social Movements: Values, Culture, and Cognitive Mobilization."
30  For example, see Alain Touraine, *The Voice and the Eye: An Analysis of Social Movements,* trans. Alan Duff (Cambridge: Cambridge University Press, 1981); and Alberto Melucci, *Nomads of the Present: Social Movements and Individual Needs in Contemporary Society,* ed. John Keane and Paul Mier (Philadelphia: Temple University Press, 1989).
31  David Plotke, "What's So New About New Social Movements?" *Socialist Review* 20 (1990): 81-102.
32  For example, see Mayer N. Zald and John D. McCarthy, *Social Movements in an Organizational Society: Collected Essays* (New Brunswick, NJ: Transaction Publishers, 1987).

33  Darren W. Davis and Christian Davenport, "Assessing the Validity of the Post-materialism Index," *American Political Science Review* 93 (1999): 649-63; Valerie Braithwaite, Toni Makkai, and Yvonne Pittelkow, "Inglehart's Materialism-Postmaterialism Concept: Clarifying the Dimensionality Debate through Rokeach's Model of Social Values," *Journal of Applied Social Psychology* 26 (1996): 1536-55.

34  Gary N. Marks, "The Formation of Materialist and Postmaterialist Values," *Social Science Research* 26 (1997): 52-68; and Paul V. Warwick, "Disputed Cause, Disputed Effect: The Postmaterialist Thesis Re-examined," *Public Opinion Quarterly* 62 (1998): 583-609.

35  Brent S. Steel et al., "The Inglehart-Flanagan Debate over Postmaterialist Values: Some Evidence from a Canadian–American Case Study," *Political Psychology* 13 (1992): 61-77; James Savage, "Postmaterialism of the Left and Right: Political Conflict in Postindustrial Society," *Comparative Political Studies* 17 (1985): 431-51.

36  New Politics opinion surveys gauge support for postmaterialism by asking respondents if they support the following priorities: having more say in government decisions, enjoying freedom of speech, having more say in community and workplace decisions, beautifying cities and the countryside, developing a friendlier society, and valuing ideas over money. See Inglehart, *Culture Shift*, 74-75.

37  A good discussion of the latter point is Herbert Kitschelt, *The Transformation of European Social Democracy* (Cambridge: Cambridge University Press, 1994).

38  For examples of textbook accounts, see Keith Archer et al., *Parameters of Power: Canada's Political Institutions*, 3rd ed. (Scarborough, ON: Nelson, 2002), 34; Stephen Brooks, *Canadian Democracy: An Introduction*, 4th ed. (Don Mills, ON: Oxford University Press, 2004), 61; and Mark O. Dickerson and Thomas Flanagan, *An Introduction to Government and Politics: A Conceptual Approach*, 6th ed. (Scarborough, ON: Nelson Thomson Learning, 2002), 69-70.

39  Miriam Smith, "Ghosts of the Judicial Committee of the Privy Council: Group Politics and Charter Litigation in Canadian Political Science," *Canadian Journal of Political Science* 35 (March 2002): 25.

40  Donatella della Porta and Mario Diani, *Social Movements: An Introduction* (Oxford: Blackwell, 1999), 367.

41  Nevitte, "New Politics," 356.

42  Nevitte, *Decline of Deference*, 9, 84.

43  Janet Ajzenstat, "Constitution Making and the Myth of the People," in *Constitutional Predicament: Canada after the Referendum of 1992*, ed. Curtis Cook (Montreal and Kingston: McGill-Queen's University Press, 1994), 125.

44  Leslie A. Pal, *Beyond Policy Analysis: Public Issue Management in Turbulent Times*, 3rd ed. (Scarborough, ON: Nelson, 2006), 67, 69.

45  Anthony A. Peacock, "Introduction: The Necessity of Rethinking the Constitution," in *Rethinking the Constitution: Perspectives on Canadian Constitutional Reform, Interpretation, and Theory*, ed. Anthony A. Peacock (Don Mills, ON: Oxford University Press, 1996), xiii; Rainer Knopff and F.L. Morton, "Canada's Court Party," in ibid., 68-71.

46  Inglehart, *Culture Shift*, 171, 373.

**Chapter 2: Searching for a Forum**

1  Dennis Guest, *The Emergence of Social Security in Canada* (Vancouver: UBC Press, 1979), 87-91.

2  See Richard Simeon and Ian Robinson, *State, Society, and the Development of Canadian Federalism* (Toronto: University of Toronto Press, 1990), 82.
3  F.R. Scott, "Centralization and Decentralization in Canadian Federalism," *Canadian Bar Review* 29 (1951): 1095-1125.
4  J.R. Mallory, *Social Credit and the Federal Power in Canada* (Toronto: University of Toronto Press, 1976), 52-53.
5  On constitutional politics in this period, see Peter Russell, *Constitutional Odyssey: Can Canadians Become a Sovereign People?* 3rd ed. (Toronto: University of Toronto Press, 2004), 57-61.
6  On the role of intellectuals, see Doug Owram, *The Government Generation: Canadian Intellectuals and the State, 1900-1945* (Toronto: University of Toronto Press, 1986), chap. 9, "The Problem of National Unity and the Rowell-Sirois Report, 1935-40."
7  Quoted in James Struthers, *No Fault of Their Own: Unemployment and the Canadian Welfare State, 1914-1941* (Toronto: University of Toronto Press, 1983), 162.
8  Donald V. Smiley, ed., *The Rowell-Sirois Report* (Toronto: McClelland and Stewart, 1963), 2.
9  Presentation of the Communist Party of Canada, Royal Commission on Dominion-Provincial Relations, *Report of Hearings*, Vol. 24, Brief 401, 31 May 1938, 9718. The records of the Hearings are available at Special Collections, Main Library, University of British Columbia, Vancouver. Subsequent references in this chapter to presentations from the Hearings will read, Presentation to the 1938 Royal Commission, and will be preceded by the name of the relevant organization or speaker.
10  Trades and Labour Congress of Canada, Presentation to the 1938 Royal Commission, Vol. 17, Brief 106, 21 January 1938, 3086.
11  Cf. Mallory, *Social Credit*, 51.
12  TLC, Presentation to the 1938 Royal Commission, 3086, 3102.
13  Ibid., 3114.
14  See Ivan Avakumovic, *The Communist Party in Canada: A History* (Toronto: McClelland and Stewart, 1975), 85-86; Desmond Morton and Terry Copp, *Working People*, rev. ed. (Ottawa: Deneau, 1984), 159.
15  Even Walter Tarnopolsky's extensive account misses this role. See his *The Canadian Bill of Rights*, 2nd ed. (Toronto: McClelland and Stewart, 1975). For the traditional left's charter demands, see TLC, Presentation to the 1938 Royal Commission, 3107, and CP, Presentation to the 1938 Royal Commission, 9723. The CP also called for Senate abolition and proportional representation, ibid.
16  TLC, Presentation to the 1938 Royal Commission, 3107.
17  CP, Presentation to the 1938 Royal Commission, 9826. On Buck's 1931 imprisonment for leading an "unlawful association," see Avakumovic, *Communist Party*, 87-90.
18  CP, Presentation to the 1938 Royal Commission, 9720.
19  TLC, Presentation to the 1938 Royal Commission, 3093.
20  Ibid., 3102.
21  Gad Horowitz, *Canadian Labour in Politics* (Toronto: University of Toronto Press, 1968), 63. On craft unionism more generally, see Eric Hobsbawm, "Artisans and Labour Aristocrats," in *Worlds of Labour: Further Studies in the History of Labour* (London: Weidenfeld and Nicholson, 1984), chap. 14.

22 On the new industrial unions, see Morton and Copp, *Working People*, chap. 15, "Industrial Unionism."

23 American Teamster President James Tobin, quoted in Irving Abella, *Nationalism, Communism and Canadian Labour: The CIO, the Communist Party, and the Canadian Congress of Labour, 1935-1956* (Toronto: University of Toronto Press, 1973), 4.

24 Jack Williams, *The Story of Unions in Canada* (Toronto: J.M. Dent and Sons, 1975), 190; Horowitz, *Canadian Labour*, 63.

25 Horowitz, *Canadian Labour*, 58-59.

26 TLC, Presentation to the 1938 Royal Commission, 3086, 3113, 3093, 3123.

27 Karl Marx and Friedrich Engels, *Manifesto of the Communist Party*, in *The Marx-Engels Reader*, ed. Robert C. Tucker (New York: Norton, 1978), 488; CP, Presentation to the 1938 Royal Commission, 9720, 9720, 9828.

28 Marx and Engels, *Manifesto*, 487; CP, Presentation to the 1938 Royal Commission, 9822.

29 Ruth Roach Pierson, "Gender and the Unemployment Insurance Debates in Canada, 1934-1940," *Labour/le Travail* 25 (1990): 78.

30 CP, Presentation to the 1938 Royal Commission, 9718-9719, 9811.

31 League for Women's Rights, Presentation to the 1938 Royal Commission, 13 May 1938, 8310.

32 LWR, Presentation to the 1938 Royal Commission, 8309. On Casgrain and the CCF, see Susan Mann Trofimenkoff, "Thérèse Casgrain and the CCF in Quebec," *Canadian Historical Review* 66 (1985): 125-53.

33 LWR, Presentation to the 1938 Royal Commission, 8303-5, 8299.

34 Ibid., 8306.

35 Ibid., 8301.

36 Ibid., 8317, 8318.

37 Ibid., 8309.

38 Ibid., 8309-10.

39 Ibid., 8308.

40 Sirois, in LWR, Presentation to the 1938 Royal Commission, 8317. This remark suggests that the acting chairman was not following the LWR's presentation. The LWR did not have a "number of ... proposals." It had only one: to amend the BNA Act to force Quebec to enfranchise women. The rest of the presentation consisted of examples in support of this proposal.

41 St. Laurent, in LWR, Presentation to the 1938 Royal Commission, 8318. On St. Laurent's Royal Commission role, see Dale C. Thomson, *Louis St. Laurent: Canadian* (Toronto: Macmillan, 1967), 95-102.

42 LWR, Presentation to the 1938 Royal Commission, 8319.

43 Sirois in ibid., 8317; Sirois in CP, Presentation to the 1938 Royal Commission, 9725.

44 Pierson, "Gender and Unemployment."

45 Catherine Lyle Cleverdon, *The Woman Suffrage Movement in Canada* (Toronto: University of Toronto Press, 1950), 232.

46 Erving Goffman, *The Presentation of Self in Everyday Life* (Garden City, NY: Anchor Books, 1959), 38.

47 Thérèse F. Casgrain, *A Woman in a Man's World*, trans. Joyce Marshall (Toronto: McClelland and Stewart, 1972), 62-63; LWR, Presentation to the 1938 Royal Commission, 8317.

48 Ibid., 8310, 8317.
49 Alison Prentice et al., *Canadian Women: A History*, 2nd ed. (Toronto: Harcourt Brace, 1996), 189.
50 LWR, Presentation to the 1938 Royal Commission, 8315. On the emphasis on infant mortality, see Carol Lee Bacchi, *Liberation Deferred? The Ideas of the English-Canadian Suffragists, 1877-1918* (Toronto: University of Toronto Press, 1983), 106.
51 St. Laurent, in LWR, Presentation to the 1938 Royal Commission, 8321.
52 See Paul Gérin-Lajoie, *Constitutional Amendment in Canada* (Toronto: University of Toronto Press, 1950), 265.
53 National Council of Women of Canada, Presentation to the 1938 Royal Commission, 26 May 1938, 9236-38; 9248.
54 Veronica Strong-Boag, "The Roots of Modern Canadian Feminism," in *Canadian History Since Confederation: Essays and Interpretations*, ed. Bruce Hodgins and Robert Page, 2nd ed. (Georgetown, ON: Irwin-Dorsey, 1979), 400, 401.
55 N.E.S. Griffiths, *The Splendid Vision: Centennial History of the National Council of Women of Canada, 1893-1993* (Ottawa: Carleton University Press, 1993), 184-204.
56 National Council of Women of Canada, *Year Book for 1938* (n.p., 1938), 34.
57 NCW, Presentation to the 1938 Royal Commission, 9229.
58 Ibid., 9229; 9230.
59 Ibid., 9230.
60 NCW, *Year Book for 1938*, 34.
61 NCW, Presentation to the 1938 Royal Commission, 9231.
62 Smiley, ed., *Rowell-Sirois*, 2.
63 A. Paul Pross, *Group Politics and Public Policy* (Toronto: Oxford University Press, 1986), chap. 2, "Beginnings: Space versus Sector."
64 Erving Goffman, *Stigma: Notes on the Management of Spoiled Identity* (New York: Touchstone, 1986), 130.
65 Mary Poovey, *Uneven Developments: The Ideological Work of Gender in Mid-Victorian England* (Chicago: University of Chicago Press, 1988), 10.
66 Ronald Inglehart, "The Silent Revolution in Europe: Intergenerational Change in Post-Industrial Societies," *American Political Science Review* 65 (1971): 993; Inglehart, *Culture Shift in Advanced Industrial Society* (Princeton, NJ: Princeton University Press, 1990), 160, 11.
67 LWR, Presentation to the 1938 Royal Commission, 8317, 8318.

### Chapter 3: Wartime

1 On the amendment, see Paul Gérin-Lajoie, *Constitutional Amendment in Canada* (Toronto: University of Toronto Press, 1950), 104-9.
2 James Struthers, *No Fault of Their Own: Unemployment and the Canadian Welfare State, 1914-1941* (Toronto: University of Toronto Press, 1983), 202.
3 Doug Owram, *The Government Generation: Canadian Intellectuals and the State, 1900-1945* (Toronto: University of Toronto Press, 1986), 303.
4 D.V. Smiley, "The Rowell-Sirois Report, Provincial Autonomy, and Post-war Canadian Federalism," *Canadian Journal of Economics and Political Science* 28 (1962): 54-69.
5 A partial exception was Maurice Duplessis' Quebec. See Dale Posgate and Kenneth McRoberts, *Quebec: Social Change and Political Crisis* (Toronto: McClelland and Stewart, 1976), 87-88.

6 Jane Jenson, "'Different' But Not 'Exceptional': Canada's Permeable Fordism," *Canadian Review of Sociology and Anthropology* 26 (1989): 69-94.

7 Desmond Morton and Terry Copp, *Working People,* rev. ed. (Ottawa: Deneau, 1984), 180. On reconstruction planning, see Donald Creighton, *The Forked Road: Canada, 1939-1957* (Toronto: McClelland and Stewart, 1976), chap. 5, "The Coming of the Planners."

8 See Ruth Roach Pierson, *"They're Still Women After All": The Second World War and Canadian Womanhood* (Toronto: McClelland and Stewart, 1986), chap. 4, "Wartime Jitters over Femininity."

9 See Pierson, *They're Still Women,* chap. 1, "Women's Emancipation and the Recruitment of Women into the War Effort"; and Pierson, "Gender and the Unemployment Insurance Debates in Canada, 1934-1940," *Labour/le Travail* 25 (1990): 77-103.

10 Jane Jenson, "Fated to Live in Interesting Times: Canada's Changing Citizenship Regimes," *Canadian Journal of Political Science* 30 (1997): 634.

11 On trade union influence on the design of UI, see Pierson, "Gender and Unemployment," 83, 88, 97.

12 H.A. Logan, *Trade Unions in Canada: Their Development and Functioning* (Toronto: Macmillan, 1948), 400; All-Canadian Congress of Labour, Presentation to the House of Commons Special Committee on Bill No. 98 Respecting Unemployment Insurance, *Minutes of Proceedings and Evidence,* No. 2, 23 July 1940, 150. Subsequent references in this chapter to presentations from these hearings will read, Presentation to the 1940 House Committee on UI, and will be preceded by the name of the relevant organization or speaker.

13 Presentation of the Communist Party of Canada, Royal Commission on Dominion-Provincial Relations, *Report of Hearings,* Vol. 24, Brief 401, 31 May 1938, 9819. On the ban, see Ivan Avakumovic, *The Communist Party in Canada: A History* (Toronto: McClelland and Stewart, 1975), 139-48.

14 For more details, see Leslie A. Pal, *State, Class, and Bureaucracy: Canadian Unemployment Insurance and Public Policy* (Kingston and Montreal: McGill-Queen's University Press, 1988), 39-50.

15 Dennis Guest, *The Emergence of Social Security in Canada* (Vancouver: UBC Press, 1979), 107.

16 Pierson, "Gender and Unemployment," 103. On the dependants' allowances, see ibid., 94-95.

17 The ACCL delegation also included representatives from the Congress of Industrial Organizations, with which it was then merging to create the new Canadian Congress of Labour. See Irving Abella, *Nationalism, Communism, and Canadian Labour: The CIO, the Communist Party, and the Canadian Congress of Labour, 1935-1956* (Toronto: University of Toronto Press, 1973), chap. 3, "The Merger, 1939-40."

18 Jack Williams, *The Story of Unions in Canada* (Toronto: J.M. Dent and Sons, 1975), 190; Trades and Labour Congress, Presentation to the 1940 House Committee on UI, No. 2, 23 July 1940, 110.

19 TLC, Presentation to the 1940 House Committee on UI, 122.

20 Williams, *Unions in Canada,* 190; ACCL, Presentation to the 1940 House Committee on UI, 154.

21 Eric Hobsbawm, "Debating the Labour Aristocracy," in *Worlds of Labour: Further Studies in the History of Labour* (London: Weidenfeld and Nicholson, 1984), chap. 12.

22 Kim Moody, *An Injury to All: The Decline of American Unionism* (London: Verso, 1988), xvi-xviii.

23 ACCL, Presentation to the 1940 House Committee on UI, 151; TLC, Presentation to the 1940 House Committee on UI, 110.

24 TLC, Presentation to the 1940 House Committee on UI, 117.

25 Jeffrey Haydu, *Between Craft and Class: Skilled Workers and Factory Politics in the United States and Britain, 1890-1922* (Berkeley: University of California Press, 1988), 56; Eric Hobsbawm, "The Aristocracy of Labour Reconsidered," in *Worlds of Labour,* 238.

26 ACCL, Presentation to the 1940 House Committee on UI, 151.

27 Ibid.

28 Pierson, "Gender and Unemployment," 98-99; ACCL, Presentation to the 1940 House Committee on UI, 153.

29 ACCL, Presentation to the 1940 House Committee on UI, 151; 153.

30 Stuart Jamieson, *Times of Trouble: Labour Unrest and Industrial Conflict in Canada, 1900-66* (Ottawa: Information Canada, 1968), 279-80; Walter D. Young, *The Anatomy of a Party: The National CCF, 1932-61* (Toronto: University of Toronto Press, 1969), 113.

31 Laurel Sefton MacDowell, "The Formation of the Canadian Industrial Relations System," in *Canadian Working Class History: Selected Readings,* ed. Laurel Sefton MacDowell and Ian Radforth (Toronto: Canadian Scholars' Press, 1992), 580-86.

32 Logan, *Trade Unions in Canada,* 521-25.

33 Trades and Labour Congress, Presentation to the House of Commons Special Committee on Reconstruction and Re-establishment, *Minutes of Proceedings and Evidence,* No. 24, 7 July 1943, 640, 639. Subsequent references in this chapter to presentations from these hearings will read, Presentation to the 1943 House Reconstruction Committee, and will be preceded by the name of the relevant organization or speaker.

34 Logan, *Trade Unions,* 522; Morton and Copp, *Working People,* 183. On the merger, see Abella, *Nationalism, Communism,* chap. 3, "The Merger, 1939-40."

35 TLC, Presentation to the 1943 House Reconstruction Committee, 644, 642. On the Marsh Report, see Guest, *Social Security,* 124-26.

36 TLC, Presentation to the 1943 House Reconstruction Committee, 641.

37 McDonald, in ibid., 646; Purdy, in ibid., 647.

38 TLC, Presentation to the 1943 House Reconstruction Committee, 639, 640.

39 McDonald, in ibid., 643; TLC, ibid.

40 TLC, ibid., 647-48.

41 Morton and Copp, *Working People,* 204.

42 Turgeon, in TLC, Presentation to the 1943 House Reconstruction Committee, 659; Gillis, in ibid.

43 TLC, quoted in Logan, *Trade Unions in Canada,* 523.

44 Canadian Congress of Labour, Presentation to the 1943 House Reconstruction Committee, No. 26, 15 July 1943, 695; ibid., 688.

45 Ibid.

46 Ibid., 693, 697, 692, 696.

47 Hill, in ibid., 701.

48 Purdy, in TLC, Presentation to the 1943 House Reconstruction Committee, 647; McNiven, in CCL, Presentation to the 1943 House Reconstruction Committee,

705; McDonald, in TLC, Presentation to the 1943 House Reconstruction Committee, 646; McDonald, in CCL, Presentation to the 1943 House Reconstruction Committee, 709.

49 Forsey cited the following authorities: the United States National Resources Planning Board, Canada's Wartime Prices and Trade Board, the Canadian Chamber of Commerce, Progressive Conservative leader John Bracken, academics A.A. Berle and Gardiner Means, the Canadian House of Commons Special Committee on Banking and Commerce, the Bank of Canada, academic H.A. Logan, the trade journal *Industrial Canada,* Sir William Beveridge, the Brookings Institution, the League of Nations, the Marsh Report, the Canadian Pacific Railway, and the United States National Resources Planning Board. See CCL, Presentation to the 1943 House Reconstruction Committee, 688-93.

50 See the remarks of various committee members, in ibid., 705-6.

51 Guest, *Social Security,* 138-40.

52 See Owram, *Government Generation,* 290, 308.

53 National Council of Women of Canada, *Year Book for 1943* (n.p., 1943), 16.

54 In Arthur Beauchesne, *Rules and Forms of the House of Commons of Canada: A Compendium of Canadian Parliamentary Practice* (Toronto: Canada Law Book Company, 1943), 193.

55 NCW, *Year Book for 1943,* 16.

56 Gail Cuthbert Brandt, "'Pigeon-Holed and Forgotten': The Work of the Subcommittee on the Post-War Problems of Women, 1943," *Histoire sociale/Social History* 29 (1982): 241.

57 Ibid., esp. 254.

58 N.E.S. Griffiths, *The Splendid Vision: Centennial History of the National Council of Women of Canada, 1893-1993* (Ottawa: Carleton University Press, 1993), 229.

59 Ibid., 229-32. The program is reprinted in NCW, *Year Book for 1943,* 78-85.

60 Quoted in Griffiths, *Splendid Vision,* 233. Hardy's address appears in NCW, *Year Book for 1943,* 40-44.

61 National Council of Women, Presentation to the House of Commons Special Committee on Social Security, *Minutes of Proceedings and Evidence,* No. 15, 28 May 1943, 407-8.

62 Ibid., 408.

63 Ibid.

64 NCW, Presentation to the 1943 House Social Security Committee, 408.

65 NCW, ibid.

66 NCW, *Year Book for 1943,* 41.

67 Erving Goffman, *Stigma: Notes on the Management of Spoiled Identity* (New York: Touchstone, 1986), 12.

68 TLC, Presentation to the 1943 House Reconstruction Committee, 641.

69 CCL, Presentation to the 1943 House Reconstruction Committee, 688.

70 TLC, Presentation to the 1940 House Committee on UI, 117.

71 ACCL, Presentation to the 1940 House Committee on UI, 153; 151.

72 On these positions, see Brandt, "Pigeon-Holed and Forgotten," 247-51, 258; and Griffiths, *Splendid Vision,* 229-32.

73 Ann Shola Orloff, "Gender and the Social Rights of Citizenship: The Comparative Analysis of Gender Relations and Welfare States," *American Sociological Review* 58 (1993): 322.

74  MacNicol, in CCL, Presentation to the 1943 House Reconstruction Committee, 703.
75  NCW, *Year Book for 1943*, 41.
76  Griffiths, *Splendid Vision*, 234.
77  Ibid., 227.

**Chapter 4: The Postwar Identity Emphasis**

1  Edwin R. Black and Alan C. Cairns, "A Different Perspective on Canadian Federalism," *Canadian Public Administration* 1 (1966): 27-44.
2  For a summary of the themes discussed in this paragraph, see Ronald Inglehart, *Culture Shift in Advanced Industrial Society* (Princeton, NJ: Princeton University Press, 1990), 3-14.
3  A good discussion is A.H. Robertson and J.G. Merrills, *Human Rights in the World: An Introduction to the Study of the International Protection of Human Rights* (Manchester: Manchester University Press, 1989).
4  Canada, Minister of Public Works and Government Services, *A History of the Vote in Canada* (Ottawa: Minister of Public Works and Government Services, 1997), 79-83; Darlene Johnston, "First Nations and Canadian Citizenship," in *Belonging: The Meaning and Future of Canadian Citizenship*, ed. William Kaplan (Montreal: McGill-Queen's University Press, 1993), 349-67.
5  Axel Honneth, *The Struggle for Recognition: The Moral Grammar of Social Conflicts*, trans. Joel Anderson (Cambridge: Polity Press, 1995), 109-11. Also see Kenneth Minogue, "The History of the Idea of Human Rights," in *The Human Rights Reader*, ed. Walter Lacqueur and Barry Rubin (New York: New American Library, 1979), 3-16.
6  Walter Tarnopolsky, *The Canadian Bill of Rights*, 2nd ed. (Toronto: McClelland and Stewart, 1975), 9.
7  Senate, Special Committee on Human Rights and Fundamental Freedoms, *Minutes of Proceedings and Evidence*, No. 1, 25 April 1950, iii.
8  Irving M. Abella and Harold M. Troper, *None Is Too Many: Canada and the Jews of Europe, 1933-1948* (Toronto: Lester, 1991).
9  Presentation of the Canadian Jewish Congress to the Senate Special Committee on Human Rights and Fundamental Freedoms, *Minutes of Proceedings and Evidence*, No. 3, 27 April 1950, 70. Subsequent references in this chapter to presentations from these hearings will read, Presentation to the 1950 Senate Committee on Human Rights, and will be preceded by the name of the relevant organization or speaker.
10  Kinley, in CJC, Presentation to the 1950 Senate Committee on Human Rights, 74.
11  CJC, ibid., 74-75.
12  Yaacov Glickman, "Political Socialization and the Social Protest of Canadian Jewry: Some Historical and Contemporary Perspectives," in *Ethnicity, Power and Politics in Canada*, ed. Jorgen Dahlie and Tissa Fernando (Toronto: Methuen, 1981), 129.
13  CJC, Presentation to the 1950 Senate Committee on Human Rights, 76.
14  Ibid., 77, 76, 75, 75.
15  Kinley, in ibid., 76.
16  CJC, ibid., 76.
17  Kinley, in ibid.

18  CJC, ibid., 74.
19  National Japanese-Canadian Citizens' Association, Presentation to the 1950 Senate Committee on Human Rights, No. 8, 10 May 1950, 270, 269.
20  Ibid., 271, 270.
21  Ibid., 277, 270, 271, 277.
22  Ibid., 271.
23  Ibid., 276, 271, 276.
24  Kinley, in ibid., 273; Roebuck, ibid.
25  From ibid.: Roebuck, 273; Kinley, 272; Ross, 275; Roebuck, 273; Ross, 275; Ross, 274; Kinley, 273; Kinley, 273; Ross, 275.
26  NJCCA, ibid., 274, 273.
27  Ann Gomer Sunahara, *The Politics of Racism: The Uprooting of Japanese Canadians during the Second World War* (Toronto: James Lorimer, 1981), 147. The internment of more than 20,000 innocent individuals also included the widespread and largely uncompensated confiscation of property, the virtual destruction of the Japanese-Canadian community in British Columbia, and the forcible "repatriation" of thousands of Canadian citizens to Japan.
28  After its May 1950 Senate Committee appearance, the NJCCA wrote a final letter to Prime Minister Louis St. Laurent in 1951 protesting the disappointing recommendations of the Bird Commission on the wartime disposition of Japanese-Canadian property. It then entered "a long dormant period," failing to even meet for more than a decade. See Roy Miki, *Redress: Inside the Japanese-Canadian Call for Justice* (Vancouver: Raincoast Books, 2004), 217-18.
29  Ivan Avakumovic, *The Communist Party in Canada: A History* (Toronto: McClelland and Stewart, 1975), 209.
30  David, in League for Democratic Rights, Presentation to the 1950 Senate Committee on Human Rights, No. 3, 27 April 1950, 106.
31  Karl Marx and Friedrich Engels, *Manifesto of the Communist Party,* in *The Marx-Engels Reader,* ed. Robert C. Tucker (New York: Norton, 1978), 473.
32  LDR, Presentation to the 1950 Senate Committee on Human Rights, 106.
33  Ibid.
34  Ibid., 112, 113.
35  Ibid., 113.
36  See ibid., 109.
37  David and Roebuck, in ibid., 100.
38  David, ibid.
39  LDR, ibid., 112.
40  Karl Marx, "On the Jewish Question," in *Marx-Engels Reader,* esp. 34-35.
41  National Council of Women of Canada, Presentation to the 1950 Senate Committee on Human Rights, No. 2, 26 April 1950, 53.
42  Ibid.
43  Ibid, 53-54.
44  Ibid., 55-56.
45  Ibid., 54.
46  Ibid., 55.
47  See Ruth Roach Pierson, *"They're Still Women After All": The Second World War and Canadian Womanhood* (Toronto: McClelland and Stewart, 1986).
48  NCW, Presentation to the 1950 Senate Committee on Human Rights, 54.
49  Reid, in ibid., 52.

50  From ibid.: Kinley, 56; Reid, 57; Kinley, 56; Baird, 57; Kinley, 56.

51  LDR, ibid., 57.

52  Richard Simeon and Ian Robinson, *State, Society, and the Development of Canadian Federalism* (Toronto: University of Toronto Press, 1990), 132; Jack Williams, *The Story of Unions in Canada* (Toronto: J.M. Dent and Sons, 1975), 170-73.

53  T.H. Marshall, *Class, Citizenship and Social Development,* ed. Seymour Martin Lipset (Garden City, NY: Doubleday, 1964), 94.

54  Gad Horowitz, *Canadian Labour in Politics* (Toronto: University of Toronto Press, 1968), 179.

55  Canadian Congress of Labour, Presentation to the 1950 Senate Committee on Human Rights, No. 3, 27 April 1950, 103; Trades and Labour Congress, Presentation to the 1950 Senate Committee on Human Rights, No. 5, 2 May 1950, 172.

56  CCL, Presentation to the 1950 Senate Committee on Human Rights, 102.

57  Ibid., 79.

58  For example, see Bryan Palmer, *Working-Class Experience: The Rise and Reconstitution of Canadian Labour, 1800-1980* (Toronto: Butterworth, 1983), 111.

59  CCL, Presentation to the 1950 Senate Committee on Human Rights, 83.

60  TLC, ibid., 165.

61  On these positions, see CCL, ibid., 98-105; and TLC, ibid., 167, 173, 175.

62  Kinley, in TLC, ibid., 174; Baird, in CCL, ibid., 104; Kinley, in TLC, ibid., 175; David, in ibid., 176.

63  TLC, ibid., 165. Cf. Richard Sennett and Jonathan Cobb, *The Hidden Injuries of Class* (New York: Vintage, 1973).

64  CCL, Presentation to the 1950 Senate Committee on Human Rights, 98-105; Kinley, ibid., 104.

65  TLC, ibid., 173; CCL, ibid., 88.

66  On this point, see Donald Creighton, *The Forked Road: Canada, 1939-1957* (Toronto: McClelland and Stewart, 1976), 127-31.

67  Ibid., 180.

68  Leslie A. Pal, *Interests of State: The Politics of Language, Multiculturalism, and Feminism in Canada* (Montreal: McGill-Queen's University Press, 1993), 91. Also see Alan C. Cairns, *Reconfigurations: Canadian Citizenship and Constitutional Change,* ed. Douglas E. Williams (Toronto: McClelland and Stewart, 1995), 113, 82.

69  For a frank statement of this lack of interest, see Justice Minister Davie Fulton's comments in Canadian Labour Congress, Presentation to the House of Commons Special Committee on Human Rights and Fundamental Freedoms, *Minutes of Proceedings and Evidence,* No. 3, 19 July 1960, 219-23. Subsequent references in this chapter to presentations from these hearings will read, Presentation to the 1960 House Committee on Human Rights, and will be preceded by the name of the relevant organization or speaker.

70  Tarnopolsky, *Canadian Bill of Rights,* 13-14.

71  Quoted in Peter C. Newman, *Renegade in Power: The Diefenbaker Years* (Toronto: McClelland and Stewart, 1963), 230.

72  CLC, Presentation to the 1960 House Committee on Human Rights, 191.

73  Ibid., 192, 196.

74  Ibid., 192, 194.

75  CCL, Presentation to the 1950 Senate Committee on Human Rights, 102.

76  CLC, Presentation to the 1960 House Committee on Human Rights, 200.

77  Canadian Jewish Congress, Presentation to the 1960 House Committee on Human Rights, No. 1, 12-15 July 1960, 87, 89.
78  Ibid., 90.
79  Ibid., 89. On the Diefenbaker initiatives see Cairns, *Reconfigurations,* 112-13.
80  CJC, Presentation to the 1960 House Committee on Human Rights, 93.
81  Ibid., 88, 87.
82  Evelyn Kallen, *Ethnicity and Human Rights in Canada* (Toronto: Gage, 1982), 198.
83  J.L. Granatstein, *Canada, 1957-1967: The Years of Uncertainty and Innovation* (Toronto: McClelland and Stewart, 1986), 6; Pal, *Interests of State,* 114.
84  Erving Goffman, "On Face-Work: An Analysis of Ritual Elements in Social Interaction," in *Language, Culture, and Society: A Book of Readings,* ed. Ben G. Blount (Cambridge, MA: Winthrop, 1974), 224-26.
85  Cairns, *Reconfigurations,* 42.
86  Hugh R. Innis, *Bilingualism and Biculturalism: An Abridged Version of the Royal Commission Report* (Toronto: McClelland and Stewart, 1973), "Foreword."
87  Granatstein, *Years of Uncertainty,* 253.
88  Ibid., 6.
89  Ukrainian Canadian Committee (Winnipeg Section), Presentation to the Royal Commission on Bilingualism and Biculturalism, Preliminary Hearing, Cathedral Hall, Ottawa, Ontario, 7-8 November 1963, 84; Canadian Polish Congress, "Brief Presented to the Royal Commission on Bilingualism and Biculturalism," n.d., 10-11, 10, 12; Canadian Jewish Congress, Presentation to the Royal Commission on Bilingualism and Biculturalism, Preliminary Hearing, Cathedral Hall, Ottawa, Ontario, 7-8 November 1963, 257, 261. The presentations dealt with in this section are all from the Preliminary Hearings of 7-8 November 1963. They are all available at Government Publications, Walter Koerner Library, University of British Columbia, Vancouver. Presentations from the Preliminary Hearings will be referred to hereafter by the designation, Presentation to the B&B Commission. In order to sample fully the reaction of ethnic minorities, this chapter also analyzes written briefs submitted to the commission, which it will identify by their specific titles.
90  CJC, Presentation to the B&B Commission, 264.
91  UCC, ibid., 84, 82-83.
92  CPC, "Brief Presented to the Royal Commission on Bilingualism and Biculturalism," 11.
93  Ibid., 11, 20.
94  Ibid., 7, 12. On loyalty as the oldest citizen virtue, see Derek Heater, *Citizenship: The Civic Ideal in World History, Politics and Education* (London: Longman, 1990), 2.
95  UCC, Presentation to the B&B Commission, 85, 86. On military service and citizenship, see Heater, *Citizenship,* 16-17.
96  UCC, Presentation to the B&B Commission, 81.
97  CPC, ibid., 184.
98  All quotations in this paragraph are from CP, "Brief Presented to the Royal Commission," 3-5.
99  UCC, Presentation to the B&B Commission, 87.
100 CLC, "Submission to the Royal Commission on Bilingualism and Biculturalism," 13 December 1965, 12.

101  Marshall, *Class, Citizenship and Social Development,* 119. For further discussion see Will Kymlicka, *Contemporary Political Philosophy: An Introduction,* 2nd ed. (Oxford: Oxford University Press, 2002), 328-29.
102  CLC, "Submission to the Royal Commission on Bilingualism and Biculturalism," 3-4.
103  Ibid., 7.
104  Ibid., 9, 5, 12.
105  CP, "Submission to the Royal Commission on Bilingualism and Biculturalism by the Communist Party of Canada," 24 June 1964, 24.
106  Presentation of the CPC, Royal Commission on Dominion-Provincial Relations, *Report of Hearings,* Vol. 24, Brief 401, 31 May 1938, 9718.
107  CP, "Submission to the Royal Commission on Bilingualism and Biculturalism," 27.
108  On the NCW's dedication to unity, see Veronica Strong-Boag, "The Roots of Modern Canadian Feminism," in *Canadian History Since Confederation: Essays and Interpretations,* ed. Bruce Hodgins and Robert Page, 2nd ed. (Georgetown, ON: Irwin-Dorsey, 1979), 399.
109  NCW, Presentation to the B&B Commission, 446.
110  Ibid., 447-48.
111  Ibid., 455.
112  For example, the council executive would soon go on record as unanimously opposed to the idea of "founding races," NCW, *Yearbook 1964* (n.p., 1964), 38.
113  NCW, Presentation to the B&B Commission, 446.
114  Strong-Boag, "Modern Canadian Feminism," 399, 408.
115  NCW, Presentation to the B&B Commission, 449.
116  CCL, Presentation to the 1950 Senate Committee on Human Rights, 102.
117  NJCCA, ibid., 271.
118  CJC, Presentation to the 1960 House Committee on Human Rights, 90; NJCCA, Presentation to the 1950 Senate Committee on Human Rights, 271; CLC, Presentation to the 1960 House Committee on Human Rights, 78.
119  In NCW, Presentation to the 1950 Senate Committee on Human Rights, 56; in NJCCA, ibid., 274, 273; in CJC, ibid., 76.
120  See esp. Bohdan Bociurkiw, "The Federal Policy of Multiculturalism and the Ukrainian-Canadian Community," in *Ukrainian Canadians, Multiculturalism, and Separatism,* ed. Manoly R. Lupul (Edmonton: University of Alberta Press, 1978), 102-4.
121  Yasmeen Abu-Laban and Christina Gabriel, *Selling Diversity: Immigration, Multiculturalism, Employment Equity, and Globalization* (Peterborough, ON: Broadview Press, 2002).
122  On the theoretical underpinnings of this point, see Ronald Inglehart, *Modernization and Postmodernization: Cultural, Economic, and Political Change in 43 Societies* (Princeton: Princeton University Press, 1997), 11-12. For Canadian evidence, see Neil Nevitte, "New Politics, the Charter, and Political Participation," in *Representation, Integration, and Political Parties in Canada,* ed. Herman Bakvis (Toronto: Dundurn Press, 1992), 394-95.
123  Nevitte, "New Politics," 361.
124  CJC, Presentation to the B&B Commission, 258; NJCCA, Presentation to the 1950 Senate Committee on Human Rights, 274; NCW, ibid., 54.

125 CPC, "Brief Presented to the Royal Commission on Bilingualism and Biculturalism," 5.
126 Ronald Inglehart, "The Silent Revolution in Europe: Intergenerational Change in Post-Industrial Societies," *American Political Science Review* 65 (1971): 991.
127 CJC, Presentation to the 1950 Senate Committee on Human Rights, 75.
128 Janine Brodie and Jane Jenson, *Crisis, Challenge and Change: Party and Class in Canada* (Toronto: Methuen, 1980), 226.
129 Kim Moody, *An Injury to All: The Decline of American Unionism* (London: Verso, 1988), xiv.

**Chapter 5: Charter Politics as Materialist Politics**

1 Peter H. Russell, *Constitutional Odyssey: Can Canadians Become a Sovereign People?* 3rd ed. (Toronto: University of Toronto Press, 2004), 72-79.
2 Alan C. Cairns, *Disruptions: Constitutional Struggles, from the Charter to Meech Lake,* ed. Douglas E. Williams (Toronto: McClelland and Stewart, 1991), chap. 1, "Recent Federalist Constitutional Proposals"; and Peter H. Russell, "The Political Purposes of the Canadian Charter of Rights and Freedoms," *Canadian Bar Review* 61 (1983): 30-54.
3 Hon. Pierre Elliott Trudeau, Minister of Justice, *A Canadian Charter of Human Rights* (Ottawa: Queen's Printer, 1968), 14, 11.
4 H.D. Forbes, "Trudeau's Moral Vision," in *Rethinking the Constitution: Perspectives on Canadian Constitutional Reform, Interpretation, and Theory,* ed. Anthony A. Peacock (Don Mills, ON: Oxford University Press, 1996).
5 See A.H. Robertson and J.G. Merrills, *Human Rights in the World: An Introduction to the Study of the International Protection of Human Rights* (Manchester: Manchester University Press, 1989), 25.
6 Trudeau, *Canadian Charter,* 12.
7 Leslie A. Pal, *Interests of State: The Politics of Language, Multiculturalism, and Feminism in Canada* (Montreal: McGill-Queen's Press, 1993).
8 Special Joint Committee of the Senate and of the House of Commons on the Constitution of Canada, *Final Report* (Ottawa: Queen's Printer, 1972), 4.
9 Bohdan Bociurkiw, "The Federal Policy of Multiculturalism and the Ukrainian-Canadian Community," in *Ukrainian Canadians, Multiculturalism, and Separatism: An Assessment,* ed. Manoly R. Lupul (Edmonton: University of Alberta Press, 1978), 104.
10 Walter Tarnopolsky, *The Canadian Bill of Rights,* 2nd ed. (Toronto: McClelland and Stewart, 1975), 20.
11 Russell, *Constitutional Odyssey,* 113.
12 Cairns, *Disruptions,* 83.
13 Cf. Donald Smiley, "A Dangerous Deed: The Constitution Act, 1982," in *And No One Cheered,* ed. Keith Banting and Richard Simeon (Toronto: Methuen, 1983); and Cairns, *Disruptions,* 226-36.
14 Robert Sheppard and Michael Valpy, *The National Deal: The Fight for a Canadian Constitution* (Toronto: Fleet, 1982), 138.
15 Ibid., 138-40.
16 Desmond Morton and Terry Copp, *Working People,* rev. ed. (Ottawa: Deneau, 1984), 275.
17 Desmond Morton, *The New Democrats, 1961-1986: The Politics of Change,* rev. ed. (Toronto: Copp Clark Pitman, 1986), 59, 76.

18  Ivan Avakumovic, *The Communist Party in Canada: A History* (Toronto: McClelland and Stewart, 1975), 278-81.

19  Communist Party of Canada, Presentation to the Special Joint Committee of the Senate and of the House of Commons on the Constitution of Canada, *Minutes of Proceedings and Evidence*, No. 81, 27 May 1971, 15. Subsequent references in this chapter to presentations from these hearings will read, Presentation to the 1970-72 Special Joint Committee, and will be preceded by the name of the relevant organization or speaker.

20  Breau, in CP, Presentation to the 1970-72 Special Joint Committee, 15.

21  On the Pearson opt-out, which would be a key influence on the later Meech Lake and Charlottetown Accords, see Richard Simeon and Ian Robinson, *State, Society, and the Development of Canadian Federalism* (Toronto: University of Toronto Press, 1990), 188.

22  CP, Presentation to the 1970-72 Special Joint Committee, 14.

23  Ibid., 22.

24  Ibid., 5.

25  Jill Vickers, Pauline Rankin, and Christine Appelle, *Politics as if Women Mattered: A Political Analysis of the National Action Committee on the Status of Women* (Toronto: University of Toronto Press, 1993), chap. 1, "The Intellectual and Political Context for the Development of NAC."

26  National Council of Women, Presentation to the 1970-72 Special Joint Committee, No. 74, 4 May 1971, 35.

27  Ibid., 37, 38, 42.

28  Ibid., 37, 38.

29  As quoted in Peter C. Newman, *Renegade in Power: The Diefenbaker Years* (Toronto: McClelland and Stewart, 1963), 230.

30  As quoted in Beverley Baines, "Law, Gender, Equality," in *Changing Patterns: Women in Canada,* ed. Sandra Burt, Lorraine Code, and Lindsay Dorney, 2nd ed. (Toronto: McClelland and Stewart, 1993), 259.

31  As quoted in Canadian Advisory Council on the Status of Women, Presentation to the Special Joint Committee of the Senate and of the House of Commons on the Constitution of Canada, *Minutes of Proceedings and Evidence*, No. 9, 20 November 1980, 126.

32  NCW, Presentation to the 1970-72 Special Joint Committee, 38, 35.

33  Ibid., 38. On jury duty and civic virtue, see Frank Henderson Stewart, *Honor* (Chicago: University of Chicago Press, 1994), 55-56.

34  Hogarth, in NCW, Presentation to the 1970-72 Special Joint Committee, 39-40.

35  Prud'homme, in ibid., 45.

36  Fergusson, in ibid., 46.

37  Allmand, in ibid., 43-44.

38  For unknown reasons, high-profile organizations such as the Canadian Jewish Congress and the National Congress of Italian Canadians did not appear or send written briefs. The only visible minority groups to do so were local or provincial associations beyond the purview of this study.

39  Canadian Polish Congress, Presentation to the 1970-72 Special Joint Committee, No. 72, 28 April 1971, 27; Ukrainian Canadian Committee (Montreal), ibid., No. 73, 29 April 1971, 49.

40  Pierre Elliott Trudeau, Statement by the Prime Minister in the House of Commons, October 8, 1971, reprinted in Augie Fleras and Jean Leonard Elliott,

*Multiculturalism in Canada: The Challenge of Diversity* (Scarborough, ON: Nelson, 1992), 282.

41 UCC (Toronto), Presentation to the 1970-72 Special Joint Committee, No. 19, 7 December 1970, 119 (for similar positions, see CPC, ibid., 27-28); Trudeau, Statement, in Fleras and Elliott, *Multiculturalism,* 282.

42 Raymond Breton, "The Production and Allocation of Symbolic Resources: An Analysis of the Linguistic and Ethnocultural Fields in Canada," *Canadian Review of Sociology and Anthropology* 21 (1984): 134.

43 CPC, Presentation to the 1970-72 Special Joint Committee, 27.

44 UCC (Toronto), ibid., 130.

45 Ibid., 130; CPC, ibid., 24; ibid., 29.

46 UCC (Toronto), ibid., 118; ibid., 129, 119; CPC, ibid., 25, 26, 29.

47 Yasmeen Abu-Laban and Christina Gabriel, *Selling Diversity: Immigration, Multiculturalism, Employment Equity, and Globalization* (Peterborough, ON: Broadview Press, 2002), 124.

48 Ryan, in UCC (Toronto), Presentation to the 1970-72 Special Joint Committee, 120.

49 See Roy Romanow, John Whyte, and Howard Leeson, *Canada ... Notwithstanding: The Making of the Constitution, 1976-1982* (Toronto: Carswell, 1984); and Ronald James Zukowsky, *Struggle Over the Constitution: From the Quebec Referendum to the Supreme Court* (Kingston: Queen's University Institute of Intergovernmental Relations, 1981).

50 On these revisions, see Zukowsky, *Struggle Over the Constitution,* 71-86.

51 James B. Kelly, *Governing with the Charter: Legislative and Judicial Activism and Framers' Intent* (Vancouver: UBC Press, 2005), 88.

52 John Richards, "The NDP in the Constitutional Drama," in *Canada: The State of the Federation 1992,* ed. Douglas Brown and Robert Young (Kingston: Queen's University Institute of Intergovernmental Relations, 1992), 172-73; Tarnopolsky, *Bill of Rights,* 7-9.

53 Pierre Elliott Trudeau, *Memoirs* (Toronto: McClelland and Stewart, 1993), 62-68.

54 Canadian Congress of Labour, Presentation to the Senate Special Committee on Human Rights and Fundamental Freedoms, No. 3, 27 April 1950, 102.

55 Canadian Labour Congress, Presentation to the House of Commons Special Committee on Human Rights and Fundamental Freedoms, No. 3, 19 July 1960, 200.

56 Canadian Congress of Labour, Presentation to the Senate Special Committee on Human Rights and Fundamental Freedoms, No. 3, 27 April 1950, 79. Cf. then Justice Minister Jean Chrétien in 1980: "Entrenchment is ... not a redistribution of powers between governments, rather it is a redistribution from governments to the people," quoted in Kelly, *Governing with the Charter,* 66.

57 Leo Panitch and Donald Swartz, *The Assault on Trade Union Freedoms: From Wage Controls to Social Contract,* rev. ed. (Toronto: Garamond, 1993), 147.

58 "While the Canadian Labour Congress has refrained from taking a formal position on the Constitutional issue, we are making one exception ... The CLC ... calls upon the ... Committee ... to ensure the entrenchment of aboriginal and treaty rights in the revised Constitution." CLC, Brief to the Joint House-Senate Committee on the Constitution, 26 November 1980, on file with author.

59 Panitch and Swartz, *Assault.* On this point, see Joel Bakan, *Just Words: Constitutional Rights and Social Wrongs* (Toronto: University of Toronto Press, 1997), chap. 5, "Freedom of Association and the Dissociation of Workers."

60  Robert Sheppard and Michael Valpy, *The National Deal: The Fight for a Canadian Constitution* (Toronto: Fleet, 1982), 138. On the television coverage, see Kelly, *Governing*, 22.

61  See esp. Canadian Congress of Labour, Presentation to the 1950 Senate Committee on Human Rights, No. 3, 27 April 1950, 98-106.

62  Canadian Polish Congress, Presentation to the Special Joint Committee of the Senate and of the House of Commons on the Constitution of Canada, *Minutes of Proceedings and Evidence*, No. 9, 20 November 1980, 104. Subsequent references in this chapter to presentations from these hearings will read, Presentation to the 1980-81 Special Joint Committee, and will be preceded by the name of the relevant organization or speaker.

63  Ukrainian Canadian Committee, Presentation to the 1980-81 Special Joint Committee, No. 14, 27 November 1980, 58.

64  National Congress of Italian Canadians, ibid., No. 23, 10 December 1980, 20.

65  UCC, ibid., 62; CPC, ibid., 103.

66  Council of National Ethnocultural Organizations of Canada, ibid., No. 22, 9 December 1980, 75.

67  CPC, ibid., 103, 106, 108.

68  Mackasey, in UCC, ibid., 69.

69  See Zukowsky, *Struggle Over the Constitution*, 79-80.

70  For example, see Raymond Breton, "Multiculturalism and Canadian Nation-Building," in *The Politics of Gender, Ethnicity, and Language in Canada*, ed. Alan C. Cairns and Cynthia Williams (Toronto: University of Toronto Press, 1985), 56; Pal, *Interests of State*, 203.

71  Afro-Asian Foundation of Canada, Presentation to the 1980-81 Special Joint Committee, No. 32, 6 January 1981, 32, 40; National Black Coalition of Canada, ibid., No. 22, 9 December 1980, 11, 9.

72  NBCC, ibid., 20, 15.

73  AAFC, Presentation to the 1980-81 Special Joint Committee, 33, 32.

74  Ibid., 33.

75  NBCC, ibid., 23, 20, 17.

76  AAFC, ibid., 31, 32, 31.

77  NBCC, ibid., 7, 15, 12.

78  National Japanese Canadian Citizens' Association, Presentation to the Senate Special Committee on Human Rights and Fundamental Freedoms, No. 8, 10 May 1950, 270.

79  UCC, Presentation to the 1980-81 Special Joint Committee, 54; CPC, ibid., 109.

80  Canadian Jewish Congress, ibid., No. 7, 18 November 1980, 80, 84.

81  National Association of Japanese Canadians, ibid., No. 13, 26 November 1980, 7, 9, 8, 7, 9.

82  Robinson, in ibid., 15; Mackasey, in ibid., 17; Fraser, in ibid., 12, 11.

83  For example, see Mackasey, in UCC, ibid., 67; Nystrom, in CPC, ibid., 119; Nystrom, in CJC, ibid., 107-9; Joyal, in NBCC, ibid., 23-24; Crombie, in AAFC, ibid., 37.

84  Kelly, *Governing with the Charter*, 92.

85  Fraser, in NAJC, Presentation to the 1980-81 Special Joint Committee, 13.

86  N.E.S. Griffiths, *The Splendid Vision: Centennial History of the National Council of Women of Canada, 1893-1993* (Ottawa: Carleton University Press, 1993), 325-26.

87 Vickers et al., *Politics as if Women Mattered*, 27. Cf. Veronica Strong-Boag, *The Parliament of Women: The National Council of Women of Canada, 1893-1929* (Ottawa: National Museums of Canada, 1976).

88 Naomi Black, "The Canadian Women's Movement: The Second Wave," in *Changing Patterns: Women in Canada*, ed. Sandra Burt, Lorraine Code, and Lindsay Dorney, 2nd ed. (Toronto: McClelland and Stewart, 1993), 158; Monique Bégin, "The Royal Commission on the Status of Women in Canada: Twenty Years Later," in *Challenging Times: The Women's Movement in Canada and the United States*, ed. Constance Backhouse and David H. Flaherty (Montreal and Kingston: McGill-Queen's University Press, 1992), 23.

89 Griffiths, *Splendid Vision*, 314.

90 Vickers et al., *Politics as if Women Mattered*, 73-74; Nancy Adamson, Linda Briskin, and Margaret McPhail, *Feminist Organizing for Change: The Contemporary Women's Movement in Canada* (Toronto: Oxford University Press, 1988), 52.

91 Vickers et al., *Politics as if Women Mattered*, 92.

92 The draft Charter of 2 October 1980 is reprinted in Edward McWhinney, *Canada and the Constitution, 1979-1982: Patriation and the Charter of Rights* (Toronto: University of Toronto Press, 1982), 141-48.

93 National Action Committee on the Status of Women, Presentation to the 1980-81 Special Joint Committee, No. 9, 20 November 1980, 58-59.

94 Ibid., 58-60.

95 Ibid., 73, 64, 59.

96 AAFC, ibid., 30; NAJC, ibid., 5; NAC, ibid., 57.

97 Vickers et al., *Politics as if Women Mattered*, 94, 104, 97.

98 NAC, Presentation to the 1980-81 Special Joint Committee, 57.

99 Ibid., 59, 64, 72, 73. On McDonald's views, see Lynn McDonald, "The Supreme Court of Canada and the Equality Guarantee in the Charter," *Socialist Studies* 2 (1984): 45-65.

100 NAC, Presentation to the 1980-81 Special Joint Committee, 73.

101 See Naomi Black, "Ripples in the Second Wave: Comparing the Contemporary Women's Movement in Canada and the United States," in *Challenging Times*, 104.

102 NAC, Presentation to the 1980-81 Special Joint Committee, 59, 60.

103 Hays, in ibid., 75.

104 Alexandra Dobrowolsky, *The Politics of Pragmatism: Women, Representation, and Constitutionalism in Canada* (Don Mills, ON: Oxford University Press, 2000), 47.

105 Penney Kome, *The Taking of Twenty-Eight: Women Challenge the Constitution* (Toronto: Women's Press, 1983), 40.

106 Vickers et al., *Politics as if Women Mattered*, 105.

107 Alexandra Dobrowolsky, "Of 'Special Interest': Interest, Identity, and Feminist Constitutional Activism in Canada," *Canadian Journal of Political Science* 31 (1998): 707-42; Kome, *Taking of Twenty-Eight*, 75-77.

108 Section 33 applies to Sections 2 and 7-15 of the Charter, and can be successively reinvoked after the end of each five-year period. For an account of its creation, see Romanow et al., *Canada ... Notwithstanding*, 208-12.

109 Cairns, *Disruptions*, 82.

110 Kome, *Taking of Twenty-Eight*.

111 Adamson et al., *Feminist Organizing*, 71. Also see Rosemary Billings, "Introduction," in Kome, *Taking of Twenty-Eight*, 13, 16; and Vickers et al., *Politics as if Women Mattered*, 104.

112   Black, "Ripples in the Second Wave," 101.
113   On disappointment, see Keith Banting and Richard Simeon, ed., *And No One Cheered* (Toronto: Methuen, 1983).
114   Doug Owram, *The Government Generation: Canadian Intellectuals and the State, 1900-1945* (Toronto: University of Toronto Press, 1986).
115   On the transitory character of multiculturalism recognition, see Yasmeen Abu-Laban and Tim Nieguth, "Reconsidering the Constitution, Minorities and Politics in Canada," *Canadian Journal of Political Science* 33 (2000): 465-98. On the contradictory effect of Charter symbolism, see Bakan, *Just Words,* chap. 8, "Rights as Political Discourse: The Charter Meets the Charlottetown Accord."
116   Dobrowolsky, *Politics of Pragmatism,* chap. 3, "Earthquakes and Aftershocks: The Tremors of Early 1980s Equality Struggles."
117   Kelly, *Governing with the Charter,* chap. 2, "Constitutional Politics and the Charter."
118   Cairns, *Disruptions,* chap. 4, "Citizens (Outsiders) and Governments (Insiders) in Constitution-Making: The Case of Meech Lake."
119   For example, see Neil Nevitte, "New Politics, the Charter, and Political Participation," in *Representation, Integration, and Political Parties in Canada,* ed. Herman Bakvis (Toronto: Dundurn Press, 1992), 356.
120   Ronald Inglehart, *Culture Shift in Advanced Industrial Society* (Princeton: Princeton University Press, 1990), 11-12.
121   F.L. Morton and Rainer Knopff, "The Supreme Court as the Vanguard of the Intelligentsia: The Charter Movement as Postmaterialist Politics," in *Canadian Constitutionalism: 1791-1991,* ed. Janet Ajzenstat (Ottawa: Canadian Study of Parliament Group, 1992); Morton and Knopff, *The Charter Revolution and the Court Party* (Peterborough, ON: Broadview Press, 2000), chap. 3, "The Court Party"; Ian Brodie and Neil Nevitte, "Evaluating the Citizens' Constitution Theory," *Canadian Journal of Political Science* 26 (1993): 234-59; and Nevitte, "New Politics, the Charter, and Political Participation." Also see Michael Lusztig and J. Matthew Wilson, "A New Right? Moral Issues and Partisan Change in Canada," *Social Science Quarterly* 86 (2005): 117; and C.L. Ostberg, Matthew E. Wetstein, and Craig R. Ducat, "Attitudes, Precedents, and Cultural Change: Explaining the Citation of Foreign Precedents by the Supreme Court of Canada," *Canadian Journal of Political Science* 34 (June 2001): 399.
122   Morton and Knopff, "Supreme Court," 76.
123   On Quebec nationalism as postmaterialism, see Robert Anderson and Anthony Heath, "Social Identities and Political Cleavages: The Role of Political Context," *Journal of the Royal Statistical Society, Series A* 166 (2003): 302-3.
124   Morton and Knopff, "Supreme Court," 67, 76.
125   Ibid., 66, 78.
126   NAC, Presentation to the 1980-81 Special Joint Committee, 73.
127   The CJC's focus on hate crime was a notable exception. See CJC, ibid., 84.
128   AAFC, ibid., 33.
129   NBCC, ibid., 20; AAFC, ibid., 31, 32.
130   Black, "Ripples in the Second Wave," 101.
131   Kome, *Taking of Twenty-Eight,* 23.

### Chapter 6: From Meech Lake to Charlottetown

1   See esp. Pierre Bourdieu, *Distinction: A Social Critique of the Judgement of Taste,* trans. Richard Nice (Cambridge, MA: Harvard University Press, 1984), 480.

2 Alan C. Cairns, *Disruptions: Constitutional Struggles, from the Charter to Meech Lake,* ed. Douglas E. Williams (Toronto: McClelland and Stewart, 1991), chap. 4, "Citizens (Outsiders) and Governments (Insiders) in Constitution-Making: The Case of Meech Lake"; Anthony A. Peacock, ed., *Rethinking the Constitution: Perspectives on Canadian Constitutional Reform, Interpretation, and Theory* (Don Mills, ON: Oxford University Press, 1996).

3 Premier René Lévesque, quoted in Alan C. Cairns, *Reconfigurations: Canadian Citizenship and Constitutional Change,* ed. Douglas E. Williams (Toronto: McClelland and Stewart, 1995), 286.

4 The following account relies on Leslie A. Pal and Robert M. Campbell, *The Real Worlds of Canadian Politics: Cases in Process and Policy,* 2nd ed. (Peterborough, ON: Broadview, 1991), chap. 5, "The Rise and Fall of the Meech Lake Accord"; Peter H. Russell, *Constitutional Odyssey: Can Canadians Become a Sovereign People?* 3rd ed. (Toronto: University of Toronto Press, 2004), chap. 9, "Round Four: Meech Lake"; and Raymond Breton, *Why Meech Failed: Lessons for Canadian Constitutionmaking* (Toronto: C.D. Howe Institute, 1992).

5 Russell, *Constitutional Odyssey,* 138.

6 Garth Stevenson, "Federalism and Intergovernmental Relations," in *Canadian Politics in the 21st Century,* ed. Michael Whittington and Glen Williams (Scarborough, ON: Nelson, 2000), 99-101.

7 Cairns, *Disruptions,* 135.

8 See Russell, *Constitutional Odyssey,* 163.

9 Patrick J. Monahan, "The Sounds of Silence," in *The Charlottetown Accord, the Referendum, and the Future of Canada,* ed. Kenneth McRoberts and Patrick J. Monahan (Toronto: University of Toronto Press, 1993), 225.

10 Russell, *Constitutional Odyssey,* 165-67.

11 Ibid., 176; David Milne, "Innovative Constitutional Processes: Renewal of Canada Conferences, January-March 1992," in *Canada: The State of the Federation, 1992,* ed. Douglas Brown and Robert Young (Kingston: Queen's University Institute of Intergovernmental Relations, 1992), 30.

12 Government of Canada, *Shaping Canada's Future Together* (Ottawa: Minister of Supply and Services, 1991).

13 Richard Johnston, André Blais, Elisabeth Gidengil, and Neil Nevitte, *The Challenge of Direct Democracy: The 1992 Canadian Referendum* (Montreal and Kingston: McGill-Queen's University Press, 1996).

14 Cairns, *Disruptions,* "Insiders and Outsiders."

15 Government of Canada, *Strengthening the Canadian Federation: The Constitution Amendment* (Ottawa: Minister of Supply and Services, 1987), 9, quoted in ibid., 159.

16 Kathy Brock, *A Mandate Fulfilled: Constitutional Reform and the Manitoba Task Force on Meech Lake* (Winnipeg: University of Manitoba Outreach Fund, 1990), 77.

17 For example, see Coalition of Visible Minority Women (joint presentation with the Ad Hoc Committee of Women on the Constitution), Presentation to the Special Joint Committee of the Senate and of the House of Commons on the 1987 Constitutional Accord, *Minutes of Proceedings and Evidence,* No. 15, 31 August 1987; and National Association of Canadians of Origins in India, ibid., No. 7, 13 August 1987. Subsequent references in this chapter to presentations from these hearings will read, Presentation to the 1987 Special Joint Committee, and will be preceded by the name of the relevant organization or speaker.

18  Ukrainian Canadian Committee, Presentation to the 1987 Special Joint Committee, No. 7, 13 August 1987, 100, 108.
19  Cairns, *Disruptions,* 109.
20  UCC, Presentation to the 1987 Special Joint Committee, 99.
21  Chinese Canadian National Council, ibid., No. 7, 13 August 1987, 62.
22  On this ambivalence, see Jill Vickers, Pauline Rankin, and Christine Appelle, *Politics as if Women Mattered: A Political Analysis of the National Action Committee on the Status of Women* (Toronto: University of Toronto Press, 1993), 94, 97, 104.
23  NAC, Presentation to the 1987 Special Joint Committee, No. 13, 26 August 1987, 38.
24  NAC, Presentation to the Special Joint Committee of the Senate and of the House of Commons on the Constitution of Canada, *Minutes of Proceedings and Evidence,* No. 9, 20 November 1980, 57-58; NAC, Presentation to the 1987 Special Joint Committee, 22.
25  NAC, Presentation to the 1987 Special Joint Committee, 23, 40.
26  CCNC, ibid., 63-64.
27  National Association of Canadians of Origins in India, ibid., 80.
28  Canadian Ethnocultural Council, ibid., No. 7, 13 August 1987, 53; NAC, ibid., 29.
29  Ad Hoc Committee of Women on the Constitution, ibid., 128; ibid., 131; UCC, ibid., 107.
30  Layton, in Canadian Ethnocultural Council, ibid., 52; Turner, in ibid., 53; Blais-Grenier, in ibid., 59.
31  UCC, Presentation to the 1987 Special Joint Committee, 108; ibid.; Coalition of Visible Minority Women, ibid., 135.
32  Brian Lee Crowley, *The Road To Equity: Gender, Ethnicity and Language – Impolitic Essays* (Toronto: Stoddart, 1994), 118; Rainer Knopff and F.L. Morton, *Charter Politics* (Scarborough, ON: Nelson, 1992), 79.
33  See Cairns, *Disruptions,* "Insiders and Outsiders."
34  Cairns, "A Defence of the Citizens' Constitution Theory: A Response to Ian Brodie and Neil Nevitte," *Canadian Journal of Political Science* 26 (1993): 262-63.
35  Deborah Coyne, "Commentary," in *After Meech Lake: Lessons for the Future,* ed. David E. Smith, Peter MacKinnon, and John C. Courtney (Saskatoon: Fifth House Publishers, 1991), 139, 141, 139.
36  Ibid., 139.
37  Donald Johnston, "Conclusion," in Pierre Elliott Trudeau, *Pierre Trudeau Speaks Out on Meech Lake,* ed. Donald Johnston (Toronto: General Paperbacks, 1990), 108.
38  Frank McKenna, quoted in Legislative Assembly of New Brunswick, Select Committee on the 1987 Constitutional Accord, *Final Report on the Constitution Amendment 1987* (Fredericton: Legislative Assembly of New Brunswick, 1989), 14.
39  Brock, *Mandate Fulfilled,* 43-45.
40  Pal and Campbell, *Real Worlds,* 104.
41  Manitoba Task Force on Meech Lake, *Report on the 1987 Constitutional Accord* (Winnipeg: Legislative Assembly of Manitoba, 1989), 26.
42  Ibid.; Trudeau, *Pierre Trudeau Speaks Out,* 34; unnamed citizen presenter, quoted in Manitoba Task Force, *Report,* 5-6.
43  Unnamed citizen presenter, quoted in Manitoba Task Force, *Report,* 5-6.
44  On exchange theory, see Stewart Clegg and David Dunkerley, *Organization, Class, and Control* (London: Routledge and Keagan Paul, 1980), 381-85, 449-51.

45 Leo Panitch and Donald Swartz, *The Assault on Trade Union Freedoms: From Wage Controls to Social Contract*, rev. ed. (Toronto: Garamond, 1993), 147.
46 Vickers et al., *Politics as if Women Mattered*, 105.
47 Fédération des femmes du Québec, Presentation to the 1987 Special Joint Committee, No. 13, 26 August 1987, 44, 43.
48 Vickers et al., *Politics as if Women Mattered*, 276.
49 Ibid., 9.
50 Canadian Labour Congress, Presentation to the 1987 Special Joint Committee, 6, 9-10, 5.
51 National Union of Provincial Government Employees, ibid., No. 3, 5 August 1987, 95.
52 United Electrical, Radio and Machine Workers of Canada, ibid., No. 10, 20 August 1987, 112; Public Service Alliance of Canada, ibid., No. 6, 12 August 1987, 48.
53 CLC, ibid., 18; 10.
54 On the CLC's "sovereignty-association" relationship with the Quebec labour movement, see Tom McIntosh, "Organized Labour in a Federal Society: Solidarity, Coalition Building, and Canadian Unions," in *Canada: The State of the Federation, 1998/99: How Canadians Connect*, ed. Harvey Lazar and Tom McIntosh (Montreal and Kingston: McGill-Queen's University Press, 1999).
55 Cairns, *Disruptions*, 156.
56 Milne, "Innovative Constitutional Processes," 30.
57 Russell, *Constitutional Odyssey*, 176.
58 Ibid., 173. For more information on the proposals, see ibid., 171-74.
59 Stephen McBride and John Shields, *Dismantling a Nation: The Transition to Corporate Rule in Canada* (Halifax: Fernwood, 1997), 101.
60 Alexandra Dobrowolsky, *The Politics of Pragmatism: Women, Representation, and Constitutionalism in Canada* (Don Mills, ON: Oxford University Press, 2000), 124.
61 Ibid., 160.
62 Russell, *Constitutional Odyssey*, 181.
63 See esp. Peter H. Russell, "The End of Mega Constitutional Politics in Canada?" and Jeffrey Simpson, "The Referendum and Its Aftermath," in *The Charlottetown Accord, the Referendum, and the Future of Canada*, ed. Kenneth McRoberts and Patrick J. Monahan (Toronto: University of Toronto Press, 1993). On the referendum campaign, see Johnston et al., *Challenge of Direct Democracy*.
64 Cairns, *Reconfigurations*, 289, 281.
65 National Action Committee on the Status of Women, Presentation to the Special Joint Committee of the Senate and of the House of Commons on a Renewed Canada, *Minutes of Proceedings and Evidence*, No. 10, 28 October 1991, 17, 20; 18. Subsequent references in this chapter to presentations from these hearings will read, Presentation to the 1991-92 Renewed Canada Committee, and will be preceded by the name of the relevant organization or speaker.
66 Canadian Labour Congress, ibid., No. 59, 4 February 1992, 19.
67 Jeremy Webber, *Reimagining Canada: Language, Culture, Community, and the Canadian Constitution* (Kingston and Montreal: McGill-Queen's University Press, 1994), 7.
68 Canadian Jewish Congress, National Congress of Italian Canadians, and Hellenic Canadian Congress, Presentation to the 1991-92 Renewed Canada Committee, No. 58, 3 February 1992, 41, 36.
69 Canadian Ethnocultural Council, ibid., No. 14, 31 October 1991, 11, 6.

70   National Black Coalition of Canada, ibid., No. 16, 4 November 1991, 49.
71   Canadian Association of Visible Minorities (joint presentation with the Afro-Canadian Caucus of Nova Scotia and the Black United Front of Nova Scotia), ibid., No. 44, 16 January 1992, 24; National Association of Japanese Canadians, ibid., No. 29, 11 December 1991, 19-20.
72   Cairns, *Reconfigurations*, 290.
73   Marjorie Griffin Cohen, "The Canadian Women's Movement and Its Efforts to Influence the Canadian Economy," in *Challenging Times: The Women's Movement in Canada and the United States*, ed. Constance Backhouse and David H. Flaherty (Montreal and Kingston: McGill-Queen's University Press, 1992), 215-24. Also see Dobrowolsky, *Politics of Pragmatism*, 101-3.
74   A.W. Johnson, "A National Government in a Federal State," in *Constitutional Politics: The Canadian Forum Book on the Federal Constitutional Proposals, 1991-92*, ed. Duncan Cameron and Miriam Smith (Toronto: Lorimer, 1992), 79-91.
75   CLC, Presentation to the 1991-92 Renewed Canada Committee, 6, 17; 19-20.
76   Public Service Alliance of Canada and National Union of Provincial Government Employees, ibid., No. 30, 12 December 1991, 50.
77   NAC, ibid., 18.
78   Canada, *Shaping Canada's Future*, quoted in Russell, *Constitutional Odyssey*, 173.
79   CLC, Presentation to the 1991-92 Renewed Canada Committee, 13; NAC, ibid., 23.
80   CEC, ibid., 11. The CJC et al. also endorsed the economic union proposals, Presentation to the 1991-92 Renewed Canada Committee, 38. The other ethnocultural minority organizations neglected to comment.
81   CEC, ibid., 7
82   NAC, ibid., 28; CAVM, ibid., 26.
83   Ibid., 27; 26. On the social charter, see Joel Bakan and David Schneiderman, ed., *Social Justice and the Constitution: Perspectives on a Social Charter for Canada* (Ottawa: Carleton University Press, 1992).
84   CJC et al., Presentation to the 1991-92 Renewed Canada Committee, 37.
85   Ibid., 6.
86   NBCC, ibid., 52; CEC, ibid., 6-7.
87   Philip Resnick, *Thinking English Canada* (Toronto: Stoddart, 1994).
88   Panitch and Swartz, *Assault*. Cf. Kim Moody, *An Injury to All: The Decline of American Unionism* (London: Verso, 1988).
89   PSAC/NUPGE, Presentation to the 1991-92 Renewed Canada Committee, 47; 49.
90   Ibid., 47, 48.
91   Barootes, in ibid., 52; PSAC/NUPGE, ibid., 53; 48.
92   Ibid., 53; ibid., 54.
93   Vickers et al., *Politics as if Women Mattered*, 272.
94   Simone Chambers, "New Constitutionalism: Democracy, Habermas, and Canadian Exceptionalism," *Canadian Political Philosophy: Contemporary Reflections*, ed. Ronald Beiner and Wayne Norman (Don Mills, ON: Oxford University Press, 2002), 63-77.
95   Cairns, *Reconfigurations*, 281.
96   Anthony A. Peacock, "Introduction: The Necessity of Rethinking the Constitution," in *Rethinking the Constitution*, Peacock, ed., ix; Tom Darby and Peter C. Emberley, "'Political Correctness' and the Constitution: Nature and Convention Re-examined," in ibid., 233-48.

97 Gerald Kernerman, *Multicultural Nationalism: Civilizing Difference, Constituting Community* (Vancouver: UBC Press, 2005).
98 Unnamed citizen presenter, quoted in Manitoba Task Force, *Report,* 5-6.
99 Manitoba Task Force, *Report,* 26.
100 CEC, Presentation to the 1991-92 Renewed Canada Committee, 7, 9.
101 Ronald Inglehart, *The Silent Revolution: Changing Values and Political Styles Among Western Publics* (Princeton: Princeton University Press, 1977), 13.
102 For example, see Peacock, "Introduction," ix; F.L. Morton, "The Effect of the Charter of Rights on Canadian Federalism," *Publius* 25 (1995): 187-88; and Janet Ajzenstat, "Constitution Making and the Myth of the People," in *Constitutional Predicament: Canada after the Referendum of 1992,* ed. Curtis Cook (Montreal and Kingston: McGill-Queen's University Press, 1994), 118.
103 Ian Brodie and Neil Nevitte, "Evaluating the Citizens' Constitution Theory," *Canadian Journal of Political Science* 26 (1993): 241.
104 For example, see Ronald Inglehart, *Culture Shift in Advanced Industrial Society* (Princeton: Princeton University Press, 1990), 373.
105 Ronald Inglehart, *Modernization and Postmodernization: Cultural, Economic, and Political Change in 43 Societies* (Princeton: Princeton University Press, 1997), 40.

**Chapter 7: Conclusion**
1 Christopher P. Manfredi, "On the Virtues of a Limited Constitution: Why Canadians Were Right to Reject the Charlottetown Accord," in *Rethinking the Constitution: Perspectives on Canadian Constitutional Reform, Interpretation, and Theory,* ed. Anthony A. Peacock (Don Mills, ON: Oxford University Press, 1996), 48; Janet Ajzenstat, "Two Forms of Democracy: A Response to Mendelsohn's 'Public Brokerage': Constitutional Reform and the Accommodation of Mass Publics," *Canadian Journal of Political Science* 33 (September 2000): 590.
2 Trades and Labour Congress of Canada, Presentation to the 1938 Royal Commission on Dominion-Provincial Relations, Vol. 17, Brief 106, 21 January 1938, 3102.
3 Augie Fleras and Jean Leonard Elliott, *Multiculturalism in Canada: The Challenge of Diversity* (Scarborough, ON: Nelson, 1992), 102.
4 Alan C. Cairns, *Reconfigurations: Canadian Citizenship and Constitutional Change,* ed. Douglas E. Williams (Toronto: McClelland and Stewart, 1995), 20.
5 An early statement of this coexistence in the Canadian context is Raymond Breton, "The Production and Allocation of Symbolic Resources: An Analysis of the Linguistic and Ethnocultural Fields in Canada," *Canadian Review of Sociology and Anthropology* 21 (1984): 123-44.
6 Axel Honneth, *The Struggle for Recognition: The Moral Grammar of Social Conflicts,* trans. Joel Anderson (Cambridge: Polity Press, 1995), 173.
7 Charles Taylor, "The Politics of Recognition," in *Multiculturalism: Examining the Politics of Recognition,* ed. Charles Taylor and Amy Gutmann, 2nd ed. (Princeton: Princeton University Press, 1994), 25.
8 For a critique of the culturalist approach, see Nancy Fraser, "Rethinking Recognition," *New Left Review* 3 (May/June 2000): 110-13.
9 William J. Goode, *The Celebration of Heroes: Prestige as a Social Control System* (Berkeley: University of California Press, 1978), vii.
10 Erving Goffman, "On Face-Work: An Analysis of Ritual Elements in Social Interaction," in *Language, Culture, and Society: A Book of Readings,* ed. Ben G. Blount (Cambridge, MA: Winthrop, 1974), 239.

11  Pierre Bourdieu, *Outline of a Theory of Practice,* trans. Richard Nice (Cambridge: Cambridge University Press, 1977), 182-83.

12  Karl Marx and Frederick Engels, *Manifesto of the Communist Party,* in *The Marx-Engels Reader,* ed. Robert C. Tucker (New York: Norton, 1978), 475; Max Weber, *Economy and Society: An Outline of Interpretive Sociology,* trans. Ephraim Fischoff et al., vol. 1 (New York: Bedminster Press, 1968), 215.

13  Peter L. Berger, Brigitte Berger, and Hansfried Kellner, *The Homeless Mind: Modernization and Consciousness* (New York: Vintage Books, 1973), 83.

14  Progressive Conservative Justice Minister Davie Fulton on why the Diefenbaker Bill of Rights was not an attempt to change the social status of Canadian women, quoted in Canadian Advisory Council on the Status of Women, Presentation to the Special Joint Committee of the Senate and of the House of Commons on the Constitution of Canada, *Minutes of Proceedings and Evidence,* No. 9, 20 November 1980, 126.

15  Council of National Ethnocultural Organizations, Presentation to the Special Joint Committee of the Senate and of the House of Commons on the Constitution of Canada, *Minutes of Proceedings and Evidence,* No. 22, 9 December 1980, 74-75.

16  National Japanese Canadian Citizens' Association, Presentation to the Special Senate Committee on Human Rights and Fundamental Freedoms, *Minutes of Proceedings and Evidence,* No. 8, 10 May 1950, 271.

17  Ad Hoc Committee of Women on the Constitution, Presentation to the Special Joint Committee of the Senate and of the House of Commons on the 1987 Constitutional Accord, *Minutes of Proceedings and Evidence,* No. 15, 31 August 1987, 144.

18  Ibid., 136.

19  Progressive Conservative MP Leo Duguay, in ibid., 140-41.

20  Hon. Pierre Elliott Trudeau, Minister of Justice, *A Canadian Charter of Human Rights* (Ottawa: Queen's Printer, 1968), 12.

21  Manitoba Task Force on Meech Lake, *Report on the 1987 Constitutional Accord* (Winnipeg: Legislative Assembly of Manitoba, 1989), 26.

22  Deborah Coyne, "Commentary," in *After Meech Lake: Lessons for the Future,* ed. David E. Smith, Peter MacKinnon, and John C. Courtney (Saskatoon: Fifth House Publishers, 1991), 139.

23  Brian Lee Crowley, *The Road To Equity: Gender, Ethnicity and Language – Impolitic Essays* (Toronto: Stoddart, 1994), 118; Rainer Knopff and F.L. Morton, *Charter Politics* (Scarborough, ON: Nelson, 1992), 79.

24  Gerald Kernerman, *Multicultural Nationalism: Civilizing Difference, Constituting Community* (Vancouver: UBC Press, 2005). Also see Jo-Anne Lee and Linda Cardinal, "Hegemonic Nationalism and the Politics of Feminism and Multiculturalism in Canada," in *Painting the Maple: Essays on Race, Gender, and the Construction of Canada,* ed. Veronica Strong-Boag et al. (Vancouver: UBC Press, 1998).

25  Leslie A. Pal, *Interests of State: The Politics of Language, Multiculturalism, and Feminism in Canada* (Montreal: McGill-Queen's Press, 1993).

26  Yasmeen Abu-Laban and Christina Gabriel, *Selling Diversity: Immigration, Multiculturalism, Employment Equity, and Globalization* (Peterborough, ON: Broadview Press, 2002).

27  Matt James, "The Permanent-Emergency Compensation State: A 'Postsocialist' Tale of Political Dystopia," in *Critical Policy Studies: Contemporary Canadian*

*Approaches,* ed. Michael Orsini and Miriam Smith (Vancouver: UBC Press, forthcoming).

28 Miriam Smith, "Resisting and Reinforcing Neoliberalism: Lesbian and Gay Organizing at the Federal and Local Levels in Canada," *Policy and Politics* 1 (2005): 75-93.

29 Harvey Lazar, "Non-Constitutional Renewal: Toward a New Equilibrium in the Federation," in *Canada: The State of the Federation 1997 – Non-Constitutional Renewal,* ed. Harvey Lazar (Kingston, ON: Queen's University Institute of Intergovernmental Relations, 1998).

# Bibliography

**Government Documents**

Canada. Department of Labour. *Labour Organization in Canada*. Thirty-third Annual Report for the Calendar Year 1943. Ottawa: King's Printer, 1944.

–. Government of Canada. *Shaping Canada's Future Together*. Ottawa: Minister of Supply and Services, 1991.

–. Government of Canada. *Strengthening the Canadian Federation: The Constitution Amendment*. Ottawa: Minister of Supply and Services, 1987.

–. Hon. Pierre Elliott Trudeau, Minister of Justice. *A Canadian Charter of Human Rights*. Ottawa: Queen's Printer, 1968.

–. Minister of Public Works and Government Services. *A History of the Vote in Canada*. Ottawa: Minister of Public Works and Government Services, 1997.

–. Parliament. House of Commons. House of Commons Special Committee on Bill No. 98 Respecting Unemployment Insurance. *Minutes of Proceedings and Evidence*. Nos. 2-3. Ottawa: King's Printer, 1940. Microfiche.

–. Parliament. House of Commons. House of Commons Special Committee on Human Rights and Fundamental Freedoms. *Minutes of Proceedings and Evidence*. Nos. 1, 3. Ottawa: Queen's Printer, 1960.

–. Parliament. House of Commons. House of Commons Special Committee on Reconstruction and Re-Establishment. *Minutes of Proceedings and Evidence*. Nos. 24, 26. Ottawa: King's Printer, 1943.

–. Parliament. House of Commons. House of Commons Special Committee on Social Security. *Minutes of Proceedings and Evidence*. No. 15. Ottawa: King's Printer, 1943.

–. Parliament. Senate. Special Senate Committee on Human Rights and Fundamental Freedoms. *Minutes of Proceedings and Evidence*. Nos. 1-3, 5, 8. Ottawa: King's Printer, 1950.

–. Parliament. Senate and House of Commons. Special Joint Committee of the Senate and of the House of Commons on the Constitution of Canada. *Final Report*. 28th Parl., 4th sess. Ottawa: Queen's Printer, 1972.

–. Parliament. Senate and House of Commons. Special Joint Committee of the Senate and of the House of Commons on the Constitution of Canada. *Minutes of Proceedings and Evidence*. 28th Parl., 3d sess. Nos. 8, 19, 72-74, 81. Hull, QC: Supply and Services Canada, 1970-71.

–. Parliament. Senate and House of Commons. Special Joint Committee of the Senate and of the House of Commons on the Constitution of Canada. *Minutes of Proceedings and Evidence*. 32d Parl., 1st sess. Nos. 7, 9, 13-14, 22-23, 32. Hull, QC: Supply and Services Canada, 1980-81.

–. Parliament. Senate and House of Commons. Special Joint Committee of the Senate and of the House of Commons on the 1987 Constitutional Accord. *Minutes of Proceedings and Evidence*. 33d Parl., 2d sess. Nos. 3, 6-7, 10, 13, 15. Ottawa: Supply and Services Canada, 1987.

–. Parliament. Senate and House of Commons. Special Joint Committee of the Senate and of the House of Commons on a Renewed Canada. *Minutes of Proceedings and Evidence*. 34th Parl., 3d sess. Nos. 10, 14, 16, 29-30, 44, 58-59. Ottawa: Supply and Services Canada, 1991-92.

–. Royal Commission on Bilingualism and Biculturalism. Preliminary Hearing of the Royal Commission on Bilingualism and Biculturalism, Cathedral Hall, Ottawa, Ontario, 7-8 November 1963. N.p. Government Publications, Walter Koerner Library, University of British Columbia, Vancouver.

–. Royal Commission on Dominion-Provincial Relations. *Report of Hearings*. Vols. 17, 21, 23-24. Briefs 106, 345, 381, 401. N.p. [1938]. Special Collections, Main Library, University of British Columbia, Vancouver.

Manitoba. Manitoba Task Force on Meech Lake. *Report on the 1987 Constitutional Accord*. Winnipeg: Legislative Assembly of Manitoba, 1989.

New Brunswick. Legislative Assembly of New Brunswick. Select Committee on the 1987 Constitutional Accord. *Final Report on the Constitution Amendment 1987*. 51st Leg., 2d sess. Fredericton: Legislative Assembly of New Brunswick, 1989.

## Unpublished Documents

Canadian Labour Congress. "Submission to the Royal Commission on Bilingualism and Biculturalism." 13 December 1965. Government Publications, Walter Koerner Library, University of British Columbia, Vancouver.

Canadian Polish Congress. "Brief Presented to the Royal Commission on Bilingualism and Biculturalism." N.d. Government Publications, Walter Koerner Library, University of British Columbia, Vancouver.

Communist Party of Canada. "Submission to the Royal Commission on Bilingualism and Biculturalism by the Communist Party of Canada." 24 June 1964. Government Publications, Walter Koerner Library, University of British Columbia, Vancouver.

## Other Primary Sources

Beauchesne, Arthur. *Rules and Forms of the House of Commons of Canada: A Compendium of Canadian Parliamentary Practice*. Toronto: Canada Law Book Company, 1943.

Casgrain, Thérèse F. *A Woman in a Man's World*. Trans. Joyce Marshall. Toronto: McClelland and Stewart, 1972.

Dowd, Norman. "Progressive Reconstruction." *The Canadian Unionist*, October 1938, 113-15.

Forsey, Eugene. *A Life on the Fringe: The Memoirs of Eugene Forsey*. Toronto: Oxford University Press, 1990.

Innis, Hugh R. *Bilingualism and Biculturalism: An Abridged Version of the Royal Commission Report*. Abridged version of Canada, Royal Commission on Bilingualism and Biculturalism, *Final Reports*, 1965-70. Toronto: McClelland and Stewart, 1973.

Kwavnick, David, ed. *The Tremblay Report*. Abridged version of Quebec, Royal Commission of Inquiry on Constitutional Problems, *Final Report*, 1953. Toronto: McClelland and Stewart, 1973.

National Council of Women of Canada. *Year Book for 1938*. N.p., 1938.

–. *Year Book for 1943*. N.p., 1943.

–. *Yearbook 1964*. N.p., 1964.

Smiley, Donald V., ed. *The Rowell-Sirois Report*. Abridged version of Canada, Royal Commission on Dominion-Provincial Relations, *Book I*, 1940. Toronto: McClelland and Stewart, 1963.

*Trades and Labour Congress Journal*. February 1942.

**Secondary Sources**

Abella, Irving Martin. *Nationalism, Communism and Canadian Labour: The CIO, the Communist Party, and the Canadian Congress of Labour, 1935-1956*. Toronto: University of Toronto Press, 1973.

Abella, Irving Martin, and Harold M. Troper. *None Is Too Many: Canada and the Jews of Europe, 1933-1948*. Toronto: Lester, 1991.

Abu-Laban, Yasmeen, and Christina Gabriel. *Selling Diversity: Immigration, Multiculturalism, Employment Equity, and Globalization*. Peterborough, ON: Broadview Press, 2002.

Abu-Laban, Yasmeen, and Tim Nieguth. "Reconsidering the Constitution, Minorities and Politics in Canada." *Canadian Journal of Political Science* 33 (2000): 465-98.

Adamson, Nancy, Linda Briskin, and Margaret McPhail. *Feminist Organizing for Change: The Contemporary Women's Movement in Canada*. Toronto: Oxford University Press, 1988.

Ajzenstat, Janet. "Constitution Making and the Myth of the People." In *Constitutional Predicament: Canada after the Referendum of 1992*, ed. Curtis Cook, 112-26. Montreal and Kingston: McGill-Queen's University Press, 1994.

–. "Two Forms of Democracy: A Response to Mendelsohn's 'Public Brokerage: Constitutional Reform and the Accommodation of Mass Publics.'" *Canadian Journal of Political Science* 33 (2000): 587-92.

Anderson, Robert, and Anthony Heath. "Social Identities and Political Cleavages: The Role of Political Context." *Journal of the Royal Statistical Society, Series A* 166 (2003): 302-3.

Archer, Keith, Roger Gibbins, Rainer Knopff, Heather MacIvor, and Leslie A. Pal. *Parameters of Power: Canada's Political Institutions*. 3d ed. Scarborough, ON: Nelson, 2002.

Avakumovic, Ivan. *The Communist Party in Canada: A History*. Toronto: McClelland and Stewart, 1975.

Bacchi, Carol Lee. *Liberation Deferred? The Ideas of the English-Canadian Suffragists, 1877-1918*. Toronto: University of Toronto Press, 1983.

Baines, Beverley. "Law, Gender, Equality." In *Changing Patterns: Women in Canada*, ed. Sandra Burt, Lorraine Code, and Lindsay Dorney, 212-42. 2d ed. Toronto: McClelland and Stewart, 1993.

Bakan, Joel. *Just Words: Constitutional Rights and Social Wrongs*. Toronto: University of Toronto Press, 1997.

Bakan, Joel, and David Schneiderman, eds. *Social Justice and the Constitution: Perspectives on a Social Charter for Canada*. Ottawa: Carleton University Press, 1992.

Banting, Keith, and Richard Simeon, eds. *And No One Cheered*. Toronto: Methuen, 1983.

Bégin, Monique. "The Royal Commission on the Status of Women in Canada: Twenty Years Later." In *Challenging Times: The Women's Movement in Canada and the United States*, ed. Constance Backhouse and David H. Flaherty, 21-38. Montreal and Kingston: McGill-Queen's University Press, 1992.

Berger, Peter L., Brigitte Berger, and Hansfried Kellner. *The Homeless Mind: Modernization and Consciousness*. New York: Vintage Books, 1973.

Black, Edwin R., and Alan C. Cairns. "A Different Perspective on Canadian Federalism." *Canadian Public Administration* 1 (1966): 27-44.

Black, Naomi. "The Canadian Women's Movement: The Second Wave." In *Changing Patterns: Women in Canada*, ed. Sandra Burt, Lorraine Code, and Lindsay Dorney, 151-76. 2d ed. Toronto: McClelland and Stewart, 1993.

–. "Ripples in the Second Wave: Comparing the Contemporary Women's Movement in Canada and the United States." In *Challenging Times: The Women's Movement in Canada and the United States*, ed. Constance Backhouse and David H. Flaherty, 94-109. Montreal and Kingston: McGill-Queen's University Press, 1992.

Bociurkiw, Bohdan. "The Federal Policy of Multiculturalism and the Ukrainian-Canadian Community." In *Ukrainian Canadians, Multiculturalism, and Separatism: An Assessment*, ed. Manoly R. Lupul, 98-128. Proceedings of the Canadian Institute of Ukrainian Studies, University of Alberta, September 1977. Edmonton: University of Alberta Press, 1978.

Bourdieu, Pierre. *Distinction: A Social Critique of the Judgement of Taste*. Trans. Richard Nice. Cambridge, MA: Harvard University Press, 1984.

–. "The Forms of Capital." In *Handbook of Theory and Research for the Sociology of Education*, ed. John G. Richardson, 241-58. New York: Greenwood Press, 1986.

–. *Outline of a Theory of Practice*. Trans. Richard Nice. Cambridge: Cambridge University Press, 1977.

–. "Social Space and Symbolic Power." *Sociological Theory* 7 (1989): 14-25.

Boyer, Patrick. "'Whose Constitution Is It, Anyway?': Democratic Participation and the Canadian Constitution." In *Challenges to Canadian Federalism*, ed. Martin Westmacott and Hugh Mellon, 79-99. Scarborough, ON: Prentice Hall, 1998.

Braithwaite, Valerie, Toni Makkai, and Yvonne Pittelkow. "Inglehart's Materialism-Postmaterialism Concept: Clarifying the Dimensionality Debate through Rokeach's Model of Social Values." *Journal of Applied Social Psychology* 26 (1996): 1536-55.

Breton, Raymond. "Multiculturalism and Canadian Nation-Building." In *The Politics of Gender, Ethnicity, and Language in Canada*, ed. Alan C. Cairns and Cynthia Williams, 27-66. Vol. 34 of the Research Studies prepared for the Royal Commission on the Economic Union and the Development Prospects for Canada. Toronto: University of Toronto Press, 1985.

–. "The Production and Allocation of Symbolic Resources: An Analysis of the Linguistic and Ethnocultural Fields in Canada." *Canadian Review of Sociology and Anthropology* 21 (1984): 123-44.

–. *Why Meech Failed: Lessons for Canadian Constitutionmaking*. No. 35 in the C.D. Howe Institute Observation Series. Toronto: C.D. Howe Institute, 1992.

Brock, Kathy. *A Mandate Fulfilled: Constitutional Reform and the Manitoba Task Force on Meech Lake.* Winnipeg: University of Manitoba Outreach Fund, 1990.

Brodie, Ian, and Neil Nevitte. "Evaluating the Citizens' Constitution Theory." *Canadian Journal of Political Science* 26 (1993): 234-59.

Brodie, Janine, and Jane Jenson. *Crisis, Challenge and Change: Party and Class in Canada.* Toronto: Methuen, 1980.

Brooks, Stephen. *Canadian Democracy: An Introduction.* 4th ed. Don Mills, ON: Oxford University Press, 2004.

Burt, Sandra. "Women's Issues and the Women's Movement in Canada Since 1970." In *The Politics of Gender, Ethnicity and Language in Canada,* ed. Alan C. Cairns and Cynthia Williams, 111-70. Vol. 34 of the Research Studies prepared for the Royal Commission on the Economic Union and the Development Prospects for Canada. Toronto: University of Toronto Press, 1985.

Cairns, Alan C. "A Defence of the Citizens' Constitution Theory: A Response to Ian Brodie and Neil Nevitte." *Canadian Journal of Political Science* 26 (1993): 261-67.

–. *Disruptions: Constitutional Struggles, from the Charter to Meech Lake.* Ed. Douglas E. Williams. Toronto: McClelland and Stewart, 1991.

–. *Reconfigurations: Canadian Citizenship and Constitutional Change.* Ed. Douglas E. Williams. Toronto: McClelland and Stewart, 1995.

*Canada's Party of Socialism: History of the Communist Party of Canada, 1921-1976.* Toronto: Progress Books, 1982.

Casgrain, Thérèse F. *A Woman in a Man's World.* Trans. Joyce Marshall. Toronto: McClelland and Stewart, 1972.

Chambers, Simone. "New Constitutionalism: Democracy, Habermas, and Canadian Exceptionalism." In *Canadian Political Philosophy: Contemporary Reflections,* ed. Ronald Beiner and Wayne Norman, 63-77. Don Mills, ON: Oxford University Press, 2001.

Clegg, Stewart, and David Dunkerley. *Organization, Class, and Control.* London: Routledge and Keagan Paul, 1980.

Cleverdon, Catherine Lyle. *The Woman Suffrage Movement in Canada.* Toronto: University of Toronto Press, 1950.

Cohen, Marjorie Griffin. "The Canadian Women's Movement and Its Efforts to Influence the Canadian Economy." In *Challenging Times: The Women's Movement in Canada and the United States,* ed. Constance Backhouse and David H. Flaherty, 215-24. Montreal and Kingston: McGill-Queen's University Press, 1992.

Coyne, Deborah. "Commentary." In *After Meech Lake: Lessons for the Future,* ed. David E. Smith, Peter MacKinnon, and John C. Courtney, 139-45. Saskatoon: Fifth House Publishers, 1991.

Creighton, Donald. *The Forked Road: Canada, 1939-1957.* Toronto: McClelland and Stewart, 1976.

Crowley, Brian Lee. *The Road To Equity: Gender, Ethnicity, and Language – Impolitic Essays.* Toronto: Stoddart, 1994.

Cuthbert Brandt, Gail. "'Pigeon-Holed and Forgotten': The Work of the Subcommittee on the Post-War Problems of Women, 1943." *Histoire sociale/Social History* 29 (1982): 239-59.

Dalton, Russell J., and Manfred Kuechler, eds. *Challenging the Political Order: New Social and Political Movements in Western Democracies.* Cambridge: Polity Press, 1990.

Darby, Tom, and Peter C. Emberley. "'Political Correctness' and the Constitution: Nature and Convention Re-examined." In *Rethinking the Constitution: Perspectives on Canadian Constitutional Reform, Interpretation, and Theory*, ed. Anthony A. Peacock, 233-48. Don Mills, ON: Oxford University Press, 1996.

Davis, Darren W., and Christian Davenport. "Assessing the Validity of the Postmaterialism Index." *American Political Science Review* 93 (1999): 649-63.

Delacourt, Susan. *United We Fall: The Crisis of Democracy in Canada*. Toronto: Viking, 1993.

della Porta, Donatella, and Mario Diani. *Social Movements: An Introduction*. Oxford: Blackwell, 1999.

Dickerson, Mark O., and Thomas Flanagan. *An Introduction to Government and Politics: A Conceptual Approach*. 6th ed. Scarborough, ON: Nelson Thomson Learning, 2002.

Dobrowolsky, Alexandra. "The Charter and Mainstream Political Science: Waves of Practical Contestation and Changing Theoretical Currents." In *Charting the Consequences: The Impact of Charter Rights on Canadian Law and Politics*, ed. David Schneiderman and Kate Sutherland, 707-42. Toronto: University of Toronto Press, 1997.

–. "Of 'Special Interest': Interest, Identity and Feminist Constitutional Activism in Canada." *Canadian Journal of Political Science* 31 (1998): 707-42.

–. *The Politics of Pragmatism: Women, Representation, and Constitutionalism in Canada*. Don Mills, ON: Oxford University Press, 2000.

Fleras, Augie, and Jean Leonard Elliott. *Multiculturalism in Canada: The Challenge of Diversity*. Scarborough, ON: Nelson, 1992.

Forbes, H.D. "Trudeau's Moral Vision." In *Rethinking the Constitution: Perspectives on Canadian Constitutional Reform, Interpretation, and Theory*, ed. Anthony A. Peacock, 17-39. Don Mills, ON: Oxford University Press, 1996.

Fraser, Nancy. *Justice Interruptus: Critical Reflections on the 'Postsocialist' Condition*. New York: Routledge, 1997.

–. "Rethinking Recognition." *New Left Review* 3 (May/June 2000): 107-20.

Gagnon, Mona-Josée. "The Quebec Labour Movement." In *Quebec Society: Critical Issues*, ed. Marcel Fournier, Michael Rosenberg, and Deena White, 142-63. Scarborough, ON: Prentice Hall, 1997.

Gérin-Lajoie, Paul. *Constitutional Amendment in Canada*. Toronto: University of Toronto Press, 1950.

Glickman, Yaacov. "Political Socialization and the Social Protest of Canadian Jewry: Some Historical and Contemporary Perspectives." In *Ethnicity, Power, and Politics in Canada*, ed. Jorgen Dahlie and Tissa Fernando, 123-50. Vol. 8 of the Canadian Ethnic Studies Association. Toronto: Methuen, 1981.

Goffman, Erving. "On Face-Work: An Analysis of Ritual Elements in Social Interaction." In *Language, Culture and Society: A Book of Readings*, ed. Ben G. Blount, 224-49. Cambridge, MA: Winthrop, 1974.

–. *The Presentation of Self in Everyday Life*. Garden City, NY: Anchor Books, 1959.

–. *Stigma: Notes on the Management of Spoiled Identity*. New York: Touchstone, 1986.

Goode, William J. *The Celebration of Heroes: Prestige as a Social Control System*. Berkeley: University of California Press, 1978.

Granatstein, J.L. *Canada, 1957-1967: The Years of Uncertainty and Innovation*. Toronto: McClelland and Stewart, 1986.

Griffiths, N.E.S. *The Splendid Vision: Centennial History of the National Council of Women of Canada, 1893-1993.* Ottawa: Carleton University Press, 1993.

Guest, Dennis. *The Emergence of Social Security in Canada.* Vancouver: UBC Press, 1979.

Haydu, Jeffrey. *Between Craft and Class: Skilled Workers and Factory Politics in the United States and Britain, 1980-1922.* Berkeley: University of California Press, 1988.

Heater, Derek. *Citizenship: The Civic Ideal in World History, Politics and Education.* London: Longman, 1990.

Heron, Craig. *The Canadian Labour Movement: A Short History.* 2d ed. Toronto: Lorimer, 1996.

Hill, Daniel G. *Human Rights in Canada: A Focus on Racism.* Ottawa: Canadian Labour Congress, 1977.

Hobsbawm, E.J. *Worlds of Labour: Further Studies in the History of Labour.* London: Weidenfeld and Nicholson, 1984.

Honneth, Axel. *The Struggle for Recognition: The Moral Grammar of Social Conflicts.* Trans. Joel Anderson. Cambridge: Polity Press, 1995.

Horowitz, Gad. *Canadian Labour in Politics.* Toronto: University of Toronto Press, 1968.

Inglehart, Ronald. *Culture Shift in Advanced Industrial Society.* Princeton: Princeton University Press, 1990.

–. *Modernization and Postmodernization: Cultural, Economic, and Political Change in 43 Societies.* Princeton: Princeton University Press, 1997.

–. "Post-Materialism in an Environment of Insecurity." *American Political Science Review* 75 (1981): 880-900.

–. *The Silent Revolution: Changing Values and Political Styles among Western Publics.* Princeton: Princeton University Press, 1977.

–. "The Silent Revolution in Europe: Intergenerational Change in Post-Industrial Societies." *American Political Science Review* 65 (1971): 991-1017.

James, Matt. "The Permanent-Emergency Compensation State: A 'Postsocialist' Tale of Political Dystopia." In *Critical Policy Studies: Contemporary Canadian Approaches*, ed. Michael Orsini and Miriam Smith. Vancouver: UBC Press, forthcoming.

–. "Redress Politics and Canadian Citizenship." In *The State of the Federation 1998: How Canadians Connect*, ed. Harvey Lazar and Tom McIntosh, 247-82. Kingston: Queen's University Institute of Intergovernmental Relations, 1999.

Jamieson, Stuart Marshall. *Times of Trouble: Labour Unrest and Industrial Conflict in Canada, 1900-66.* Study No. 22 of the Research Studies prepared for the Task Force on Labour Relations. Ottawa: Information Canada, 1968.

Jenson, Jane. "'Different' But Not 'Exceptional': Canada's Permeable Fordism." *Canadian Review of Sociology and Anthropology* 26 (1989): 69-94.

–. "Fated to Live in Interesting Times: Canada's Changing Citizenship Regimes." *Canadian Journal of Political Science* 30 (1997): 627-44.

Johnson, A.W. "A National Government in a Federal State." In *Constitutional Politics: The Canadian Forum Book on the Federal Constitutional Proposals, 1991-92*, ed. Duncan Cameron and Miriam Smith, 79-91. Toronto: Lorimer, 1992.

Johnston, Darlene. "First Nations and Canadian Citizenship." In *Belonging: The Meaning and Future of Canadian Citizenship*, ed. William Kaplan, 349-67. Montreal: McGill-Queen's University Press, 1993.

Johnston, Richard, André Blais, Elisabeth Gidengil, and Neil Nevitte. *The Challenge of Direct Democracy: The 1992 Canadian Referendum*. Montreal and Kingston: McGill-Queen's University Press, 1996.

Kallen, Evelyn. *Ethnicity and Human Rights in Canada*. Toronto: Gage, 1982.

Kelly, James B. *Governing with the Charter: Legislative and Judicial Activism and Framers' Intent*. Vancouver: UBC Press, 2005.

Kernerman, Gerald. *Multicultural Nationalism: Civilizing Difference, Constituting Community*. Vancouver: UBC Press, 2005.

Kitschelt, Herbert. *The Transformation of European Social Democracy*. Cambridge: Cambridge University Press, 1994.

Knopff, Rainer, and F.L. Morton. "Canada's Court Party." In *Rethinking the Constitution: Perspectives on Canadian Constitutional Reform, Interpretation, and Theory*, ed. Anthony A. Peacock, 63-81. Don Mills, ON: Oxford University Press, 1996.

–. *Charter Politics*. Scarborough, ON: Nelson, 1992.

Kome, Penney. *The Taking of Twenty-Eight: Women Challenge the Constitution*. Toronto: Women's Press, 1983.

Kymlicka, Will. *Contemporary Political Philosophy: An Introduction*. 2nd ed. Toronto: Oxford University Press, 2002.

Laforest, Guy. *Trudeau and the End of a Canadian Dream*. Trans. Paul Leduc Browne and Michelle Weinroth. Montreal and Kingston: McGill-Queen's University Press, 1995.

Larana, Enrique, Hank Johnston, and Joseph R. Gusfield, eds. *New Social Movements: From Ideology to Identity*. Philadelphia: Temple University Press, 1994.

Lazar, Harvey. "Non-Constitutional Renewal: Toward a New Equilibrium in the Federation." In *Canada: The State of the Federation 1997 – Non-Constitutional Renewal*, ed. Harvey Lazar, 3-38. Kingston: Queen's University Institute of Intergovernmental Relations, 1998.

Lee, Jo-Anne, and Linda Cardinal. "Hegemonic Nationalism and the Politics of Feminism and Multiculturalism in Canada." In *Painting the Maple: Essays on Race, Gender, and the Construction of Canada*, ed. Veronica Strong-Boag, Sherrill Grace, Avigail Eisenberg, and Joan Anderson, 215-41. Vancouver: UBC Press, 1998.

Lipset, Seymour Martin. *Consensus and Conflict: Essays in Political Sociology*. New Brunswick, NJ: Transaction Books, 1985.

Logan, H.A. *Trade Unions in Canada: Their Development and Functioning*. Toronto: Macmillan, 1948.

Luard, Evan, ed. *The International Protection of Human Rights*. London: Thames and Hudson, 1967.

Lusztig, Michael, and J. Matthew Wilson. "A New Right? Moral Issues and Partisan Change in Canada." *Social Science Quarterly* 86 (March 2005): 109-28.

McBride, Stephen, and John Shields. *Dismantling a Nation: The Transition to Corporate Rule in Canada*. Halifax: Fernwood, 1997.

McCarthy, John D., and Mayer N. Zald. "Resource Mobilization and Social Movements: A Partial Theory." *American Journal of Sociology* 82 (1977): 1212-41.

McCormack, Thelma. *Politics and the Hidden Injuries of Gender: Feminism and the Making of the Welfare State*. Research Paper No. 28 of the Canadian Research Institute for the Advancement of Women. Ottawa: Canadian Research Institute for the Advancement of Women, 1991.

McDonald, Lynn. "The Supreme Court of Canada and the Equality Guarantee in the Charter." *Socialist Studies* 2 (1984): 45-65.

MacDowell, Laurel Sefton. "The Formation of the Canadian Industrial Relations System." In *Canadian Working Class History: Selected Readings*, ed. Laurel Sefton MacDowell and Ian Radforth, 575-93. Toronto: Canadian Scholars' Press, 1992.

McIntosh, Tom. "Organized Labour in a Federal Society: Solidarity, Coalition Building and Canadian Unions." In *Canada: The State of the Federation, 1998/99: How Canadians Connect*, ed. Harvey Lazar and Tom McIntosh, 147-78. Montreal and Kingston: McGill-Queen's University Press, 1999.

McRoberts, Kenneth, and Patrick J. Monahan, eds. *The Charlottetown Accord, the Referendum, and the Future of Canada*. Toronto: University of Toronto Press, 1993.

Mallory, J.R. *Social Credit and the Federal Power in Canada*. Toronto: University of Toronto Press, 1976.

Manfredi, Christopher P. "On the Virtues of a Limited Constitution: Why Canadians Were Right to Reject the Charlottetown Accord." In *Rethinking the Constitution: Perspectives on Canadian Constitutional Reform, Interpretation, and Theory*, ed. Anthony A. Peacock, 40-60. Don Mills, ON: Oxford University Press, 1996.

Marks, Gary N. "The Formation of Materialist and Postmaterialist Values." *Social Science Research* 26 (1997): 52-68.

Marshall, T.H. *Class, Citizenship and Social Development*. Ed. Seymour Martin Lipset. Garden City, NY: Doubleday, 1964.

Marx, Karl. "On the Jewish Question." In *The Marx-Engels Reader*, ed. Robert C. Tucker, 26-52. 2d ed. New York: Norton, 1978 (first published 1843).

Marx, Karl, and Friedrich Engels. *Manifesto of the Communist Party*. In *The Marx-Engels Reader*, ed. Robert C. Tucker, 469-500. 2d ed. New York: Norton, 1978 (first published 1848).

Maslow, A. H. *Motivation and Personality*. 2d ed. New York: Harper, 1954.

Melucci, Alberto. *Nomads of the Present: Social Movements and Individual Needs in Contemporary Society*. Ed. John Keane and Paul Mier. Philadelphia: Temple University Press, 1989.

Miki, Roy. *Redress: Inside the Japanese-Canadian Call for Justice*. Vancouver: Raincoast Books, 2004.

Miki, Roy, and Cassandra Kobayashi, eds. *Justice in Our Time: Redress for Japanese Canadians*. Vancouver: National Association of Japanese Canadians, 1988.

Milne, David. "Innovative Constitutional Processes: Renewal of Canada Conferences, January-March 1992." In *Canada: The State of the Federation, 1992*, ed. Douglas Brown and Robert Young, 27-51. Kingston: Queen's University Institute of Intergovernmental Relations, 1992.

Minogue, Kenneth. "The History of the Idea of Human Rights." In *The Human Rights Reader*, ed. Walter Laqueur and Barry Rubin, 3-16. New York: New American Library, 1979.

Monahan, Patrick J. *Meech Lake: The Inside Story*. Toronto: University of Toronto Press, 1991.

-. "The Sounds of Silence." In *The Charlottetown Accord, the Referendum, and the Future of Canada*, ed. Kenneth McRoberts and Patrick J. Monahan, 222-48. Toronto: University of Toronto Press, 1993.

Moody, Kim. *An Injury to All: The Decline of American Unionism*. London: Verso, 1988.

Morton, Desmond. *The New Democrats, 1961-1986: The Politics of Change*. Rev. ed. Toronto: Copp Clark Pitman, 1986.

Morton, Desmond, and Terry Copp. *Working People*. Rev. ed. Ottawa: Deneau, 1984.

Morton, F.L. "The Effect of the Charter of Rights on Canadian Federalism." *Publius* 25 (1995): 173-88.

Morton, F.L., and Rainer Knopff. *The Charter Revolution and the Court Party*. Peterborough, ON: Broadview Press, 2000.

–. "The Supreme Court as the Vanguard of the Intelligentsia: The Charter Movement as Postmaterialist Politics." In *Canadian Constitutionalism: 1791-1991*, ed. Janet Ajzenstat, 57-80. Ottawa: Canadian Study of Parliament Group, 1992.

Nevitte, Neil. *The Decline of Deference: Canadian Value Change in Cross-National Perspective*. Peterborough, ON: Broadview Press, 1996.

–. "New Politics, the Charter, and Political Participation." In *Representation, Integration and Political Parties in Canada*, ed. Herman Bakvis, 355-418. Vol. 14 of the Research Studies prepared for the Royal Commission on Electoral Reform and Party Financing. Toronto: Dundurn Press, 1992.

Nevitte, Neil, and Herman Bakvis. "In Pursuit of Postbourgeois Man: Postmaterialism and Intergenerational Change in Canada." *Comparative Political Studies* 20 (1987): 357-89.

Nevitte, Neil, and Roger Gibbins. "The Ideological Contours of 'New Politics' in Canada: Policy, Mobilization, and Partisan Support." *Canadian Journal of Political Science* 22 (1989): 475-503.

Newman, Peter C. *Renegade in Power: The Diefenbaker Years*. Toronto: McClelland and Stewart, 1963.

Opp, Karl-Dieter. "Postmaterialism, Collective Action, and Protest." *American Journal of Political Science* 34 (1990): 212-35.

Orloff, Ann Shola. "Gender and the Social Rights of Citizenship: The Comparative Analysis of Gender Relations and Welfare States." *American Sociological Review* 58 (1993): 303-28.

Ostberg, C.L., Matthew E. Wetstein, and Craig R. Ducat. "Attitudes, Precedents, and Cultural Change: Explaining the Citation of Foreign Precedents by the Supreme Court of Canada." *Canadian Journal of Political Science* 34 (2001): 377-99.

Owram, Doug. *The Government Generation: Canadian Intellectuals and the State, 1900-1945*. Toronto: University of Toronto Press, 1986.

Pal, Leslie A. *Beyond Policy Analysis: Public Issue Management in Turbulent Times*. 3d ed. Scarborough, ON: Nelson, 2006.

–. *Interests of State: The Politics of Language, Multiculturalism, and Feminism in Canada*. Montreal: McGill-Queen's University Press, 1993.

–. *State, Class, and Bureaucracy: Canadian Unemployment Insurance and Public Policy*. Kingston and Montreal: McGill-Queen's University Press, 1988.

Pal, Leslie A., and Robert M. Campbell. *The Real Worlds of Canadian Politics: Cases in Process and Policy*. 2d ed. Peterborough, ON: Broadview, 1991.

Palmer, Bryan D. *Working-Class Experience: The Rise and Reconstitution of Canadian Labour, 1800-1980*. Toronto: Butterworth, 1983.

Panitch, Leo, and Donald Swartz. *The Assault on Trade Union Freedoms: From Wage Controls to Social Contract*. Rev. ed. Toronto: Garamond, 1993.

Peacock, Anthony A. "Introduction: The Necessity of Rethinking the Constitution." In *Rethinking the Constitution: Perspectives on Canadian Constitutional*

*Reform, Interpretation, and Theory*, ed. Anthony A. Peacock (Don Mills, ON: Oxford University Press, 1996).

Pierson, Ruth Roach. "Gender and the Unemployment Insurance Debates in Canada, 1934-1940." *Labour/le Travail* 25 (1990): 77-103.

–. *"They're Still Women After All: The Second World War and Canadian Womanhood.* Toronto: McClelland and Stewart, 1986.

Plotke, David. "What's So New about New Social Movements?" *Socialist Review* 20 (1990): 81-102.

Poovey, Mary. *Uneven Developments: The Ideological Work of Gender in Mid-Victorian England*. Chicago: University of Chicago Press, 1988.

Posgate, Dale, and Kenneth McRoberts. *Quebec: Social Change and Political Crisis.* Toronto: McClelland and Stewart, 1976.

Prentice, Alison, Paula Bourne, Gail Cuthbert Brandt, Beth Light, Wendy Mitchinson, and Naomi Black. *Canadian Women: A History*. 2d ed. Toronto: Harcourt Brace, 1996.

Pross, A. Paul. *Group Politics and Public Policy*. Toronto: Oxford University Press, 1986.

Putnam, Robert D. *Bowling Alone: The Collapse and Revival of American Community*. New York: Simon and Schuster, 2000.

Resnick, Philip. *Thinking English Canada*. Toronto: Stoddart, 1994.

Richards, John. "The NDP in the Constitutional Drama." In *Canada: The State of the Federation 1992*, ed. Douglas Brown and Robert Young, 159-82. Kingston: Queen's University Institute of Intergovernmental Relations, 1992.

Robertson, A.H., and J.G. Merrills. *Human Rights in the World: An Introduction to the Study of the International Protection of Human Rights*. Manchester: Manchester University Press, 1989.

Romanow, Roy, John Whyte, and Howard Leeson. *Canada ... Notwithstanding: The Making of the Constitution, 1976-1982*. Toronto: Carswell, 1984.

Russell, Peter H. *Constitutional Odyssey: Can Canadians Become a Sovereign People?* 3d ed. Toronto: University of Toronto Press, 2004.

–. "The End of Mega Constitutional Politics in Canada?" In *The Charlottetown Accord, the Referendum, and the Future of Canada*, ed. Kenneth McRoberts and Patrick J. Monahan, 211-21. Toronto: University of Toronto Press, 1993.

–. "The Political Purposes of the Canadian Charter of Rights and Freedoms." *Canadian Bar Review* 61 (1983): 30-54.

Savage, James. "Postmaterialism of the Left and Right: Political Conflict in Postindustrial Society." *Comparative Political Studies* 17 (1985): 431-51.

Scott, Alan. *Ideology and the New Social Movements*. London: Unwin Hyman, 1990.

Scott, F.R. "Centralization and Decentralization in Canadian Federalism." *Canadian Bar Review* 29 (1951): 1095-125.

Sheppard, Robert, and Michael Valpy. *The National Deal: The Fight for a Canadian Constitution*. Toronto: Fleet, 1982.

Simeon, Richard, and Ian Robinson. *State, Society, and the Development of Canadian Federalism*. Vol. 71 of the Research Studies prepared for the Royal Commission on the Economic Union and Development Prospects for Canada. Toronto: University of Toronto Press, 1990.

Smiley, Donald V. "A Dangerous Deed: The Constitution Act, 1982." In *And No One Cheered*, ed. Keith Banting and Richard Simeon, 74-95. Toronto: Methuen, 1983.

–. "The Rowell-Sirois Report, Provincial Autonomy, and Post-War Canadian Federalism." *Canadian Journal of Economics and Political Science* 28 (1962): 54-69.

Smith, Lynn. "A New Paradigm for Equality Rights?" In *Righting the Balance: Canada's New Equality Rights*, ed. Lynn Smith, 351-407. Saskatoon: Canadian Human Rights Reporter, 1986.

Smith, Miriam. "Ghosts of the Judicial Committee of the Privy Council: Group Politics and Charter Litigation in Canadian Political Science." *Canadian Journal of Political Science* 35 (2002): 3-30.

–. *Lesbian and Gay Rights in Canada: Social Movements and Equality Seeking, 1971-1995*. Toronto: University of Toronto Press, 1999.

–. "Resisting and Reinforcing Neoliberalism: Lesbian and Gay Organizing at the Federal and Local Levels in Canada." *Policy and Politics* 1 (2005): 75-93.

–. "Social Movements and Equality-Seeking: The Case of Gay Liberation in Canada." *Canadian Journal of Political Science* 31 (1998): 285-309.

Steel, Brent S., Rebecca L. Warner, Nicholas P. Lovrich, and John C. Pierce. "The Inglehart-Flanagan Debate over Postmaterialist Values: Some Evidence from a Canadian-American Case Study." *Political Psychology* 13 (1992): 61-77.

Stevenson, Garth. "Federalism and Intergovernmental Relations." In *Canadian Politics in the 21st Century*, ed. Michael Whittington and Glen Williams, 79-104. Scarborough, ON: Nelson, 2000.

Stewart, Frank Henderson. *Honor*. Chicago: University of Chicago Press, 1994.

Strong-Boag, Veronica. *The Parliament of Women: The National Council of Women of Canada, 1893-1929*. Ottawa: National Museums of Canada, 1976.

–. "The Roots of Modern Canadian Feminism." In *Canadian History Since Confederation: Essays and Interpretations*, ed. Bruce Hodgins and Robert Page, 398-408. Georgetown, ON: Irwin-Dorsey, 1979.

Strong-Boag, Veronica, Sherrill Grace, Avigail Eisenberg, and Joan Anderson, eds. *Painting the Maple: Essays on Race, Gender, and the Construction of Canada*. Vancouver: UBC Press, 1998.

Struthers, James. *No Fault of Their Own: Unemployment and the Canadian Welfare State, 1914-1941*. Toronto: University of Toronto Press, 1983.

Sunahara, Ann Gomer. *The Politics of Racism: The Uprooting of Japanese Canadians during the Second World War*. Toronto: James Lorimer, 1981.

Tarnopolsky, Walter. *The Canadian Bill of Rights*. 2d ed. Toronto: McClelland and Stewart, 1975.

Tarrow, Sidney. *Power in Movement: Social Movements, Collective Action, and Politics*. New York: Cambridge University Press, 1994.

Taylor, Charles. "The Politics of Recognition." In *Multiculturalism: Examining the Politics of Recognition*, ed. Charles Taylor and Amy Gutmann, 25-73. 2d ed. Princeton: Princeton University Press, 1994.

Thompson, John B. *Studies in the Theory of Ideology*. Cambridge: Polity Press, 1984.

Thomson, Dale C. *Louis St. Laurent: Canadian*. Toronto: Macmillan, 1967.

Topper, Keith. "Not So Trifling Nuances: Pierre Bourdieu, Symbolic Violence, and the Perversions of Democracy." *Constellations* 8:1 (2001): 30-56.

Touraine, Alain. *The Voice and the Eye: An Analysis of Social Movements*. Trans. Alan Duff. Cambridge: Cambridge University Press, 1981.

Trimble, Linda. "'Good Enough Citizens': Canadian Women and Representation in Constitutional Deliberations." *International Journal of Canadian Studies* 17 (1998): 131-56.

Trofimenkoff, Susan Mann. "Thérèse Casgrain and the CCF in Quebec." *Canadian Historical Review* 66 (1985): 125-53.

Trudeau, Pierre Elliott. *Memoirs*. Toronto: McClelland and Stewart, 1993.

–. *Pierre Trudeau Speaks Out on Meech Lake*. Ed. Donald Johnston. Toronto: General Paperbacks, 1990.

Tupper, Allan. "English-Canadian Scholars and the Meech Lake Accord." *International Journal of Canadian Studies* 7-8 (1993): 347-54.

Vickers, Jill. "The Intellectual Origins of the Women's Movements in Canada." In *Challenging Times: The Women's Movement in Canada and the United States*, ed. Constance Backhouse and David H. Flaherty, 39-60. Montreal and Kingston: McGill-Queen's University Press, 1992.

–. "Why Should Women Care about Constitutional Reform?" In *Conversations among Friends/entre amies: Proceedings of an Interdisciplinary Conference on Women and Constitutional Reform*, ed. David Schneiderman, 18-22. Edmonton: University of Alberta Centre for Constitutional Studies, 1991.

Vickers, Jill, Pauline Rankin, and Christine Appelle. *Politics As If Women Mattered: A Political Analysis of the National Action Committee on the Status of Women*. Toronto: University of Toronto Press, 1993.

Warwick, Paul V. "Disputed Cause, Disputed Effect: The Postmaterialist Thesis Re-examined. *Public Opinion Quarterly* 62 (1998): 583-609.

Webber, Jeremy. *Reimagining Canada: Language, Culture, Community, and the Canadian Constitution*. Kingston and Montreal: McGill-Queen's University Press, 1994.

Weber, Max. *Economy and Society: An Outline of Interpretive Sociology*. Trans. Ephraim Fischoff et al. 3 vols. New York: Bedminster Press, 1968.

Williams, Cynthia. "The Changing Nature of Citizen Rights." In *Constitutionalism, Citizenship and Society in Canada*, ed. Alan C. Cairns and Cynthia Williams, 99-127. Vol. 33 of the Research Studies prepared for the Royal Commission on the Economic Union and the Development Prospects for Canada. Toronto: University of Toronto Press, 1985.

Williams, Jack. *The Story of Unions in Canada*. Toronto: J.M. Dent and Sons, 1975.

Young, Walter D. *The Anatomy of a Party: The National CCF, 1932-61*. Toronto: University of Toronto Press, 1969.

Zald, Mayer N., and John D. McCarthy. *The Dynamics of Social Movements*. Cambridge, MA: Winthrop, 1979.

–. *Social Movements in an Organizational Society: Collected Essays*. New Brunswick, NJ: Transaction Publishers, 1987.

Zukowsky, Ronald James. *Struggle over the Constitution: From the Quebec Referendum to the Supreme Court*. Kingston: Queen's University Institute of Intergovernmental Relations, 1981.

# Index